MTTC Learning Disabled
63 Teacher Certification Exam

By: Sharon Wynne, M.S
Southern Connecticut State University

XAMonline, INC.
Boston

Copyright © 2007 XAMonline, Inc.
All rights reserved. No part of the material protected by this copyright notice may be reproduced or utilized in any form or by any means, electronic or mechanical, including photocopying, recording or by any information storage and retrievable system, without written permission from the copyright holder.

To obtain permission(s) to use the material from this work for any purpose including workshops or seminars, please submit a written request to:

XAMonline, Inc.
21 Orient Ave.
Melrose, MA 02176
Toll Free 1-800-509-4128
Email: info@xamonline.com
Web www.xamonline.com
Fax: 1-781-662-9268

Library of Congress Cataloging-in-Publication Data

Wynne, Sharon A.
    Learning Disabled 63: Teacher Certification / Sharon A. Wynne. -2nd ed.
    ISBN 978-1-58197-953-4
    1. Learning Disabled 63.   2. Study Guides.   3. MTTC
    4. Teachers' Certification & Licensure.   5. Careers

Disclaimer:
The opinions expressed in this publication are the sole works of XAMonline and were created independently from the National Education Association, Educational Testing Service, or any State Department of Education, National Evaluation Systems or other testing affiliates.

Between the time of publication and printing, state specific standards as well as testing formats and website information may change that is not included in part or in whole within this product. Sample test questions are developed by XAMonline and reflect similar content as on real tests; however, they are not former tests. XAMonline assembles content that aligns with state standards but makes no claims nor guarantees teacher candidates a passing score. Numerical scores are determined by testing companies such as NES or ETS and then are compared with individual state standards. A passing score varies from state to state.

Printed in the United States of America   œ-1

MTTC: Learning Disabled 63
ISBN: 978-1-58197-953-4

ACKNOWLEDGEMENTS
Special Education

Recognizing the hard work in the production of our study guides we would like to thank those involved. The credentials and experience fulfilling the making of this study guide, aided by the professionalism and insight of those who expressed the subject mastery in specialized fields, is valued and appreciated by XAMonline. It results in a product that upholds the integrity and pride represented by modern educators who bear the name **TEACHER**.

Providers of foundational material
Founding authors 1996	Kathy Schinerman
	Roberta Ramsey
Pre-flight editorial review	Paul Sutliff
Pre-flight construction:	Brittany Good
	Harris
	Brooks
	Hughes
Authors 2006	Paul Sutliff
	Beatrice Jordan
	Marisha Tapera
	Kathy Gibson
	Twya Lavender
	Carol Moore
	Christi Godard
Sample test rational	Sidney Findley

XAMonline Editorial and Production acknowledgements
Project Manager	Sharon Wynne
Project Coordinator	Twya Lavender
Series Editor	Mary Collins
Editorial Assistant	Virginia Finnerty
Marketing Manager	John Wynne
Marketing support	Maria Ciampa
Cover design	Brian Messenger
Sales	Justin Dooley
Production Editor	David Aronson
Typist	Julian German
Manufacturing	Chris Morning/Midland Press
E-Books	Kristy Gipson/Lightningsource
Cover Administrator	Jenna Hamilton

TEACHER CERTIFICATION STUDY GUIDE

Table of Contents

About the Test..vi

Introduction...ix

Pre-test 1

SUBAREA I.	**HUMAN DEVELOPMENT AND THE EDUCATIONAL IMPLICATIONS OF LEARNING DISABILITIES**

Skill 1.01   Demonstrate knowledge of human development and behavior..50

Skill 1.02   Demonstrate knowledge of the characteristics of students with special needs, types of learning disabilities, and ways in which learning disabilities influence human development 61

Skill 1.03   Demonstrate knowledge of types and characteristics of receptive and expressive language disorders associated with learning disabilities...65

Skill 1.04   Demonstrate knowledge of types and characteristics of perceptual and memory disorders associated with learning disabilities 67

Skill 1.05   Demonstrate knowledge of types and characteristics of thinking disorders associated with learning disabilities 68

Skill 1.06   Demonstrate knowledge of types and characteristics of behavioral, social, and emotional disorders associated with learning disabilities...69

SUBAREA II.	EVALUATION, ASSESSMENT, AND INDIVIDUALIZED EDUCATIONAL PROGRAMS (IEPs)
Skill 2.01	Demonstrate knowledge of types and characteristics of assessment Instruments and methods 73
Skill 2.02	Demonstrate knowledge of procedures for conducting a comprehensive evaluation 78
Skill 2.03	Analyze the uses of ongoing assessment in the education of students with learning disabilities 83
Skill 2.04	Demonstrate knowledge of the development and implementation of Individualized Educational Programs (IEPs) for students with learning disabilities 84
Skill 2.05	Demonstrate knowledge of a continuum of options for program and service delivery for students with learning disabilities 89

SUBAREA III.   METHODOLOGY AND INSTRUCTION

Skill 3.01 Apply principles and methods involved in individualizing instruction for students with learning disabilities 93

Skill 3.02 Demonstrate knowledge of various instructional approaches used with students with learning disabilities 99

Skill 3.03 Demonstrate knowledge of approaches and techniques used to improve students' receptive language skills 100

Skill 3.04 Demonstrate knowledge of approaches and techniques used to improve students' reading skills 102

Skill 3.05 Demonstrate knowledge of approaches and techniques used to improve students' oral expressive language skills 107

Skill 3.06 Demonstrate knowledge of approaches and techniques used to improve students' written expression skills 113

Skill 3.07 Demonstrate knowledge of approaches and techniques used to improve students' mathematical skills 116

Skill 3.08 Demonstrate knowledge of approaches and techniques used to improve students' self-esteem and personal and social skills and to facilitate transition into adult life-roles 119

Skill 3.09 Demonstrate knowledge of the development and implementation of individual behavior management approaches 122

Skill 3.10 Apply techniques for promoting career awareness and initiating transition services for students with learning disabilities 127

SUBAREA IV. PROGRAM AND SERVICE DELIVERY

Skill 4.01 Apply knowledge of state regulations and historical trends in the delivery of special education and related services 132

Skill 4.02 Apply consultation, collaboration, and coordination procedures 143

Skill 4.03 Demonstrate knowledge of methods of communicating with and providing information for the families of students with learning disabilities.. 145

Skill 4.04 Analyze procedures for communicating with and promoting self-advocacy in students with learning disabilities 148

Sample Test 150

Rationales with Sample Questions 174

References 216

TEACHER CERTIFICATION STUDY GUIDE

ABOUT THE TEST

The Michigan Test for Teacher certification exam is designed to ensure that each certified teacher has the necessary basic skills and content knowledge to serve in Michigan public schools.

The Learning Disabled Test (63) has four subareas. The subareas and the percentage of question for each subarea is as follows:

Subarea	Approximate Percentage of Questions on Test
Human Development and the Educational Implications of Learning Disabilities	24%
Evaluation, Assessment, and Individualized Educational Programs (IEPs)	20%
Methodology and Instruction	40%
Program and Service Delivery	16%

Scores

Passing status is determined on the basis of an examinee's total test performance. All test results are reported as scaled scores. The scaled score is a conversion of the number of scorable test questions the examinee answers correctly, ranging from 100 to 300, with a score of 220 representing the passing score.

Cost:
At the time of this publication, the cost for this exam is $74 (1st subject area test) $ 59 for each additional subject area test

Location
Please go to www.mttc.nesinc.com/index.asp for current locations and other important information.

TEACHER CERTIFICATION STUDY GUIDE

Great Study and Testing Tips!

What to study in order to prepare for the subject assessments is the focus of this study guide but equally important is *how* you study.

You can increase your chances of truly mastering the information by taking some simple, but effective steps.

Study Tips:

1. Some foods aid the learning process. Foods such as milk, nuts, seeds, rice and oats help your study efforts by releasing natural memory enhancers called CCKs (*cholecystokinin*) composed of *tryptopha*n, *choline*, and *phenylalanine*. All of these chemicals enhance the neurotransmitters associated with memory. Before studying, try a light, protein-rich meal of eggs, turkey and fish. All of these foods release the memory enhancing chemicals. The better the connections, the more you comprehend.

Likewise, before you take a test, stick to a light snack of energy boosting and relaxing foods. A glass of milk, a piece of fruit or some peanuts all release various memory-boosting chemicals and help you to relax and focus on the subject at hand.

2. Learn to take great notes. A by-product of our modern culture is that we have grown accustomed to getting our information in short doses (i.e.: TV news sound bites or USA Today style newspaper articles).

Consequently, we've subconsciously trained ourselves to assimilate information better in neat little packages. If your notes are scrawled all over the paper, it fragments the flow of the information. Strive for clarity. Newspapers use a standard format to achieve clarity. Your notes can be much clearer through use of proper formatting. A very effective format is called the *"Cornell Method."*

Take a sheet of loose-leaf lined notebook paper and draw a line all the way down the paper about 1-2" from the left-hand edge.

Draw another line across the width of the paper about 1-2" up from the bottom. Repeat this process on the reverse side of the page.

Look at the highly effective result. You have ample room for notes, a left hand margin for special emphasis items or inserting supplementary data from the textbook, a large area at the bottom for a brief summary, and a little rectangular space for just about anything you want.

3. Get the concept then the details. Too often we focus on the details and don't gather an understanding of the concept; however, if you simply memorize only dates, places or names, you may well miss the whole point of the subject. A key way to understand things is to put them in your own words. If you are working from a textbook, automatically summarize each paragraph in your mind. If you are outlining text, don't simply copy the author's words.

Rephrase them in your own words. You remember your own thoughts and words much better than someone else's and subconsciously tend to associate the important details to the core concepts.

4. Ask Why? Pull apart written material paragraph by paragraph and don't forget the captions under the illustrations.

Example: If the heading is "Stream Erosion, *"flip it around to read "Why do streams erode?"* Then answer the questions.

If you train your mind to think in a series of questions and answers, not only will you learn more, but it also helps to lessen the test anxiety because you are used to answering questions.

5. Read for reinforcement and future needs. Even if you only have 10 minutes, put your notes or a book in your hand. Your mind is similar to a computer; you have to input data in order to have it processed. *By reading, you are creating the neural connections for future retrieval.* The more times you read something, the more you reinforce the learning of ideas.

Even if you don't fully understand something on the first pass, *your mind stores much of the material for later recall.*

6. Relax to learn so go into exile. Our bodies respond to an inner clock called biorhythms. Burning the midnight oil works well for some people, but not everyone.

If possible, set aside a particular place to study that is free of distractions. Shut off the television, cell phone, pager and exile your friends and family during your study period.

If you really are bothered by silence, try background music. Light classical music at a low volume has been shown to aid in concentration over other types.

Music that evokes pleasant emotions without lyrics are highly suggested. Try just about anything by Mozart. It relaxes you.

7. **Use arrows not highlighters**. At best, it's difficult to read a page full of yellow, pink, blue and green streaks.

Try staring at a neon sign for a while and you'll soon see my point, the horde of colors obscure the message.

A quick note, a brief dash of color, an underline and an arrow pointing to a particular passage is much clearer than a horde of highlighted words.

8. **Budget your study time.** Although you shouldn't ignore any of the material, *allocate your available study time in the same ratio that topics may appear on the test.*

TEACHER CERTIFICATION STUDY GUIDE

Testing Tips:

1. <u>Get smart, play dumb</u>. Don't read anything into the question. Don't make an assumption that the test writer is looking for something else than what is asked. Stick to the question as written and don't read extra things into it.

2. <u>Read the question and all the choices *twice* before answering the question</u>. You may miss something by not carefully reading, and then re-reading both the question and the answers.

If you really don't have a clue as to the right answer, leave it blank on the first time through. Go on to the other questions, as they may provide a clue as to how to answer the skipped questions.

If later on, you still can't answer the skipped ones. *Guess*.
The only penalty for guessing is that you *might* get it wrong. Only one thing is certain; if you don't put anything down, you will get it wrong!

3. <u>Turn the question into a statement</u>. Look at the way the questions are worded. The syntax of the question usually provides a clue. Does it seem more familiar as a statement rather than as a question? Does it sound strange?

By turning a question into a statement, you may be able to spot if an answer sounds right, and it may also trigger memories of material you have read.

4. <u>Look for hidden clues</u>. It's actually very difficult to compose multiple-foil (choice) questions without giving away part of the answer in the options presented.

In most multiple-choice questions you can often readily eliminate one or two of the potential answers. This leaves you with only two real possibilities and automatically your odds go to Fifty-Fifty for very little work.

5. <u>Trust your instincts</u>. For every fact that you have read, you subconsciously retain something of that knowledge. On questions that you aren't really certain about, go with your basic instincts. **Your first impression on how to answer a question is usually correct.**

6. <u>Mark your answers directly on the test booklet</u>. Don't bother trying to fill in the optical scan sheet on the first pass through the test.

Just be very careful not to miss-mark your answers when you eventually transcribe them to the scan sheet.

7. <u>Watch the clock</u>! You have a set amount of time to answer the questions. Don't get bogged down trying to answer a single question at the expense of 10 questions you can more readily answer.

LEARNING DISABLED

INTRODUCTION

This one-volume study guide was designed for professionals preparing to take a teacher competency test in special education or in any field in which the principles of special education are a part of the test content. Objectives specific to the field of special education were obtained from state departments of education and federal territories and dependencies across the nation. Educators preparing to take tests in the various areas of special education should find the manual helpful, for the objectives and the scope of the discussions concerning each objective cover a wide range of the field.

The study guide offers many benefits to the person faced with the necessity of making a qualifying score on a competency test in special education. A large number of source materials must be covered in order to study the conceptual knowledge reflected by the objectives listed in each state study guide. These objectives encompass the major content of the special education field. The term "objective" may be called "competency" in some states. These terms are synonymous and refer to an item of professional knowledge for mastery.

Many prominent textbooks used by preservice teacher training programs nationwide were researched for the content of this book. Other important resources (e.g. books, journal articles, and media) were included in the discussions about the objectives. The compilation of this research alleviates the hardship imposed on a teacher who attempts to accumulate, as one individual preparing for an examination, the vast body of professional material. This one-volume study guide highlights the current knowledge and accepted concepts of the field of special education, thus reducing the massive amount of material, which would need to be assembled if one did not have it between a single set of covers.

The book is organized by major topical sections. These topics often correspond with course titles and textbooks in pre-service teacher training programs. The objectives and discussions about them comprise the main content within each section. The discussions feature important information from textbooks in the field of special education, reported in the books in a synthesized and summarized form. Specific references have been given for charts and quoted materials, which were included to enhance understanding of conceptual discussions. Complete reference citations can be located in the reference listings. A glossary of terms is located at the end of each topical section. The definitions are stated in the contextual usage of special education.

Finally, questions specific to the discussion of each objective have been written to help determine if the reader understands that material. Correctness of responses to questions can be checked for immediate accuracy in the Answer Key section. Test questions are written as teaching mechanisms and appear in the style and format to cover those used on tests by any state.

Though this manual is comprehensive, it in no way purports to contain all the research and applied techniques in every area of exceptionality. Research generates new applications, and continuing in-service education is a requirement for all special education professionals. This manual gives the reader a one-volume summary of the fundamentals known and practiced at the time of writing.

TEACHER CERTIFICATION STUDY GUIDE

PRE-TEST

1. A ruling pertaining to the use of evaluation procedures later consolidated in Public Law 94 – 142 resulted from which court case listed?
   a. Diana v. the State Board of Education (1970)
   b. Wyatt v. Stickney
   c. Larry P. v. Riles
   d. PASE v. Hannon

Correct answer is "a."
Diana v. the State Board of Education resulted in the decision that all children must be evaluated in their native language.

2. Included in data brought to the attention of Congress regarding the evaluation procedures for education of students with disabilities was the fact that?
   a. There were a large number of children and youths with disabilities in the United States
   b. Many children with disabilities were not receiving an appropriate education
   c. Many parents of children with disabilities were forced to seek services outside of the public realm
   d. All of the above

Correct answer is "d."
All three factors, and many more, have driven Congress to act.

3. The Individuals with Disabilities Education Act (IDEA) was signed into law in and later reauthorized through second revision in what years?
   a. 1975 and 2004
   b. 1980 and 1990
   c. 1990 and 2004
   d. 1995 and 2001

Correct answer is "c."
IDEA, Public Law 101-476 is a consolidation and reauthorization of all prior Special Education mandates, with amendments. It was signed into law by President Bush on October 30, 1990. Revision of IDEA occurred in 2004, IDEA was re-authorized as the Individuals with Disabilities Education Improvement Act of 2004 (IDEIA 2004) is commonly referred to as IDEA 2004. IDEA 2004 (effective July 1, 2005).

LEARNING DISABLED

4. How was the training of Special Education teachers changed by the No Child Left Behind Act of 2002?
   a. Required all Special Education teachers to be certified in reading and math
   b. Required all Special Education teachers to take the same coursework as general education teachers
   c. If a Special Education teacher is teaching a core subject, he or she must meet the standard of a highly qualified teacher in that subject.
   d. All of the above

Correct answer is "c."
In order for special education teachers to be a students sole teacher of a core subject they must meet the professional criteria of NCLB. They must be *highly qualified*, that is certified or licensed in their area of special education and show proof of a specific level of professional development in the core subjects that they teach. As special education teachers received specific education in the core subject they teach, they will be better prepared to teach to the same level of learning standards as the general education teacher.

5. Which of the following is a specific change of language in the IDEA?
   a. The term "Disorder" changed to "Disability"
   b. The term "Children" changed to "Children and Youth"
   c. The term "Handicapped" changed to "Impairments"
   d. The term "Handicapped" changed to "With Disabilities"

Correct answer is "d."
"Children" became "individuals", highlighting the fact that some students with special needs were adolescents not just "children". The word "handicapped" was changed to "with disabilities", denoting the difference between limitations imposed by society, (handicap) and an inability to do certain things (disability). "With disabilities" also demonstrates that the person is thought of first, and the disabling condition is but one of the characteristics of the individual.

6. Which component changed with the reauthorization of the Education for all Handicapped Children Act of 1975 (EHA) 1990 EHA Amendment?
    a. Specific terminology
    b. Due Process Protections
    c. Non-Discriminatory Reevaluation Procedures
    d. Individual Education Plans

Correct answer is "a."
See Skill 1.1 Question # 5

7. The definition of Assistive technology devices was amended in the IDEA reauthorization of 2004 to exclude what?
    a. iPods other hand-held devices
    b. Computer enhanced technology
    c. Surgically implanted devices
    d. Braille and/or special learning aids

Correct answer is "c."
The definition of Assistive technology devices was amended to exclude devices that are surgically implanted (i.e. cochlear implants), and clarified that students with assistive technology devices shall not be prevented from having special education services. Assistive technology devices may need to be monitored by school personnel, but schools are not responsible for the implantation or replacement of such devices surgically.

8. Which of these factors relate to eligibility for learning disabilities?
    a. A discrepancy between potential and performance
    b. Sub-average intellectual functioning
    c. Social deficiencies or learning deficits that are not due to intellectual, sensory, or physical conditions
    d. Documented results of behavior checklists and anecdotal records of aberrant behavior

Correct answer is "a."
Tests need to show a discrepancy between potential and performance. Classroom observations and samples of student work (such as impaired reading ability) also provide indicators of possible learning disabilities. Eligibility for services in behavior disorders requires documented evidence of social deficiencies or learning deficits that are not due to intellectual, sensory, or physical conditions. Any student undergoing multidisciplinary evaluation is usually given an intelligence test, diagnostic achievement tests, and social and/or adaptive inventories. Answers b, c and d are symptoms displayed before testing for eligibility. Some students who display these symptoms do fail the tests and are not categorized as eligible to receive services.

LEARNING DISABLED

9. Which is untrue about the Americans with disabilities Act (ADA)?
    a. It was signed into law the same year as IDEA by President Bush
    b. It reauthorized the discretionary programs of EHA
    c. It gives protection to all people on the basis of race, sex, national origin, and religion
    d. It guarantees equal opportunities to persons with disabilities in employment, public accommodations, transportation, government services, and telecommunications.

Correct answer is "b."
EHA is the precursor of IDEA, the Individuals with Disabilities Education Act. ADA, however, is Public Law 101 – 336, the Americans with disabilities Act, which gives civil rights protection to all individuals with disabilities in private sector employment, all public services, public accommodations, transportation and telecommunications. It was patterned after the Rehabilitation Act of 1973.

10. Requirements for evaluations were changed in IDEA 2004 to reflect that no 'single' assessment or measurement tool can be used to determine special education qualification, furthering that a disproportionate representation of what types of students?
a. Disabled
b. Foreign
c. Gifted
d. Minority and Bilingual

Correct answer is "d."
IDEA 2004 recognized that there exists a disproportionate representation of minorities and bilingual students and that pre-service interventions that are *scientifically based on early reading programs, positive behavioral interventions and support,* and early intervening services may prevent some of those children from needing special education services.

11. IEPs continue to have multiple sections; one section, present levels now addresses what?
    a. Academic achievement and functional performance
    b. English as a second language
    c. Functional performance
    d. Academic achievement

Correct answer is "a."
Individualized Education Plans (IEPS) continue to have multiple sections. One section, present levels, now addresses academic achievement and functional performance. Annual IEP goals must now address the same areas.

12. What is true about IDEA? In order to be eligible, a student must:
    a. Have a medical disability
    b. Have a disability that fits into one of the categories listed in the law
    c. Attend a private school
    d. Be a slow learner

Correct answer is "b."
IDEA is a legal instrument, thus it is defined by law. Every aspect in the operation of IDEA is laid out in law.

13. What determines whether a person is entitled to protection under Section 504?
    a. The individual must meet the definition of a person with a disability
    b. The person must be able to meet the requirements of a particular program in spite of his or her disability
    c. The school, business or other facility must be the recipient of federal funding assistance
    d. All of the above

Correct answer is "d."
To be entitled to protection under Section 504, an individual must meet the definition of a person with a disability, which is: any person who (i) has a physical or mental impairment which substantially limits one or more of that person's major life activities, (ii) has a record of such impairment, or (iii) is regarded as having such an impairment. Major life activities are: caring for oneself, performing manual tasks, walking, seeing, hearing, speaking, breathing, learning, and working. The person must also be "otherwise qualified," which means that the person must be able to meet the requirements of a particular program in spite of the disability. The person must also be afforded "reasonable accommodations" by recipients of federal financial assistance.

14. The Free Appropriate Public Education (FAPE) describes Special Education and related services as?
    a. Public expenditure and standard to the state educational agency
    b. Provided in conformity with each student's individualized education program, if the program is developed to meet requirements of the law.
    c. Include preschool, elementary and/or secondary education in the state involved
    d. All of the above.

Correct answer is "d."
FAPE states that Special Education and related services are provided at public expense; meet the standards of the state educational agency; include preschool, elementary and/or secondary education in the state involved; and are provided in conformity with each student's IEP is the program is developed to meet requirements of the law.

15. Jane is a third grader. Mrs. Smith, her teacher, noted that Jane was having difficulty with math and reading assignments. The results from recent diagnostic tests showed a strong sight vocabulary, strength in computational skills, but a weakness in comprehending what she read. This weakness was apparent in mathematical word problems as well. The multi-disciplinary team recommended placement in a special education resource room for learning disabilities two periods each school day. For the remainder of the school day, her placement will be:
    a. In the Regular Classroom
    b. At a Special School
    c. In a Self-Contained Classroom
    d. In a Resource Room for Mental Retardation

Correct answer is "a."
The resource room is a special room inside the school environment where the child goes to be taught by a teacher who is certified in the area of disability. We hope the accommodations and services provided in the resource room will help her to catch up and perform with her peers in the regular classroom.

TEACHER CERTIFICATION STUDY GUIDE

16. Legislation in Public Law 94 – 142 attempts to:
    a. Match the child's educational needs with appropriate educational services
    b. Include parents in the decisions made about their child's education
    c. Establish a means by which parents can provide input
    d. All of the above

Correct answer is "d."
Much of what was stated in separate curt rulings and mandated legislation was brought together into what is now considered to be the "backbone" of special education. Public Law 94 – 142, (education for All Handicapped Children Act) was signed into law by President Ford in 1975. It was the culmination of a great deal of litigation and legislation from the late 1960's to the mid 1970's , that included decisions supporting the need to assure an appropriate education to all persons regardless of race, creed, or disability. In 1990, this law was reauthorized and renamed the Individuals with Disabilities education Act, IDEA.

17. Bob shows behavior problems like lack of attention, out of seat and talking out. His teacher has kept data on these behaviors and has found that Bob is showing much better self-control since he has been self-managing himself through a behavior modification program. The most appropriate placement recommendation for Bob at this time is probably:
    a. Any available part-time special education program
    b. The regular classroom solely
    c. A behavior disorders resource room for one period a day
    d. A specific learning disabilities resource room for one period a day

Correct answer is "b."
Bob is able to self-manage himself and is very likely to behave like the other children in the regular classroom. The classroom is the least restrictive environment.

18. Which is an educational characteristic common to students with mild intellectual learning and behavioral disabilities?
    a. Show interest in schoolwork
    b. Have intact listening skills
    c. Require modification in classroom instruction
    d. Respond better to passive than to active learning tasks

Correct answer is "c."
Here are some of the characteristics of students with mild learning and behavioral disabilities are as follows: Lack of interest in schoolwork; prefer concrete rather than abstract lessons; weak listening skills; low achievement; limited verbal and/or writing skills; respond better to active rather than passive learning tasks; Have areas of talent or ability often overlooked by teachers; prefer to receive special help in regular classroom; higher dropout rate than regular education students; achieve in accordance with teacher expectations; require modification in classroom instruction; and are easily distracted.

19. Michael's teacher complains that he is constantly out of his seat. She also reports that he has trouble paying attention to what is going on in class for more than a couple of minutes at a time. He appears to be trying, but his writing is often illegible, containing many reversals. Although he seems to want to please, he is very impulsive and stays in trouble with his teacher. He is failing reading, and his math grades, though somewhat better, are still below average. Michael's psychometric evaluation should include assessment for:
    a. Mild mental retardation
    b. Specific learning disabilities
    c. Mild behavior disorders
    d. Hearing impairment

Correct answer is "b."
Here are some of the characteristics of persons with learning disabilities:
- Hyperactivity: a rate o motor activity higher than normal
- Perceptual difficulties: visual, auditory, and hap tic perceptual problems
- Perceptual-motor impairments: poor integration of visual and motor systems, often affecting fine motor coordination.
- Disorders of memory and thinking: memory deficits, trouble with problem-solving, concept formation and association, poor awareness of own metacognitive skills (learning strategies)
- Impulsiveness: acts before considering consequences, poor impulse control, often followed by remorselessness.
- Academic problems in reading, math, writing or spelling; significant discrepancies in ability levels.

20. In general, characteristics of the learning disabled include:
    a. A low level of performance in a majority of academic skill areas
    b. Limited cognitive ability
    c. A discrepancy between achievement and potential
    d. A uniform pattern of academic development

Correct answer is "c."
The individual with a specific learning disability exhibits a discrepancy between achievement and potential.

21. Zero Reject requires all children with disabilities be provided with what?
    a. Total exclusion of Functional exclusion
    b. Adherence to the annual local education agency (LEA) reporting.
    c. Free, appropriate public education
    d. Both b and c.

Correct answer is "both a and c."
The principle of zero reject requires that all children with disabilities be provided with a free, appropriate public education and the LEA reporting procedure locates, identifies and evaluates children with disabilities within a given jurisdiction to ensure their attendance in public school.

22. Joey is in a mainstreamed preschool program. One of the means his teacher uses in determining growth in adaptive skills is that of observation. Some questions about Joey's behavior that she might ask include:
    a. Is he able to hold a cup?
    b. Can he call the name of any of his toys?
    d. Can he reach for an object and grasp it?
    e. All of the above

Correct answer is "d."
Here are some characteristics of individual with mental retardation or intellectual Disabilities:
- IQ of 70 or below
- Limited cognitive ability; delayed academic achievement, particularly in language-related subjects
- Deficits in memory which often relate to poor initial perception, or inability to apply stored information to relevant situations
- Impaired formulation of learning strategies
- Difficulty in attending to relevant aspects of stimuli: slowness in reaction time or in employing alternate strategies.

23. Individuals with mental retardation ca be characterized as:
    a. Often indistinguishable from normal developing children at an early age
    b. Having a higher than normal rate of motor activity
    c. Displaying significant discrepancies in ability levels
    d. Uneducable in academic skills

Correct answer is "a."
See rationale included in previous question and response.

24. Which of the following statements about children with an motional/behavioral disorder is true?
    a. They have very high IQs
    b. They display poor social skills
    c. They are poor academic achievers
    d. b and c

Correct answer is "d."
Children who exhibit mild behavioral disorders are characterized by:
- Average or above average scores o intelligence tests
- Poor academic achievement; learned helplessness
- Unsatisfactory interpersonal relationships
- Immaturity; attention seeking

Aggressive, acting-out behavior: (hitting, fighting, teasing, yelling, refusing to comply with requests, excessive attention seeking, poor anger control, temper tantrums, hostile reactions, defiant use of language) OR
Anxious, withdrawn behavior: (infantile behavior, social isolation, few friends, withdrawal into fantasy, fears, hypochondria, unhappiness, crying).

25. Which behavior would be expected at the mild level of emotional/behavioral disorders?
    a. Attention seeking
    b. Inappropriate affect
    c. Self-Injurious
    d. Poor sense of identity

Correct answer is "a."
See rationale to question 19.

26. Which of the following is true about autism?
    a. It is caused by having cold, aloof or hostile parents
    b. Approximately 4 out of 10 people have autism
    c. It is a separate exceptionality category in idea
    d. It is a form of mental illness

Correct answer is "c."
In IDEA, the 1990 Amendment to the Education for All Handicapped Children Act, autism was classified as a separate exceptionality category. It is thought to be caused by a neurological or biochemical dysfunction. It generally becomes evident before age 3. The condition occurs in about 4 of every 10,000 persons. Smith and Luckasson, 1992, describe it as a severe language disorder which affects thinking, communication, and behavior. They list the following characteristics:

- **Absent or distorted relationships with people**—inability to relate with people except as objects, inability to express affection, or ability to build and maintain only distant, suspicious or bizarre relationships.
- **Extreme or peculiar problems in communication**—absence of verbal language or language that is not functional such as echolalia (parroting what one hears), misuse of pronouns (e.g. he for you or I for her), neologisms (made-up meaningless words or sentences), talk that bears little or no resemblance to reality.
- **Self-stimulation**—repetitive stereo-typed behavior that seems to have no purposes other than providing sensory stimulation. this may take a wide variety of forms, such as swishing saliva, twirling objects, patting one's cheeks, flapping one's arms, staring,...etc.
- **Self-injury**—repeated physical self-abuse, such as biting, scratching, or poking oneself, head banging, ...etc
- **Perceptual anomalies**—unusual responses or absence of response to stimuli that seem to indicate sensory impairment or unusual sensitivity.

27. Autism is a condition characterized by:
    a. Distorted relationships with others
    b. Perceptual anomalies
    c. Self-stimulation
    d. All or the above

d. is correct.
See previous question.

28. As a separate exceptionality category in IDEA, autism:
    a. Includes emotional/behavioral disorders as defined in federal regulations
    b. Adversely affects educational performance
    c. Is thought to be a form of mental illness
    d. Is a developmental disability that affects verbal and non-verbal communication

Correct answer is "d."

29. Which of the following must be provided in a written notice to parents when proposing a child's educational placement?
    a. A list of parental due process safeguards
    b. A list of current test scores
    c. A list of persons responsible for the child's education
    d. A list of academic subjects the child has passed

Correct answer is "a."
Written notice must be provided to parents prior to a proposal or refusal or refusal to initiate or make a change in the child's identification, evaluation or educational placement. Notices must contain:
- A listing of parental due process safeguards.
- A description and a rationale for the chosen action.
- A detailed listing of components (e.g. tests, records, reports) which were
- the basis for the decision.
- Assurance that the language and content of the notices were understood by the parents.

30. Students who receive special services in a regular classroom with consultation, generally have academic and/or social-interpersonal performance deficits at which level of severity?
    a. Mild
    b. Moderate
    c. Severe
    d. Profound

Correct answer is "a."
The majority of students receiving special services are enrolled primarily in regular classes. Those with mild learning and behavior problems exhibit academic and/or social interpersonal deficits that are often evident only in a school-related setting. These students appear no different to their peers, physically.

31. The greatest number of students receiving special services are enrolled primarily in:
    a. The regular classroom
    b. The resource room
    c. Self-contained classrooms
    d. Special schools

Correct answer is "a."
See previous question.

32. The most restrictive environment in which an individual might be placed and receive instruction is that of:
    a. Institutional setting
    b. Homebound instruction
    c. Special schools
    d. Self-contained special classes

Correct answer is "a."
Individuals, who require significantly modified environments for care treatment and accommodation, are usually educated in an institutional setting. They usually have profound/multiple disorders.

TEACHER CERTIFICATION STUDY GUIDE

33. The law effects required components of the IEP, elements required by the IEP and the law are?
    a. Present level of academic and functional performance; statement of how the disability affects the student's involvement and progress; evaluation criteria and timeliness for instructional objective achievement; modifications of accommodations
    b. Projected dates for services initiation with anticipated frequency, location and duration; statement of when parent will be notified; statement of annual goals
    c. Extent to which child will not participate in regular education program; transitional needs for students age 14.
    d. All of the above.

Correct answer is "d."
IEPs state 14 elements that are required, review them in Skill 1.3 under IEP. Educators must keep themselves apprised of the changes and amendments to laws such as IDEA 2004 with addendums released in October of 2006.

34. The opportunity for persons with disabilities to live as close t the normal as possible describes:
a.   Least Restrictive Environment
    b. Normalization
    c. Mainstreaming
    d. Deinstitutionalization

Correct answer is "b."

35. Developmental Disabilities:
    a. Is the categorical name for mental retardation in IDEA
    b. Includes congenital conditions such as severe Spina Bifida, deafness, blindness or profound mental retardation
    c. Includes children who contract diseases such as polio or meningitis, and are left in an incapacitating functional state
    d. b and c

Correct answer is "d."

LEARNING DISABLED

TEACHER CERTIFICATION STUDY GUIDE

36. IDEA defines children with a disability as children evaluated in accordance with what?
a. 300.53.0200.4
b. 300.54.0200.6
c. 300.53.0300.5
d. None of the above

Correct answer is "c."
300.53.0300.5 defines disability as children who are mentally retarded, hard of hearing deaf, speech impaired, visually impaired, seriously emotionally disturbed, orthopedic ally impaired, other health impaired, deaf-blind, multi-handicapped, or as having specific learning disabilities, who, because of those impairments, need special education and related services (300.5).

37. Normality in child behavior is influenced by societies?
    a. Attitudes and cultural beliefs
    b. Religious beliefs
    c. Religious and cultural beliefs
    d. Attitudes and Victorian era motto

Correct answer is "a."

38. The CST coordinates and participates in due diligence through what process?
    a. Child study team meets first time without parents
    b. Teachers take child learning concerns to the school counselor
    c. School counselor contact parents for permission to perform screening assessments
    d. All of the above

Correct answer is "d."
The CST coordinates and participates in due diligence through a process that includes teachers or parents concerns about academic or functional development goes to the counselor who then obtain a permission for screening assessments of child's skills And, the results determine need, if needed child study team meets without parents first.

LEARNING DISABLED

39. When a student is identified as being at-risk academically or socially what does Federal law hope for first?
    a. Move the child quickly to assessment
    b. Place child in Special Education as soon as possible
    c. Observe child to determine what is wrong
    d. Perform remedial intervention in the classroom

Correct answer is "d."
Once a student is identified as being at-risk academically or socially, remedial interventions are attempted within the regular classroom. Federal legislation requires that sincere efforts be made to help the child learn in the regular classroom.

40. What do the 9th and 10th Amendments to the U.S. Constitution state about education?
    a. That education belongs to the people
    b. That education is an unstated power vested in the states
    c. That elected officials mandate education
    d. That education is free

41. The IDEA states that child assessment is?
    a. At intervals with teacher discretion
    b. Continuous on regular basis
    c. Left to the counselor
    d. Conducted annually

Correct answer is "b."
Assessments in Special Education are continuous and occur on a regular basis.

42. Safeguards against bias and discrimination in the assessment of children include:
    a. The testing of a child in Standard English
    b. The requirement for the use of one standardized test
    c. The use of evaluative materials in the child's native language or other mode of communication
    d. All testing performed by a certified, licensed, psychologist

Correct answer is "c."
The law requires that the child be evaluated in his native language, or mode of communication. The idea that a licensed psychologist evaluate the child does not meet the criteria if it is not done in the child's normal mode of communication.

43. Which is characteristic of group tests?
    a. Directions are always read to students
    b. The examiner monitors several students at the same time
    c. The teacher is allowed to probe students who almost have the correct answer
    d. Both quantitative and qualitative information may be gathered

Correct answer is "b."
In group tests, the examiner may provide directions for children up to and including fourth grade. Children write or mark their own responses. The examiner monitors the progress of several children at the same time. He cannot rephrase questions or probe or prompt responses. It is very difficult, almost impossible to obtain qualitative information in group tests. Group tests are appropriate for program evaluation, screening, and some types of program planning, such as tracking. Special consideration may need to be given if there is any motivational, personality, linguistic, or physically disabling factors that might impair the examinee's performance. When planning individual programs, individual tests should be used.

44. For which of the following uses are individual tests most appropriate?
    a. Screening students to determine possible need for special education services
    b. Evaluation of special education curricular
    c. Tracking of gifted students
    d. Evaluation of a student for eligibility and placement, or individualized program planning, in special education

Correct answer is "d."
See previous question.

45. Which of the following is an advantage of giving individual, rather than group tests?
    a. The test administrator can control the tempo of an individual test, giving breaks when needed
    b. The test administrator can clarify or rephrase questions
    c. Individual tests provide for the gathering of both qualitative and quantitative results
    d. All of the above

Correct answer is "d."

TEACHER CERTIFICATION STUDY GUIDE

46. Mrs. Stokes has been teaching her third-grade students about mammals during a recent science unit. Which of the following would be true of a criterion-referenced test she might administer at the conclusion of the unit?
    a. It will be based on unit objectives
    b. Derived scores will be used to rank student achievement.
    c. Standardized scores are effective of national performance samples
    d. All of the above

Correct answer is "a."
Criterion-referenced tests measure the progress made by individuals in mastering specific skills. The content is based on a specific set of objectives rather than on the general curriculum. Criterion-referenced tests provide measurements pertaining to the information a given student needs to know and the skills that student needs to master. Norm-referenced tests have a large advantage over criterion-referenced tests when used for screening or program evaluation. Norm-referenced tests provide a means of comparing a student's performance to the performance typically expected of others of his age.

47. For which of the following purposes is a norm-referenced test least appropriate?
    a. Screening
    b. Individual program planning
    c. Program evaluation
    d. Making placement decisions

Correct answer is "b."

48. Criterion referenced tests can provide information about:
    a. Whether a student has mastered prerequisite skills
    b. Whether a student is ready to proceed to the next level of instruction
    c. which instructional materials might be helpful in covering program objectives
    d. All of the above

Correct answer is "a."
In criterion referenced testing, the emphasis is on assessing specific and relevant behaviors that have been mastered. Items on criterion-referenced tests are often linked directly to specific instructional objectives.

LEARNING DISABLED

49. Which of the following purposes of testing calls for an informal test?
    a. Screening a group of children to determine their readiness for the first reader
    b. Measure the content of a social studies unit prepared by the classroom teacher covering one aspect of the general curriculum
    c. Evaluating the effectiveness of a fourth-grade math program at the end of its first year of use in a specific school
    d. Determining the general level of intellectual functioning of a class of fifth graders

Correct answer is "b."
Formal tests are commercially prepared standardized tests. Formal tests may be categorized as norm-referenced or as criterion-referenced. Informal tests are usually teacher-prepared. These are usually criterion referenced. b is the only teacher-made test.

50. Which of the following is **not** a true statement about informal tests?
    a. Informal tests are useful in comparing students to others of their age or grade level
    b. The correlation between curriculum and test criteria is much higher in informal tests
    c. Informal tests are useful in evaluating an individual's response to instruction
    d. Informal tests are used to diagnose a student's particular strengths and weaknesses for purposes of planning individual programs

Correct answer is "a."
Informal or teacher-made tests are usually criterion-referenced. Norm-referenced tests are usually group tests given to large populations, rather than individualized, or teacher-made.

51. For which situation might a teacher be apt to select a formal test?
    a. A pretest for studying world religions
    b. A weekly spelling test
    c. To compare student progress with that of peers of same age or grade level on a national basis
    d. To determine which content objectives outlined on the student's IEPs were mastered

Correct answer is "c."
See previous question.

LEARNING DISABLED

52. The extent to which a test measures what its authors or users claim that it measures is called its:
    a. Validity
    b. Reliability
    c. Normality
    d. Acculturation

Correct answer is "a."
Validity: degree or extent to which a test measures what it was designed or intended to measure.
Reliability: the extent to which a test is consistent in its measurements.

53. Which of the following is a factor in determining test validity?
    a. The appropriateness of the sample items chosen to measure a criterion
    b. The acculturation of the norm group as compared to that of the population being tested
    c. The reliability of the test
    d. All of the above

Correct answer is "d."
Validity can be affected by:
- The appropriateness of the sample items chosen to measure a criterion
- The cultural, environmental and language background of the norm group as compared to that of the population being tested
- The accuracy with which a person's performance on a criterion can be predicted from his test score on that criterion
- The consistency in administration and scoring of the test
- The reliability of the test

54. If a scholastic aptitude test is checked against predictive success in academic endeavors, which type of validity is one attempting to establish?
    a. Content
    b. Criterion-related
    c. Construct
    d. Confirmation

Correct answer is "b."
There are different kinds of evidence to support a particular judgment. If the purpose of a test is to measure the skills covered in a particular course or unit, then we would hope to see test questions on all the important topics and not on extraneous topics. If this condition is met, then we would have content validity. Some tests, like the SAT, are designed to predict outcomes. If SAT scores correlate with academic performance in college, as measured by GPA in the first year, then, we have criterion related validity. Construct validity is probably the most important. It is gathered over many years, and is indicated by a pattern of scores e.g. older children can answer more questions on intelligence tests than younger children. This fits with our construct of intelligence.

55. Acculturation refers to the individual's:
    a. Gender
    b. Experiential background
    c. Social class
    d. Ethnic background

Correct answer is "b."
A person's culture has little to do with gender, or social class, or ethnicity. A person is the product of his experiences. Acculturation: differences in experiential background.

56. To which aspect does fair assessment relate?
    a. Representation
    b. Acculturation
    c. Language
    d. All of the above

Correct answer is "d."
All three aspects are necessary and vital for assessment to be fair.

LEARNING DISABLED

57. Youngsters in regular classrooms receive regular testing primarily related to:
    a. Eligibility for special education
    b. Promotion by grade level
    c. IEP program planning
    d. All of the above

Correct answer is "b."
Promotion by grade level is the only reason for testing of regular students in regular classrooms.

58. Which of the following statements reflects true factors that affect the reliability of a test?
    a. Short tests tend to be more reliable than long tests
    b. The shorter the time length between two administrations of a test, the greater the possibility that the scores will change
    c. Even if guessing results in a correct response, it introduces error into a test score and into interpretation of the results
    d. All of the above

Correct answer is "c."
The reliability of a test is concerned with the extent to which the person tested will receive the same score on repeated administrations of that test. When a person's score fluctuates randomly, the test lacks reliability.

59. Mrs. Freud administered a personality traits survey to her high school psychology class. She readministered the same survey two weeks later. The method which she used to determine reliability was that of:
    a. Test-retest
    b. Split half
    c. Alternate form
    d. Kuder-Richardson formula

Correct answer is "a."
The test-retest reliability is accomplished by do the same test on a second occasion.

TEACHER CERTIFICATION STUDY GUIDE

60. Children who write poorly might be given tests which allow oral responses that are unless the purpose for giving the test is to:
    a. Assess handwriting skills
    b. Test for organization of thoughts
    c. Answer questions pertaining to math reasoning
    d. Assess rote memory

Correct answer is "a."
It is necessary to have the child write, if we are assessing his skill in that domain.

61. Which of the following types of tests is used to estimate learning potential and to predict academic achievement?
    a. Intelligence tests
    b. Achievement tests
    c. Adaptive behavior tests
    d. Personality tests

Correct answer is "a."
An intelligence test is designed to measure intellectual abilities like memory, comprehension and abstract reasoning. IQ is often used to estimate the learning capacity of a student as well as to predict academic his achievement.

62. Which skills are typically assessed by an intelligence test?
    a. Abstract reasoning, comprehension
    b. Interest, capacity
    c. Math computation, math-reasoning skills
    d. Independent functioning, language development

Correct answer is "a."
See previous question.

63. In which of the following exceptionality categories may a student be considered for inclusion if his IQ score falls more than two standard deviations below the mean?
    a. Mental retardation
    b. Specific learning disabilities
    c. Emotionally/behaviorally disordered
    d. Gifted

Correct answer is "a."
Only about 1 to 1.5% of the population fit the AAMD's definition of mental retardation. They fall outside the 2 standard deviations limit for Special Learning Disabilities and Emotionally/Behaviorally disordered.

LEARNING DISABLED

64. A test, which measures students' skill development in academic content areas, is classified as an _____ test.
    a. Achievement
    b. Aptitude
    c. Adaptive
    d. Intelligence

Correct answer is "a."
Achievement tests directly assess students' skill development in academic content areas. It measures the degree to which a student has benefited education and/or life experiences compared to others of the same age or grade level. They may be used as diagnostic tests to find strengths and weaknesses of students. They may be used for screening, placement progress evaluation, and curricular effectiveness.

65. The Key Math Diagnostic Arithmetic Test is an individually administered test of math skills. It is comprised of fourteen subtests which are classified into the major math areas of content, operations, and applications for which subtest scores are reported. The test manual describes the population sample upon which the test was normed, and reports data pertaining to reliability and validity. In addition, for each item in the test, a behavioral objective is presented. From the description, it can be determined that this achievement test is:
    a. Individually administered
    b. Criterion-referenced
    c. Diagnostic
    d. All of the above

Correct answer is "d."
The test has a limited content designed to measure to what extent the student has mastered specific areas in math. The expressions "individually administered" and "diagnostic" appear in the description of the test.

66. The best measures of a student's functional capabilities and entry level skills are:
    a. Norm-referenced tests
    b. Teacher-made post-tests
    c. Standardized I Q tests
    d. Criterion referenced measures

Correct answer is "d."
Criterion-referenced measures are useful for assessment of a student's functional capabilities and entry-level skills. unlike norm-referenced tests, which compare an individual with others of the same grade or age level, criterion-referenced tests, measures the level of functions and skills if the individual.

67. A prerequisite skill is:
    a. The lowest order skill in a hierarchy of skills, needed to perform a specific task
    b. A skill which must be demonstrated before instruction on a specific task can begin
    c. A tool for accomplishing task analysis
    d. The smallest component of any skill

Correct answer is "b."
This is an enabling skill that a student needs in order to perform an objective successfully.

68. Presentation of tasks can be altered to match the student's rate of learning by:
    a. Describing how much of a topic is presented in one day and how much practice is assigned, according to the student's abilities and learning style
    b. Using task analysis, assign a certain number of skills to be mastered in a specific amount of time
    c. Introducing a new task only when the student has demonstrated mastery of the previous task in the learning hierarchy
    d. a and c

Correct answer is "d."
Pacing is the term used for altering of tasks to match the student's rate of learning. This can be done in two ways; altering the subject content and the rate at which tasks are presented.

69. All of the following are suggestions for altering the presentation of tasks to match the student's rate of learning except:
    a. Teach in several shorter segments of time rather than a single lengthy session
    b. Continue to teach a task until the lesson is completed in order to provide more time on task
    c. Watch for nonverbal cues that indicate students are becoming confused, bored, or restless
    d. Avoid giving students an inappropriate amount of written work

Correct answer is "b."
This action taken does not alter the subject content; neither does it alter the rate at which tasks are presented.

70. In which of the following ways does an effective teacher cooperate pacing as a means of matching a student's rate of learning?
    a. Selected content is presented based upon prerequisite skills
    b. Task presentations are paced during optimum time segments
    c. Special needs students always require smaller steps and learning segments regardless of the activity or content
    d. a and b

Correct answer is "d."
C is not a true statement. A and B are true statements.

TEACHER CERTIFICATION STUDY GUIDE

71. Which of the following examples would be considered of highest priority when determining the need for the delivery of appropriate special education and related services?
    a. An eight-year-old boy is repeating first grade for the second time and exhibits problems with toileting, gross motor functions, and remembering number and letter symbols. His regular classroom teacher claims the referral forms are too time-consuming and refuses to complete them. He also refuses to make accommodations because he feels every child should be treated alike.
    b. A six-year-old girl who has been diagnosed as autistic is placed in a special education class within the local school. Her mother wants her to attend residential school next year, even though the girl is showing progress.
    c. A ten-year-old girl with profound mental retardation who is receiving education services in a state institution.
    d. A twelve-year-old boy with mild disabilities who was placed in a behavior disorders program, but displays obvious perceptual deficits (e.g. reversal of letters and symbols, and inability to discriminate sounds). He originally thought to have a learning disability, but did not meet state criteria for this exceptionality category, based on results of standard scores. He has always had problems with attending to a task, and is now beginning to get into trouble during seatwork time. His teacher feels that he will eventually become a real behavior problem. He receives social skills training in the resource room one period a day.

Correct answer is "a."
No modifications are being made, so the child is not receiving any services whatsoever.

72. Which of the following would be classified as direct rather than indirect services that a specially trained special education teacher would provide to regular education teachers?
    a. Answer questions about a particular child's academic or social-interpersonal needs
    b. Teach a math unit on measurement
    c. Assist with selecting special materials for a student
    d. Develop math worksheets tailored to meet a student's needs

Correct answer is "b."
Indirect services are those given when special education personnel consult with regular classroom teachers to assist them in teaching students with mild disabilities who are enrolled fulltime in their regular classrooms. Direct services are those in which personnel work with the students in the classroom to remediate difficulties.

LEARNING DISABLED

73. Which is a less than ideal example of collaboration in successful inclusion?
    a. Special education teachers are part of the instructional team in a regular classroom
    b. Special education teachers assist regular education teachers in the classroom
    c. Teaming approaches are used for problem solving and program implementation
    d. Regular teachers, special education teachers, and other specialists or support teachers co-teach

Correct answer is "b."
In a special education setting, the special education teacher should be the lead teacher.

74. Which of the following is an example of tactile perception?
    a. Making an angel in the snow with one's body
    b. Running a specified course
    c. Identifying a rough surface with eyes closed
    d. Demonstrating aerobic exercises

Correct answer is "c."
Tactile: having to do with touch.

75. Which of the following activities best exemplifies a kinesthetic exercise in developing body awareness?
    a. Touching materials of different textures
    b. Playing a game like "Looby Loo"
    c. Identifying geometric shapes being drawn on one's back
    d. Making a shadow-box project

Correct answer is "b."
Kinesthetic: having to do with body movement.

76. Which of the following teaching activities is least likely to enhance observational learning in students with special needs?
    a. A verbal description of the task to be performed, followed by having the children immediately attempt to perform the instructed behavior
    b. A demonstration of the behavior, followed by an immediate opportunity for the children to imitate the behavior
    c. A simultaneous demonstration and explanation of the behavior, followed by ample opportunity for the children to rehearse the instructed behavior
    d. Physically guiding the children through the behavior to be imitated, while verbally explaining the behavior

Correct answer is "a."
Students are given verbal instructions only. The children are not given a chance to observe, or see, the behavior so that they can imitate it. Some of the students may have hearing deficiencies.

77. The _____ modality is most frequently used in the learning process.
    a. Auditory
    b. Visual
    c. Tactile
    d. All of the Above

Correct answer is "d."
The auditory, visual, and tactile modalities are the ones frequently used in the learning process. We learn through an integration of these modalities (multi-sensory approach).

78. Which of the following is an example of cross-modal perception involving integrating visual stimuli to an auditory verbal process?
    a. Following spoken directions
    b. Describing a picture
    c. Finding certain objects in pictures
    d. b and c

Correct answer is "b."
We see (visual modality) the picture and use words (auditory modality) to describe it.

TEACHER CERTIFICATION STUDY GUIDE

79. Which of the following is a good example of a generalization?
    a. Jim has learned to add and is now ready to subtract
    b. Sarah adds sets of units to obtain a product
    c. Bill recognizes a vocabulary word on a billboard when traveling
    d. Jane can spell the word "net" backwards to get the word "ten"

Correct answer is "c."
Generalization is the occurrence of a learned behavior in the presence of a stimulus other than the one that produced the initial response. It is the expansion of a student's performance beyond the initial setting. Students must be able to expand or transfer what is learned to other settings (e.g., reading to math word problems, resource room to regular classroom). Generalization may be enhanced by the following:
- Use many examples in teaching to deepen application of learned skills
- Use consistency in initial teaching situations, and later introduce variety in format, procedure and use of examples
- Have the same information presented by different teachers, in different settings, and under varying conditions
- Include a continuous reinforcement schedule at first, later changing to delayed and intermittent schedules as instruction progresses
- Teach students to record instances of generalization and to reward themselves at that time
- Associate naturally occurring stimuli when possible

80. _____ is a method used to increase student engaged learning time by having students teach other students.
    a. Collaborative learning
    b. Engaged learning time
    c. Allocated learning time
    d. Teacher consultation

Correct answer is "a."
Collaborative Learning is a method for increasing student learning time by having students teach other students.

LEARNING DISABLED

81. Which is NOT included by Henley, Ramsey, and Algozzine (1993) as steps teachers use to establish cooperative learning groups in the classroom? The teacher:
    a. Selects Members of Each Learning Group
    b. Directly Teaches Cooperative Group Skills
    c. Assigns Cooperative Group Skills
    d. Has Students Self-Evaluate Group Efforts

Correct answer is "d."
According to Henley et al, there are four steps to establishing cooperative learning groups:
1. The teacher selects members of each learning group
2. The teacher directly teaches cooperative group skills
3. The teacher assigns cooperative group activities
4. The teacher evaluates group efforts

82. Some environmental elements which influence learning styles include all except:
    a. Light
    b. Temperature
    c. Design
    d. Motivation

Correct answer is "d."
Individual learning styles are influenced by environmental, emotional, sociological, and physical elements. Environmental include sound, light, temperature and design. Emotional elements such as motivation, persistence, responsibility and structure. Motivation is not an environmental element.

LEARNING DISABLED

83. When teaching a student, who is predominantly auditory, to read, it is best to:
    a. Stress sight vocabulary
    b. Stress phonetic analysis
    c. Stress the shape and configuration of the word
    d. Stress rapid reading

Correct answer is "b."
Sensory modalities are one of the physical elements that affect learning style. Some students learn best through their visual sense (sight), others through their auditory sense (hearing) and still others by doing, touching and moving (tactile-kinesthetic). Auditory learners generally listen to people, follow verbal directions, and enjoy hearing records, cassette tapes, and stories. Phonics has to do with sound, an auditory stimulus.

84. If a student is predominantly a visual learner, he may learn more effectively by:
    a. Reading aloud while studying
    b. Listening to a cassette tape
    c. Watching a film strip
    d. Using body movement

Correct answer is "c."
Visual learners use their sense of sight, which is the sense being used to watch a filmstrip.

85. Cognitive learning strategies include:
    a. Reinforcing appropriate behavior
    b. Teaching students how to manage their own behavior in school
    c. Heavily structuring the learning environment
    d. Generalizing learning from one setting to another

Correct answer is "b."
See previous question.

86. The effective teacher varies her instructional presentations and response requirements depending upon:
    a. Student needs
    b. The task at hand
    c. The learning situation
    d. All of the above

Correct answer is "d."

87. In order for a student to function independently in the learning environment, which of the following must be true?
    a. The learner must understand the nature of the content
    b. The student must be able to do the assigned task
    c. The teacher must communicate performance criteria to the learner
    d. All of the above

Correct answer is "d."
Together with the above, the child must be able to ask for and obtain assistance if necessary.

88. Cognitive modeling is an essential component of which self-training approach?
    a. Self-instructional training
    b. Self-monitoring
    c. Self-reinforcing
    d. Self-punishing

Correct answer is "a."
Cognitive modeling: The adult model performs a task while verbally instructing himself
Self-instruction: The child performs the task while instructing himself, silently or overtly
Self-monitoring: Refers to procedures by which the learner records whether or not he is engaging in certain behaviors, particularly those that would lead to increased academic achievement and/or social behavior

89. Strategies specifically designed to move the learner from dependence to independence include:
    a. Assessment, planning, implementation, and reevaluation
    b. Demonstration, imitation, assistance, prompting, and verbal instruction
    c. Cognitive modeling and self-guidance through overt, faded overt and covert stages
    d. b and c

Correct answer is "a."
Both are correct, as demonstration is a form of modeling.

90. Alan has failed repeatedly in his academic work. He needs continuous feedback in order to experience small, incremental achievements. What type of instructional material would best meet this need?
    a. Programmed materials
    b. Audiotapes
    c. Materials with no writing required
    d. Worksheets

Correct answer is "a."
Programmed materials are best suited as Alan would be able to chart his progress as he achieves each goal. He can monitor himself and take responsibility for his successes.

91. After purchasing what seemed to be a very attractive new math kit for use with her SLD (severely learning disabled) students, Ms. Davis discovered her students could not use the kit unless she read the math problems and instructions to them, as the readability level was higher than the majority of the students' functional reading capabilities. Which criterion of the materials selection did Ms. Davis most likely fail to consider when selecting this math kit?
    a. Durability
    b. Relevance
    c. Component Parts
    d. Price

Correct answer is "b."
Relevance is the only cognitive factor, listed. Since her students were severely learning disabled, she almost certainly would have considered the kit's durability and component parts. She did not have to consider price. That would be taken care of by the district.

92. Which of the following questions most directly evaluates the utility of instructional material?
    a. Is the cost within budgetary means?
    b. Can the materials withstand handling by students?
    c. Are the materials organized in a useful manner?
    d. Are the needs of the students met by the use of the materials?

Correct answer is "c."
It is a question of utility or usefulness.

93. Which of the following is descriptive of a good safety precaution when operating equipment?
    a. Reporting malfunctioning of a machine to the school's media specialist
    b. Leaving the room while a filmstrip is being shown in class
    c. Operating a machine with frayed cords
    d. Allowing an overhead projector to remain set up and plugged into a wall receptacle so the next class can view the transparencies too

Correct answer is "a."
All three others are hazardous practices, and should not be allowed to happen.

94. John learns best through the auditory channel, so his teacher wants to reinforce his listening skills. Through which of the following types of equipment would instruction be most effectively presented?
    a. Overhead projector
    b. Cassette player
    c. Microcomputer
    d. Opaque projector

Correct answer is "b."
Audio cassette player would help sharpen and further develop his listening skills as he is an auditory learner.

95. A money bingo game was designed by Ms Johnson for use with her middle grade students. Cards were constructed with different combinations of coins pasted on each of the nine spaces. Ms. Johnson called out various amounts of change (e.g. 30 cents) and students were instructed t cover the coin combinations on their cards which equaled the amount of change (e.g. two dimes and two nickels, three dimes, and so on). The student who had the first bingo was required to add the coins in each of the spaces covered and tell the amounts before being declared the winner. Five of Ms. Johnson's sixth graders played the game the ten minute free activity time following math the first day the game was constructed. Which of the following attributes are present in this game in this situation?
    a. Accompanied by simple, uncomplicated rules
    b. Of brief duration, permitting replay
    c. Age appropriateness
    d. All of the above

Correct answer is "d."
Games and puzzles should also be colorful and appealing, of relevance to individual students, and appropriate for learners at different skill levels, in order to sustain interest and motivational value.

96. For which stage of learning would computer software be utilized that allows for continued drill and practice of a skill to achieve accuracy and speed?
    a. Acquisition
    b. Proficiency
    c. Maintenance
    d. Generalization

Correct answer is "b."
Acquisition: Introduction of a new skill.
Maintenance: Continued practice without further instruction.
Proficiency: Practice under supervision to achieve accuracy and speed.
Generalization: Application of the new skills in new settings and situations.

97. In which way is a computer like an effective teacher?
    a. Provides immediate feedback
    b. Sets the pace at the rate of the average student
    c. Produces records of errors made, only
    d. Programs to skill levels at which students at respective chronological ages should be working

Correct answer is "a."

98. During which written composition stage are students encouraged to read their stories aloud to others?
    a. Planning
    b. Drafting
    c. Revising/editing
    d. Sharing/publication

Correct answer is "c."
It is encouraged at this stage as both the child and the audience will distinguish errors and make corrections. The child also learns to accept constructive criticism.

99. Which recently developed assistive device can "read' aloud sections from a newspaper received electronically?
    a. Soniguide
    b. Personal companion
    c. Closed circuit television
    d. Talking books

Correct answer is "b."
The Personal Companion can "read" aloud sections from newspapers delivered over telephone lines. This machine can maintain a daily appointment book, and turn appliances on and off.

100. Which electronic device enables persons with hearing impairments to make and receive phone calls?
    a. Personal companion
    b. Telecommunication device for the deaf
    c. Deafnet
    d. Hearing aids

Correct answer is "b."

101. Which electronic device can assist by dialing a telephone, turning book pages, and drinking from a cup?
    a. Communication boards
    b. Manipulator robots
    c. Electronic switches
    d. Crutches

Correct answer is "b."
As the name implies, a manipulator robot is a moving, electronic device that can be manipulated or controlled.

102. Behaviorists contend that all behavior is:
    a. Predictable
    b. Observed
    c. Conditioned
    d. Learned

Correct answer is "d."
Behavior modification is based on the premise that all behavior, regardless of its appropriateness, has been learned, and therefore, can be changed.

103. Procedures employed to decrease targeted behaviors include:
    a. Punishment
    b. Negative reinforcement
    c. Shaping
    d. a and b

Correct answer is "a."
Punishment and extinction may be used to decrease target behaviors.

104. Which description best characterizes primary reinforcers of an edible nature?
    a. Natural
    b. Unconditioned
    c. Innately motivating
    d. All of the above

Correct answer is "d."
Primary reinforcers are those stimuli which are of biological importance to an individual. They are natural, unlearned, unconditioned, and innately motivating. The most common and appropriate reinforcer used in the classroom is food.

105. Mrs. Chang is trying to prevent satiation from occurring, so that her reinforcers will be effective, as she is using a continuous reinforcement schedule. Which of the following ideas would be least effective in preventing satiation?
    a. Use only one type of edible rather than a variety
    b. Ask for ten vocabulary words rather than twenty
    c. Give pieces of cereal, bits of fruit, or M&Ms rather than large portions of edibles
    d. Administer a peanut then a sip of water

Correct answer is "a."
Here are some suggestions for preventing satiation:
- Vary reinforcers with instructional tasks
- Shorten the instructional sessions, and presentation of reinforcers will be decreased
- Alternate reinforcers (e.g. food, then juice)
- Decrease the size of edibles presented
- Have an array of edibles available

106. Which tangible reinforcer would Mr. Whiting find to be most effective with teenagers?
    a. Plastic whistle
    b. Winnie-the-Pooh book
    c. Poster of a current rock star
    d. Toy ring

Correct answer is "c."
This tops the list of things that teenagers crave. It is the most desirable.

107. Which is an example of a secondary reinforcer?
    a. Water
    b. Praise
    c. Hug
    d. b and c

Correct answer is "d."
Secondary reinforcers are not necessarily naturally reinforcing to most people. Their value is learned or conditioned through an association, or pairing, with primary reinforcers. Secondary reinforcers include social participation in preferred activities, praise, body language and attention.

108. Which is not a valid reason for using a secondary reinforcer?
    a. The possibility of satiation, using a primary reinforcer
    b. The pairing of a primary reinforcer with a secondary reinforcer, which requires too much time and effort
    c. The inability to assure a state of deprivation when using a primary reinforcer
    d. The possibility of student dependency upon the primary reinforcer

Correct answer is "b."
Some reasons for using secondary reinforcers are:
- The student may become temporarily satiated with the primary reinforcer
- The inability to assure a state of deprivation when using a primary reinforcer
- The possibility of student dependency upon the primary reinforcer

109. Positive reinforcer is generally effective if it is desired by the student and:
    a. Is worthwhile in size
    b. Given immediately after the desired behavior
    c. Given only upon the occurrence of the target behavior
    d. All of the above

Correct answer is "d."
Timing and quality of the reinforcer are key to encourage the individual to continue the targeted behavior.

110. Which of the following is a behavioral rule, which places emphasis on consequential events?
    a. Behavior that is reinforced tends to occur more frequently
    b. Behavior that is no longer reinforced will be extinguished
    c. Behavior that is punished occurs less frequently
    d. All of the above

Correct answer is "d."
The basic rules of behaviorism are stated in a, b, and c.

111. Dispensing school supplies is a component associated with which type of reinforcement system?
    a. Activity reinforcement
    b. Tangible reinforcement
    c. Token reinforcement
    d. b and c

Correct answer is "a."
The Premack Principle states that any activity in which a student voluntarily participates on a frequent basis can be used as a reinforcer for any activity in which the student seldom participates. Running errands, decorating bulletin boards, leading group activities, passing out books or papers, collecting materials, or operating equipment, all provide activity reinforcement.

112. Which type of reinforcement system is most easily generalized into other settings?
    a. Social reinforcement
    b. Activity reinforcement
    c. Tangible reinforcement
    d. Token reinforcement

Correct answer is "a."
There are many advantages to social reinforcement. It is easy to use, takes little of the teacher's time or effort, and is available in any setting. It is always positive, unlikely to satiate, and can be generalized to most situations.

113. Bill talks out in class an average of 15 times an hour. Other youngsters sometimes talk out, but Bill does so as a higher:
    a. Rate
    b. Intensity
    c. Volume
    d. Degree

Correct answer is "a."
Rate or frequency is the number of times the behavior is displayed in a given period.

114. Which category of behaviors would most likely be found on a behavior rating scale?
    a. Disruptive, acting out
    b. Shy, withdrawn
    c. Aggressive (physical or verbal)
    d. All of the above

Correct answer is "d."
These are all possible problem behaviors that can adversely impact the student or the class, thus they may be found on behavior rating scales.

115. The social skills of students in mental retardation programs are likely to be appropriate for children of their mental age, rather than chronological age. This means that the teacher will need to do all of the following except:
    a. Model desired behavior
    b. Provide clear instructions
    c. Expect age appropriate behaviors
    d. Adjust the physical environment when necessary

Correct answer is "c."
Age appropriate means mental age appropriate, not chronological age appropriate.

116. Target behaviors must be:
    a. Observable
    b. Measurable
    c. Definable
    d. All of the above

Correct answer is "d."
Behaviors must be observable, measurable and definable in order to be assessed and changed.

117. The Carrow Elicited Language Inventory is a test designed to give the examiner diagnostic information about a child's expressive grammatical competence. Which of the following language components is being assessed?
    a. Phonology
    b. Morphology
    c. Syntax
    d. b and c

Correct answer is "c."
- Morphology and syntax refer to refer to understanding grammatical structure of language in the receptive channel, and using the grammatical structure of language in the expressive channel.
- Assessment of morphology refers to linguistic structure of words.
- Assessment of syntax includes grammatical usage of word classes, word order, and transformational rules for the variance of word order.

118. In the Grammatic Closure subtest of the Illinois Test of Psycholinguistic Abilities, the child is presented with a picture representing statements such as the following: "Here is one die; here are two ____." This test is essentially a test of:
    a. Phonology
    b. Morphology
    c. Syntax
    d. Semantics

c. is correct.

119. Five-year-old Tom continues to substitute the "w" sound for the "r" sound when pronouncing words; therefore, he often distorts words e.g., "wabbit" for "rabbit" and "wat" for "rat." His articulation disorder is basically a problem in:
    a. Phonology
    b. Morphology
    c. Syntax
    d. Semantics

Correct answer is "a."
Phonology: the study of significant units of speech sounds
Morphology: The study of the smallest units of language that convey meaning.
Syntax: A system of rules for making grammatically correct sentences
Semantics: the study of the relationships between words and grammatical forms in a language, and their underlying meaning

120. Which of the following is untrue about the ending "er?"
   a. It is an example of a free morpheme
   b. It represents one of the smallest units of meaning within a word
   c. It is called an inflectional ending
   d. When added to a word, it connotes a comparative status

Correct answer is "a."
Morpheme: the smallest unit of meaningful language. "Er" on its own, has no meaning.

121. Which component of language involves **language content** rather than the form of language?
   a. Phonology
   b. Morphology
   c. Semantics
   d. Syntax

c. is correct.

122. Matthew's conversational speech is adequate, but when he tries to speak before a group of more than two listeners, his speech becomes mumbling and halting. which of the following activities would be least helpful in strengthening Matthew's self-expression skills?
   a. Having him participate in show-and-tell time
   b. Asking him comprehension questions about a story that was read to the class
   c. Having him recite a poem in front of the class, with two other children
   d. Asking him to tell a joke to the rest of the class

Correct answer is "a."
This exercise helps him to speak before a group larger than two listeners but smaller than the class.

123. Which of the following language skills involve encoding?
   a. Application
   b. Interpretation
   c. Comprehension
   d. Self-Expression

Correct answer is "d."
The child who has difficulty in verbalizing his thoughts and feelings (self-expression) has a problem **encoding** language. The child who has difficulty understanding what is said to him, relating it to situations with which he is familiar, or applying it to a new or different situation, may have a problem **decoding** language.

124. The child who has a problem decoding language, may exhibit difficulty:
    a. Understanding what is said to him
    b. Relating what was said, to familiar situations or objects
    c. Generalizing what was stated to new and appropriate situations
    d. All of the above

Correct answer is "d."
See previous rationale.

125. Which of the following is a language disorder?
    a. Articulation problems
    b. Stuttering
    c. Aphasia
    d. Excessive Nasality

Correct answer is "c."
Language disorders are often considered just one category of speech disorder. The problem is really different, with its own origins and causes. Persons with language disorders exhibit one or more of the following traits:
- Difficulty in comprehending questions, commands or statements (receptive language problems)
- Inability to adequately express their own thoughts (expressive language problems).
- Language that is below the level expected for the child's chronological age (delayed language)
- Interrupted language development (dysphasia)
- Qualitatively different language
- Total absence of language.

126. Which of the following is a speech disorder?
    a. Disfluency
    b. Aphasia
    c. Delayed language
    d. Comprehension difficulties

Correct answer is "a."

Persons with speech disorders exhibit one or more of the following traits:
- Unintelligible speech or speech that is difficult to understand, and articulation disorders (distortions, omissions, substitutions).
- Speech-flow disorders (sequence, duration, rate, rhythm, fluency)
- Unusual voice quality (nasality, breathiness, hoarseness, pitch, intensity, quality disorders)
- Obvious emotional discomfort when trying to communicate (stuttering, cluttering)
- Damage to nerves or brain centers which control muscles used in speech (dysarthria).

127. Children with disabilities can be taught social-interpersonal skills by:
    a. Developing sensitivity to other people
    b. Making behavioral choices in social situations
    c. Developing social maturity
    d. All of the above

Correct answer is "d."

Social-interpersonal skills: the ability to build and maintain interdependent relationships between persons. These skills are considered the domain of affective education and classroom management.

128. Children are engaged in a game of charades. Which type of social-interpersonal skill is the teacher most likely attempting to develop?
    a. Sensitivity to others
    b. Making behavioral choices in social situations
    c. Social maturity
    d. All of the above

Correct answer is "a."

Children with disabilities often perceive facial expressions and gestures differently to their nondisabled peers, due to their impairment. The game of charades, a guessing game, would help them develop sensitivity to others.

129. Social maturity may be evidenced by the student's:
    a. Recognition of rights and responsibilities (his own and others)
    b. Display of respect for legitimate authority figures
    c. Formulation of a valid moral judgment
    d. Demonstration of all of the above

Correct answer is "d."
Some additional evidence of social maturity:
- The ability to cooperate
- Following procedures formulated by an outside party
- Schieving appropriate levels of independence

130. Mrs. Right has noticed that Stevie typically plays alone and is seldom seen playing with other children. Today, Stevie is one of the last children in her room to be chosen by a team captain as a member of his group. One way in which Mrs. Wright can find out how Stevie is accepted by his peers would be to administer:
    a. Burk's behavior rating scale
    b. The walker problem behavior identification checklist
    c. A class play
    d. A self-test

Correct answer is "c."
A class play is the best choice as it gives the teacher a chance to assess the behavior through all of its five phases.

131. The work-study movement:
    a. Evolved primarily during the 1970s
    b. Focused upon the delivery of services within a specific type of interagency agreement
    c. Was declared a top priority by the U.S. Office of Education by Sidney Maryland, the Commissioner of Education
    d. Was implemented in both regular and special education settings

Correct answer is "b."
This program was conducted cooperatively between the schools and the local state rehabilitation services, when it emerged in the 1960s. The general goal was to create an integrated, academic social and vocational curriculum that included appropriate work experience. Programs were to be designed in such a way that students with mild disabilities would become prepared for eventual community adjustment. Cooperative agreements between the schools and the rehabilitation agencies were made in order to administer these programs.

132. The career education movement:
    a. Had its inception during the 1960s
    b. Maintained a cooperative agreement between the schools and the rehabilitation agencies
    c. Was funded by federal monies generated by rehabilitation agencies
    d. Was targeted for the general populace of students but included special education students as well

Correct answer is "d."
This movement had its inception in 1970, and focused upon the integration and of readiness for a life career throughout a student's education, from kindergarten to 12th grade. It targeted the general populace of students, and did not mention students with disabilities. However, when the Career Education Implementation Incentive Act, P.L. 95-207, was passed in 1977, it specifically mentioned people with disabilities as an appropriate target population for services.

133. Effective transition was included in:
    a. President Bush's 1990 State of the Union Message
    b. Public Law 101-476
    c. Public Law 95-207
    d. a and b

Correct answer is "d."
With the enactment of P. L. 101-476, (IDEA) transition services became a right.

134. Vocational training programs are based on all of the following ideas except:
    a. Students obtain career training from elementary through high school
    b. Students acquire specific training in job skills prior to exiting school
    c. Students need specific training and supervision in applying skills learned in school to requirements in job situations
    d. Students obtain needed instruction and field-based experiences that help them to be able to work in specific occupations

Correct answer is "a."
Vocational education programs or transition programs prepare students for entry into the labor force. They are usually incorporated into the work-study at the high school or post-secondary levels. They are usually focused on job skills, job opportunities, skill requirements for specific jobs, personal qualifications in relation to job requirements, work habits, money management, and academic skills needed for specific jobs.

135. In career education specific training and preparation required for the world of work occurs during the phase of:
    a. Career Awareness
    b. Career Exploration
    c. Career Preparation
    d. Daily Living and Personal-Social Interaction

Correct answer is "c."
Curricular aspects of career education include:
- career awareness: diversity of available jobs
- career exploration: skills needed for occupational groups
- career preparation: specific training and preparation required for the world of work

136. What is most descriptive of vocational training in special education?
    a. Trains students in intellectual disabilities solely
    b. Segregates students with and without disabilities in vocational training programs
    c. Only includes students capable of moderate supervision
    d. Instruction focuses upon self-help skills, social-interpersonal skills, motor skills, rudimentary academic skills, simple occupational skills, and lifetime leisure and occupational skills

Correct answer is "d."
Persons with disabilities are mainstreamed with nondisabled students where possible. Special sites provide training for those persons with more severe disabilities who are unable to be successfully taught in an integrated setting. Specially trained vocational counselors monitor and supervise student work sites.

137. An individual with disabilities in need of employability training, as well a job, would go to which community service agency for assistance?
    a. State Health Department
    b. Rehabilitation Services
    c. Social Services Agency
    d. Social Security Administration

Correct answer is "b."

TEACHER CERTIFICATION STUDY GUIDE

SUBAREA I.   **HUMAN DEVELOPMENT AND THE EDUCATIONAL IMPLICATIONS OF LEARNING DISABILITIES**

Skill 1.01   Demonstrate knowledge of human development and behavior

Social Emotional
Children whose behavior deviates from society's standards for normal behavior for certain ages and stages of development. Behavioral expectations vary from setting to setting; for example, it is acceptable to yell on the football field, but not as the teacher is explaining a lesson to the class. Different cultures have their standards of behavior, further complicating the question of what constitutes a behavioral problem. People have their personal opinions and standards for what is tolerable and what is not. Some behavioral problems are openly expressed; others are inwardly directed and not very obvious. As a result of these factors, the terms behavioral disorders and emotional disturbance have become almost interchangeable.

While almost all children at times exhibit behaviors that are aggressive, withdrawn or otherwise inappropriate, the IDEA definition of serious emotional disturbance focuses on behaviors that persist over time, are intense and impair a child's ability to function in society. The behaviors must not be caused by temporary stressful situations or other causes (i.e.: depression over the death of a grandparent or anger over the parents' impending divorce). In order for a child to be considered seriously emotionally disturbed, he or she must exhibit one or more of the following characteristics over a **long period of time** and to a **marked degree** that **adversely affects** a child's educational performance.

- Inability to learn, that cannot be explained by intellectual, sensory or health factors.
- Inability to maintain satisfactory interpersonal relationships.
- Inappropriate types of behaviors.
- General pervasive mood of unhappiness or depression.
- Physical symptoms or fears associated with personal or school problems.
- Schizophrenic children are covered under this definition, and social maladjustment by itself does not satisfy this definition unless it is accompanied by one of the other conditions of SED.

The diagnostic categories and definitions used to classify mental disorders come from the American Psychiatric Association's publication Diagnostic and Statistical Manual of Mental Disorders (DSM-IV), the handbook that is used by psychiatrists and psychologists. The DSM-IV is a multiaxial classification system consisting of dimensions (axes) coded along with the psychiatric diagnosis. The axes are:

- **Axis I** - principal psychiatric diagnosis (e.g., overanxious disorder)
- **Axis II** - developmental problems (e.g., developmental reading disorder)
- **Axis III** - physical disorders (e.g., allergies)
- **Axis IV** - psychosocial stressors (e.g., divorce)
- **Axis V** - rating of the highest level of adaptive functioning (includes intellectual and social). Rating is called Global Assessment Functioning (GAF) score.

While the DSM-IV diagnosis is one way of diagnosing serious emotional disturbance, there are other ways of classifying the various forms that behavior disorders manifest themselves. The following tables summarize some of these classifications.

Externalizing Behaviors	**Internalizing Behaviors**
Aggressive behaviors expressed outwardly toward others.	Withdrawing behaviors that are directed inward to oneself.
Manifested as hyperactivity, persistent aggression, irritating behaviors that are impulsive and distractible.	Social withdrawal.
Examples: hitting, cursing, stealing, arson, cruelty to animals or hyperactivity.	Depression, fears, phobias, elective mutism, withdrawal, anorexia and bulimia.

Well-known instruments used to assess children's behavior have their own categories (scales) to classify behaviors. The table on the following page illustrates the scales used in some of the widely used instruments.

LEARNING DISABLED

Walker Problem Identification Checklist	Burks' Behavior Rating Scales (BBRS)	Devereux Behavior Rating Scale (Adolescent)	Revised Behavior Problem Checklist (Quay & Peterson)
Acting out	Excessive self-blame	Unethical behavior	Major scales
Withdrawal	Excessive anxiety	Defiant-resistive	Conduct Disorder
Distractibility	Excessive withdrawal	Domineering-sadistic	Socialized aggression
Disturbed peer Relations	Excessive dependency	Heterosexual interest	Attention-problems-immaturity
Immaturity	Poor ego strength	Hyperactive expansive	Anxiety-withdrawal
	Poor physical strength	Poor emotional control	
	Poor coordination	Need approval, dependency	Minor scales
	Poor intellectuality	Emotional disturbance	Psychotic behavior
	Poor academics	Physical inferiority-timidity	Motor excess
	Poor attention	Schizoid withdrawal	
	Poor impulse control	Bizarre speech and cognition	
	Poor reality contact	Bizarre actions	
	Poor sense of identity		
	Excessive suffering		
	Poor anger control		
	Excessive sense of persecution		
	Excessive aggressiveness		
	Excessive resistance		
	Poor social conformity		

Disturbance may also be categorized in degrees: mild, moderate or severe. The degree of disturbance will affect the type and degree of interventions and services required by emotionally handicapped students. Degree of disturbance also must be considered when determining the least restrictive environment and the services named fro free, appropriate education for these students. An example of a set of criteria for determining the degree of disturbance is the one developed by P.L. Newcomer[1]:

CRITERIA	DEGREE OF DISTURBANCE		
	Mild	Moderate	Severe
Precipitating events	Highly stressful	Moderately stressful	Not stressful
Destructiveness	Not destructive	Occasionally destructive	Usually destructive
Maturational appropriateness	Behavior typical for age	Some behavior untypical for age	Behavior too young or too old
Personal functioning	Cares for own needs	Usually cares for own needs	Unable to care for own needs
Social functioning	Usually able to relate to others	Usually unable to relate to others	Unable to relate to others
Reality index	Usually sees events as they are	Occasionally sees events as they are	Little contact with reality
Insight index	Aware of behavior	Usually aware of behavior	Usually not aware of behavior
Conscious control	Usually can control behavior	Occasionally can control behavior	Little control over behavior
Social responsiveness	Usually acts appropriately	Occasionally acts appropriately	Rarely acts appropriately

Language Development and Behavior Components of Language

Language learning is composed of five components. Children progress through developmental stages through each component.

Phonology

Phonology is the system of rules about sounds and sound combinations for a language. A phoneme is the smallest unit of sound that combines with other sounds to make words. A phoneme, by itself, does not have a meaning; it must be combined with other phonemes. Problems in phonology may be manifested as developmental delays in acquiring consonants, or reception problems, such as misinterpreting words because a different consonant was substituted.

---

[1] Source: Understanding and Teaching Emotionally Disturbed Children and Adolescents, (2nd ed., p. 139), by P.L. Newcomer, 1993, Austin, TX: Pro-De. Copyright 1993. Reprinted with permission.

LEARNING DISABLED

Morphology

Morphemes are the smallest units of language that convey meaning. Morphemes are root words, or free morphemes that can stand alone (e.g., walk), and affixes (e.g., ed, s or ing). Content words carry the meaning in a sentence and functional words join phrases and sentences. Generally, students with problems in this area may not use inflectional endings in their words, may not be consistent in their use of certain morphemes or may be delayed in learning morphemes such as irregular past tenses.

Syntax

Syntax rules, commonly known as grammar, govern how morphemes and words are correctly combined, Wood (1976) describes six stages of syntax acquisition (Mercer, p 347).

- **Stages 1 and 2**: birth to about 2 years: individual is learning the semantic system.
- **Stage 3 - ages 2 to 3 years**: simple sentences contain subject and predicate.
- **Stage 4 - ages 2 ½ to 4 years**: elements such as question words are added to basic sentences (e.g., where) word order is changed to ask questions. The individual begins to use "and" to combine simple sentences and the individual begins to embed words within the basic sentence.
- **Stage 5 - about 31/2 to 7 years**: the individual uses complete sentences that include word classes of adult language. The individual is becoming aware of appropriate semantic functions of words and differences within the same grammatical class.
- **Stage 6- about 5 to 20 years**: the individual begins to learn complex sentences and sentences that imply commands, requests and promises.

Syntactic deficits are manifested by the child using sentences that lack length or complexity for a child that age. The child may have problems understanding or creating complex sentences and embedded sentences.

Semantics

Semantics is language content: objects, actions and relations between objects. As with syntax, Wood (1976) outlines stages of semantic development:

- **Stage 1 - birth to about 2 years**: the child is learning meaning while learning his first words. Sentences are one-word, but the meaning varies according to the context. Therefore, "doggie" may mean, "This is my dog," or, "There is a dog," or "The dog is barking."
- **Stage 2 - about 2 to 8 years**: the child progresses to two-word sentences about concrete actions. As more words are learned, the child forms longer sentences, until about age 7, things are defined in terms of visible actions. The child begins to respond to prompts (e.g., pretty/flower) and at about age 8 the child can respond to a prompt with an opposite (e.g., pretty/ugly).

- **Stage 3 - begins at about age 8**: the child's word meanings relate directly to experiences, operations and processes. Vocabulary is defined by the child's experiences, not the adult's. At about age 12, the child begins to give "dictionary" definitions and the semantic level approaches that of adults.

Semantic problems take the form of:

- Limited vocabulary.
- Inability to understand figurative language or idioms; interprets literally.
- Failure to perceive multiple meanings of words, changes in word meaning from changes in context, resulting in incomplete understanding of what is read.
- Difficulty understanding linguistic concepts (e.g., before/after), verbal analogies and logical relationships such as possessives, spatial and temporal.
- Misuse of transitional words such as "although," "regardless."

Pragmatics

Commonly known as the speaker's intent, pragmatics is used to influence or control actions or attitudes of others. **Communicative competence** depends on how well one understands the rules of language, as well as the social rules of communication such as taking turns and using the correct tone of voice.

Pragmatic deficits are manifested by failures to respond properly to indirect requests after age 8 (e.g., "Can't you turn down the TV"? elicits a response of "No" instead of "Yes" and the child turning down the volume). Children with these deficits have trouble reading cues that indicate the listener does not understand them. Whereas a person would usually notice this and adjust one's speech to the listener's needs the child with pragmatic problems does not do this. Pragmatic deficits are also characterized by inappropriate social behaviors such as interruptions or monopolizing conversations. Children may use immature speech and have trouble sticking to a topic. These problems can persist into adulthood, affecting academic, vocational and social interactions. Problems in language development often require long-term interventions, and can persist into adulthood. Certain problems are associated with different grade levels:

Preschool and Kindergarten: the child's speech may sound immature, the child may not be able to follow simple directions, and often cannot name things such as the days of the week and colors. The child may not be able to discriminate between sounds and the letters associated with the sounds. The child might substitute sounds and have trouble responding accurately to certain types of questions. The child may play less with his peers or participate in non-play or parallel play.

Elementary School: problems with sound discrimination persist, and the child may have problems with temporal and spatial concepts (e.g., before/after). As the child progresses through school, he may have problems making the transition from narrative to expository writing. Word retrieval problems may not be very evident because the child begins to devise strategies such as talking around the word he cannot remember, or using fillers, and descriptors. The child might speak more slowly, have problems sounding out words, and get confused with multiple-meaning words. Pragmatic problems show up in social situations such as failure to correctly interpret social cues and adjust to appropriate language, inability to predict consequences, and inability to formulate requests to obtain new information.

Secondary School: at this level, difficulties become more subtle. The child lacks the ability to use and understand higher-level syntax, semantics and pragmatics. If the child has problems with auditory language, he may also have problems with short-term memory and/or expressive language delays impair the child's ability to learn effectively. The child often lacks the ability to organize/categorize the information received in school. Problems associated with pragmatic deficiencies persist but because the child is aware of them, he becomes inattentive, withdrawn or frustrated.

Cognitive Development
Children go through patterns of learning beginning with pre-operational thought processes and move to concrete operational thoughts. Eventually they begin to acquire the mental ability to think about and solve problems in their head because they can manipulate objects symbolically. Children of most ages can use symbols such as words and numbers to represent objects and relations, but they need concrete reference points. It is essential children be encouraged to use and develop the thinking skills that they possess in solving problems that interest them. The content of the curriculum must be relevant, engaging and meaningful to the students.

The teacher of special needs students must have a general knowledge of cognitive development. Although children with special needs cognitive development rate maybe different than other children, a teacher needs to be aware of some of the activities of each stage as part of the basis to determine what should be taught and when it should be taught.

The following information about cognitive development was taken from the Cincinnati Children's Hospital Medical Center at www.cincinattichildrens.org

Some common features indicating a progression from more simple to more complex cognitive development include the following:

Children (ages 6-12)
Begin to develop the ability to think in concrete ways:

- Concrete operations are operations performed in the presence of the object and events that are to be used.
- Examples: how to combine (addition), separate (subtract or divide), order (alphabetize and sort/categorize) and transform (change things such as 25 pennies=1 quarter) objects and actions.

Adolescence (ages 12-18)
Adolescence marks the beginning development of more complex thinking skills, including abstract thinking, the ability to reason from known principles (form own new ideas or questions), the ability to consider many points of view according to varying criteria (compare or debate ideas or opinions), and the ability to think about the process of thinking.

What cognitive developmental changes occur during adolescence?
During adolescence (between 12 and 18 years of age), the developing teenager acquires the ability to think systematically about all logical relationships within a problem. The transition from concrete thinking to formal logical operations occurs over time. Every adolescent progresses at varying rates in developing his / her ability to think in more complex ways. Each adolescent develops his / her own view of the world. Some adolescents may be able to apply logical operations to school work long before they are able to apply them to personal dilemmas. When emotional issues arise, they often interfere with an adolescent's ability to think in more complex ways. The ability to consider possibilities, as well as facts, may influence decision making, in either positive or negative ways.

Some common features indicating a progression from more simple to more complex cognitive development include the following:

- Early adolescence - during early adolescence, the use of more complex thinking is focused on personal decision making in school and home environments, including the following:
- Begins to demonstrate use of formal logical operations in schoolwork.
- Begins to question authority and society standards.
- Begins to form and verbalize his / her own thoughts and views on a variety of topics, usually more related to his / her own life, such as:
- Which sports are better to play.
- Which groups are better to be included in.
- What personal appearances are desirable or attractive.
- What parental rules should be changed.

LEARNING DISABLED

- Middle adolescence - with some experience in using more complex thinking processes, the focus of middle adolescence often expands to include more philosophical and futuristic concerns, including the following:
- Begins to think long term.
- Often analyzes more extensively.
- Often questions more extensively.
- Thinks about and begins to form his / her own code of ethics.
- Thinks about and begins to make his / her own plans.
- Thinks about and begins to systematically consider possible future goals.
- Thinks about different possibilities and begins to develop own identity.
- Use of systematic thinking begins to influence relationships with others.
- Late adolescence – during late adolescence, complex thinking processes are used to focus on less self-centered concepts as well as personal decision making, including the following:
- Begins to focus thinking on emerging role in adult society.
- Begins to focus thinking on making career decisions.
- Debate and develop intolerance of opposing views.
- Develops idealistic views on specific topics or concerns.
- Increased thoughts about more global concepts such as justice, history, politics and patriotism.

What encourages healthy cognitive development during adolescence?
The following suggestions will help to encourage positive and healthy cognitive development in the adolescent:
- Assist adolescents in re-evaluating poorly made decisions for themselves.
- Assist adolescents in setting their own goals.
- Compliment and praise adolescents for well thought out decisions.
- Encourage adolescents to share ideas and thoughts with adults.
- Encourage adolescents to think independently and develop their own ideas.
- Include adolescents in discussions about a variety of topics, issues, and current events.
- Stimulate adolescents to think about possibilities of the future.

Physical Development, Including Motor and Sensory
It is important for the teacher to be aware of the physical stage of development and how the child's physical growth and development affect the child's learning.

Factors determined by the physical stage of development include:
- Ability to sit and attend.
- The need for activity.
- The relationship between physical skills and self-esteem.
- The degree to which physical involvement in an activity (as opposed to being able to understand an abstract concept) affects learning.

Children with physical impairments possess a variety of disabling conditions. Although there are significant differences among these conditions, similarities also exist. Each condition usually affects one particular system of the body: the cardiopulmonary system (i.e.: blood vessels, heart and lungs), the musculoskeletal system (i.e.: spinal cord and brain nerves). Some conditions develop during pregnancy, birth or infancy because of the known or unknown factors, which may affect the fetus or newborn infant. Other conditions occur later due to injury (trauma), disease or factors not fully understood.

In addition to motor disorders, individuals with physical disabilities may have multi-disabling conditions such as concomitant hearing impairments, visual impairments, perceptual disorders, speech defects, behavior disorders or mental handicaps, performance and emotional responsiveness. Some characteristics in which may occur with individuals with physical disabilities and other health impairments are:

1. Lack of physical stamina; fatigue.
2. Chronic illness; poor endurance.
3. Deficient motor skills; normal movement may be prevented.
4. May cause physical limitations or impede motor development; a prosthesis or an orthosis may be required.
5. Mobility and exploration of one's environment may be limited.
6. Limited self-care abilities.
7. Progressive weakening and degeneration of muscles.
8. Frequent speech and language defects; communication may be prevented; echolatia orthosis may be present.
9. May experience pain and discomfort throughout the body.
10. May display emotional (psychological) problems, which require treatment.
11. Social adjustments may be needed; may display maladaptive social behavior.
12. May necessitate long-term medical treatment.
13. May have embarrassing side effects from certain diseases or treatment.
14. May exhibit erratic or poor attendance patterns.

In IDEA, the 1990 Amendment to the Education for All Handicapped Children Act, autism was classified as a separate exceptionality category. It is thought to be caused by a neurological or biochemical dysfunction. It generally becomes evident before age 3. The condition occurs in about 4 of every 10,000 persons. Smith and Luckasson, 1992, describe it as a severe language disorder which affects thinking, communication and behavior. They list the following characteristics:

- **Absent or distorted relationships with people**—inability to relate with people except as objects, inability to express affection, or ability to build and maintain only distant, suspicious or bizarre relationships.
- **Extreme or peculiar problems in communication**—absence of verbal language or language that is not functional such as echolalia (parroting what one hears),misuse of pronouns (e.g. he for you or I for her), neologisms (made-up meaningless words or sentences), talk that bears little or no resemblance to reality.
- **Self-stimulation**—repetitive stereo-typed behavior that seems to have no purposes other than providing sensory stimulation. this may take a wide variety of forms, such as swishing saliva, twirling objects, patting one's cheeks, flapping one's arms, staring,…etc.
- **Self-injury**—repeated physical self-abuse, such as biting, scratching, or poking oneself, head banging, …etc
- **Perceptual anomalies**—unusual responses or absence of response to stimuli that seem to indicate sensory impairment or unusual sensitivity.

Skill 1.02 Demonstrate knowledge of the characteristics of students with special needs, types of learning disabilities, and ways in which learning disabilities influence human development.

CHARACTERISTICS OF STUDENTS WITH LEARNING DISABLITIES
The individual with a specific learning disability exhibits a discrepancy between achievement and potential. Deficiencies can occur within a spectrum of skill areas. The youngster typically shows a low level of performance in one of several skill areas: rarely is a uniform pattern of academic development demonstrated. The cause of delayed academic performance is not due to limited cognitive ability, sensory and physical impairments, emotional disturbances or environmental deprivation. The child or youth with a disability is characterized by:

1. **Hyperactivity**: a rate of motor activity higher than normal.
2. **Perceptual difficulties**: visual, auditory and haptic perceptual problems.
3. **Perceptual-motor impairments**: poor integration of visual and motor systems, often affecting fine motor coordination.
4. **General coordination deficits**: clumsiness in physical activities.
5. **Disorders of memory and thinking**: memory deficits, trouble with Problem solving, concept formation, and association: poor awareness of own metacognitive skills (learning strategies).

6. **Disorders of attention**: short attention span, distractibility, lack of selective attention, perseveration.
7. **Emotional lability**: frequent changes in mood, low tolerance for frustration, sensitive to others.
8. **Impulsiveness**: acts before considering consequences, poor impulse control, often followed by remorsefulness.
9. **Academic problems in reading, math, writing or spelling**: significant discrepancies in ability levels.
10. **Disorders in speech, hearing and sight**: high proportion of auditory and visual perceptual difficulties.
11. **Equivocal neurological signs**: and electroencephalogram (EEG) irregularities, neurological abnormalities (soft signs), which may or may not be due to brain injury.
12. **Social adjustment: frequently poor adjustment**: low self-esteem, social isolation or reckless and uninhibited, learned helplessness, poor motivation, external focus of control, poor reaction to environmental changes.
13. **Interpersonal problems**: over-excitable in a group, better relations with limited number of peers, frequently poor judgment exhibited: often overly affectionate and clinging.
14. **Problems in achievement**: academic disability, poor graphics (wiring), disorganized or slow in finishing work.
15. **Intraindividual discrepancies**: uneven development between different areas on functioning.

"Student with a disability" means a student with a disability who has not attained the age of 21 prior to September 1st and who is entitled to attend public schools and who, because of mental, physical or emotional reasons, has been identified as having a disability and who requires special services and programs approved by the department. The terms used in this definition are defined as follows:

1. *Autism* means a developmental disability significantly affecting verbal and nonverbal communication and social interaction, generally evident before age 3, that adversely affects a student's educational performance. Other characteristics often associated with autism are engagement in repetitive activities and stereotyped movements, resistance to environmental change or change in daily routines, and unusual responses to sensory experiences. The term does not apply if a student's educational performance is adversely affected primarily because the student has an emotional disturbance. A student who manifests the characteristics of autism after age 3 could be diagnosed as having autism if the criteria in this paragraph are otherwise satisfied.
2. *Deafness* means a hearing impairment that is so severe that the student is impaired in processing linguistic information through hearing, with or without amplification, that adversely affects a student's educational performance.

TEACHER CERTIFICATION STUDY GUIDE

3. 3. *Deaf-blindness* means concomitant hearing and visual impairments, the combination of which causes such severe communication and other developmental and educational needs that they cannot be accommodated in special education programs solely for students with deafness or students with blindness.

4. *Emotional disturbance* means a condition exhibiting one or more of the following characteristics over a long period of time and to a marked degree that adversely affects a student's educational performance:
   i. An inability to learn that cannot be explained by intellectual, sensory, or health factors.
   ii. An inability to build or maintain satisfactory interpersonal relationships with peers and teachers.
   iii. Inappropriate types of behavior or feelings under normal circumstances.
   iv. A generally pervasive mood of unhappiness or depression.
   v. A tendency to develop physical symptoms or fears associated with personal or school problems.

   The term includes schizophrenia. The term does not apply to students who are socially maladjusted, unless it is determined that they have an emotional disturbance.

5. *Hearing impairment* means an impairment in hearing, whether permanent or fluctuating, that adversely affects the child's educational performance but that is not included under the definition of deafness in this section.

6. *Learning disability* means a disorder in one or more of the basic psychological processes involved in understanding or in using language, spoken or written, which manifests itself in an imperfect ability to listen, think, speak, read, write, spell or to do mathematical calculations. The term includes such conditions as perceptual disabilities, brain injury, minimal brain dysfunction, dyslexia and developmental aphasia. The term does not include learning problems that are primarily the result of visual, hearing or motor disabilities, of mental retardation, of emotional disturbance or of environmental, cultural or economic disadvantage.

7. *Mental retardation* means significantly sub-average general intellectual functioning, existing concurrently with deficits in adaptive behavior and manifested during the developmental period, that adversely affects a student's educational performance.

8. *Multiple disabilities* means concomitant impairments (such as mental retardation-blindness, mental retardation-orthopedic impairment and etc.), the combination of which cause such severe educational needs that they cannot be accommodated in a special education program solely for one of the impairments. The term does not include deaf-blindness..

LEARNING DISABLED

9. *Orthopedic impairment* means a severe orthopedic impairment that adversely affects a student's educational performance. The term includes impairments caused by congenital anomaly (*e.g.*, clubfoot, absence of some member and etc.), impairments caused by disease (*e.g.*, poliomyelitis, bone tuberculosis and etc.), and impairments from other causes (*e.g.*, cerebral palsy, amputation and fractures or burns, which cause contractures).

10. *Other health-impairment* means having limited strength, vitality or alertness, including a heightened alertness to environmental stimuli, that results in limited alertness with respect to the educational environment, that is due to chronic or acute health problems, including but not limited to a heart condition, tuberculosis, rheumatic fever, nephritis, asthma, sickle cell anemia, hemophilia, epilepsy, lead poisoning, leukemia, diabetes, attention deficit disorder or attention deficit hyperactivity disorder or Tourettes syndrome, which adversely affects a student's educational performance.

11. *Speech or language impairment* means a communication disorder, such as stuttering, impaired articulation, a language impairment or a voice impairment, that adversely affects a student's educational performance.

12. *Traumatic brain injury* means an acquired injury to the brain caused by an external physical force or by certain medical conditions such as stroke, encephalitis, aneurysm, anoxia or brain tumors with resulting impairments that adversely affect educational performance. The term includes open or closed head injuries or brain injuries from certain medical conditions resulting in mild, moderate or severe impairments in one or more areas, including cognition, language, memory, attention, reasoning, abstract thinking, judgment, problem solving, sensory, perceptual and motor abilities, psychosocial behavior, physical functions, information processing, and speech. The term does not include injuries that are congenital or caused by birth trauma.

13. *Visual impairment including blindness* means an impairment in vision that, even with correction, adversely affects a student's educational performance. The term includes both partial sight and blindness.

Skill 1.03 **Demonstrate knowledge of types and characteristics of receptive and expressive language disorders associated with learning disabilities**

Typical, Delayed And Disordered Communication Patterns Among Individuals With Disabilities

Language is the means whereby people communicate their thoughts, make requests and respond to others. Communication competence is an interaction of cognitive competence, social knowledge and language competence. Communication problems may result from, in any or all of these areas, which directly impact the student's ability to interact with others. Language consists of several components each of which follows a sequence of development. Brown and colleagues were the first to describe language as a function of developmental stages rather than age (Reid, 1988 p 44). He developed a formula to group the mean length of utterances (sentences) into stages. Counting the number of morphemes per 100 utterances, one can calculate a mean length of utterance, MLU. Total number of morphemes / 100 = MLU (e.g., 180/100 = 1.8).

Summary of Brown's findings about MLU and language development:

Stage	MLU	Developmental Features
L	1.5-2.0	14 basic morphemes (e.g. in, on, articles, possessives)
LI	2.0-2.5	Beginning of pronoun use, auxiliary verbs
LII	2.5-3.0	Language form approximate adult forms. Beginning of questions and negative statements
Lv	3.0-3.5	Use of complex (embedded)sentences
V	3.5-4.0	Use of compound sentences.

Please refer to skill 1.01 for more information on language development.

Characteristics of Students with Speech/Language Impairments

As a group, youngsters with speech and language impairments generally score below normal children on measures of intelligence, achievement and adaptive social skills; however, this is in part attributable to the fact that a large percentage of children with mental, physical, behavioral and learning disabilities exhibit speech and language disorders secondary to their major disability. Children with markedly deviant or delayed speech and language generally have concurrent difficulties with severe intellectual disabilities, chronic emotionally/behavioral disturbances or acute hearing problems and function at a delayed developmental level.

Children with speech impairments who have no observable organic defects perform slightly lower than average on tests of motor proficiency. Problems are most likely to occur in the areas of coordination, application of strength and rhythm. Children with communication disorders tend to demonstrate less interaction with peers.

In addition to these general characteristics, children with cleft palates tend to be underachieving and to show more personality problems (e.g., shyness, inhibition and social withdrawal) then normal children. Children who stutter severely exhibit much anxiety and have low self-esteem.

Speech Disorders

Identification and Characteristics
Children with speech disorders are characterized by one or more of the following:
1. Unintelligible speech, or speech that is difficult to understand, and articulation disorders (distortions, omissions and substitutions).
2. Speech-flow disorders (sequence, duration, rate, rhythm and fluency).
3. Unusual voice quality (nasality, breathiness, hoarseness, pitch, intensity and quality disorders.
4. Peculiar physical mannerisms when speaking.
5. Obvious emotional discomfort when trying to communicate (particularly stutterers and clutterers).
6. Damage to nerves or brain centers which control muscles used in speech (dysarthria).

Language Disorders
Language disorders are often considered just one category of speech disorder, but the problem is really a separate one with different origins and causes. Language-disordered children exhibit one or more of the following characteristics.
1. Difficulty in comprehending questions, commands or statements (receptive language problems).
2. Inability to adequately express their own thoughts (expressive language problems).
3. Language that is below the level expected for the child's chronological age (delayed language).
4. Interrupted language development (dysphasia).
5. Qualitatively different language.
6. Total absence of language (aphasia).

Skill 1.04 Demonstrate knowledge of types and characteristics of perceptual and memory disorders associated with learning disabilities

Perceptual disorders refer to visual processing problems that occur when an individual has problems making sense of information that is seen through the eyes. This is not to be confused with problems that result from sight or sharpness of vision. People that have perceptual disorders have problems processing visual information and not seeing.

Students with perceptual disorders have problems identifying the position of objects in space. They cannot precisely view objects in space when placed next to other objects.

The problems of spatial relationships are significant in reading and math. Both math and reading require the use of symbols, letters, numbers, punctuation and signs. Some examples of problems associated with perception include not being able to view words and numbers as separate entities, confusion with letters that resemble each other such as b, d and p and having problems with directions in reading and math.

The significance of having perceptual acuity is present throughout math. In order to fully master mathematical concepts, individuals have to be able to ascertain that certain digits go together to create a single number such as 25 and that other digits are single digit numbers and the addition, subtraction and multiplication signs are separate from the numbers but show a relationship between the numbers.

There are three different types of memories that are significant in the learning process. Working memory is the ability to hold on to parts of information until the pieces come together to formulate a complete thought or concept. An example of this is when you read a sentence and at the end of it are able to comprehend the full context.

Short-term memory is the active process of storing and retaining information for a brief limited period of time. The information is available for a short period of time and is not yet stored for long-term memorization.

Long-term memory is information that has been stored and is available for use over a long period of time. Some people may have problems with auditory or visual memory. Auditory memory is being able to store and recall information that is received verbally. Visual memory is being able to store and recall information that is received visually or through the eyes.

Sequencing problems stem from people having problems learning information in the correct sequence. For example, a student can have problems memorizing the order of the alphabet or the months of the year.

Abstraction problems occur when an individual has problems deducing the meaning of words or concepts. Someone with abstraction problems would have difficulty understanding jokes, sarcasm, idioms, or words with different meanings. Organization problems occur when an individual has problems keeping his things organized. They may constantly lose, forget, or misplace homework, school assignments, and papers. They also have problems keeping their work environment organized and have difficulty with projects that may be due on a particular date.

Skill 1.05 Demonstrate knowledge of types and characteristics of thinking disorders associated with learning disabilities

Thinking disorders associated with learning disabilities include problems forming concepts and solving problems. Problem solving is the systematic use of a step-by-step system to respond to hard questions. Concept formation is the process of combining a series of features that group together to create a class of ideas or objects.

If there were no formation of concepts then people would have to learn and recall the word that stands for every unique thing in the world. For example, each type of chair, flower or truck would require its own name in order to learn and communicate about it in any significant manner.

Difficulties with higher order thinking skills are problematic for students studying mathematics because these skills are needed for many problems in upper level math classes. Students must determine the solution to questions that are asked indirectly and many have problems correctly identifying the problem and how to go about finding the solution. Students also have difficulty with problems with many steps. Students with disabilities sometimes cannot determine how to begin working on the problem or cannot finish the problem once they have completed some of the steps, leaving an incomplete resolution.

Students' underdeveloped processing skills may also lead to problems deducing important information from insignificant information when resolving word problems. Numerous problems that the student's are faced with entail too much or too little information, which then requires the student to deduce what information is required to solve the problem. This makes it even harder for students who have problems with multi-step problem solving and higher order thinking skills.

Skill 1.06 Demonstrate knowledge of types and characteristics of behavioral, social, and emotional disorders associated with learning disabilities

Identify the Characteristics of Emotionally Disturbed Children

Children with emotional disturbances or behavioral disorders are not always easy to identify. It is, of course, easy to identify the acting-out child who is constantly fighting, who cannot stay on task for more than a few minutes, or who shouts obscenities when angry. It is not always easy to identify the child who internalizes his or her problems, on the other hand, or may appear to be the "model" student, but suffers from depression, shyness or fears. Unless the problem becomes severe enough to impact school performance, the internalizing child may go for long periods without being identified or served. Studies of children with behavioral and emotional disorders, share some general characteristics:

- **Lower academic performance**: while it is true that some emotionally disturbed children have average or above average IQ scores, the majority are behind their peers in measures of intelligence and school achievement. Most score in the "slow learner" or "mildly mentally retarded" range on IQ tests, averaging about 90. Many have learning problems that exacerbate their acting out or "giving-up" behavior. As the child enters secondary school, the gap between her and nondisabled peers widens until the child may be as many as 2 to 4 years behind in reading and/or math skills by high school. As the students fall further and further behind their peers, it is difficult to weed out true learning disabilities from those academic issues directly related to the behavior issues. On the other hand, behavioral problems can be the direct result of unidentified learning disabilities. Some children become so frustrated and overwhelmed that they begin to act out behaviorally.

- **Social skills deficits**: students with these deficits may be uncooperative, selfish in dealing with others, unaware of what to do in social situations, or ignorant of the consequences of their actions. This may be a combination of lack of prior training, lack of opportunities to interact, or again frustration students experience as a result of learning disabilities undiagnosed and treated, and dysfunctional value systems and beliefs learned from their family.

- Classroom behaviors: often, emotionally disturbed children display classroom behavior that is highly disruptive to the classroom setting. Emotionally disturbed children are often out of their seat or running around the room, hitting, fighting or disturbing their classmates, stealing or destroying property, defiant and noncompliant, and/or verbally disruptive. They do not follow directions and often do not complete assignments. Additionally, students may use these outwardly disruptive behaviors to cover up other issues they may be experiences. In their minds, students sometimes believe it is more socially acceptable to their peers to become mouthy with the teacher than to demonstrate they are unable to read a simple passage.

- **Aggressive behaviors**: aggressive children often fight or instigate their peers to strike back at them. Aggressiveness may also take the form of vandalism or destruction of property. Aggressive children also engage in verbal abuse.

- **Delinquency**: as emotionally disturbed, acting-out children enter adolescence; they may become involved in socialized aggression (i.e.: gang membership) and delinquency. Delinquency is a legal term rather than a medical one that describes truancy and actions that would be criminal if adults committed them. Not every delinquent is classified as emotionally disturbed, but children with behavioral and emotional disorders are especially at risk for becoming delinquent because of their problems at school (the primary place for socializing with peers), deficits in social skills that may make them unpopular at school, and/or dysfunctional homes.

- **Withdrawn behaviors**: children who manifest withdrawn behaviors may consistently act in an immature fashion or prefer to play with younger children. They may daydream or complain of being sick in order to "escape." They may also cry often, cling to the teacher, ignore those who attempt to interact, or suffer from fears or depression. This escapist attitude can also sometimes be due to difficulties with the academic work presented.

- **Schizophrenia and psychotic behaviors**: children may have bizarre delusions, hallucinations, incoherent thoughts and disconnected thinking. Schizophrenia typically manifests itself between the ages of 15 and 45, and the younger the onset, the more severe the disorder. These behaviors usually require intensive treatment beyond the scope of the regular classroom setting.

- **Gender**: many more boys than girls are identified as having emotional and behavioral problems, especially hyperactivity and attention Deficit disorder, autism, childhood psychosis and problems with under control (aggression, socialized aggression). Girls, on the other hand, have more problems with over control (i.e.: withdrawal and phobias). Boys are much more prevalent than girls in problems with mental retardation and language and learning disabilities.

LEARNING DISABLED

- **Age Characteristics**: when they enter adolescence, girls tend to experience affective or emotional disorders such as anorexia, depression, bulimia and anxiety at twice the rate of boys, which mirrors the adult prevalence pattern.
- **Family Characteristics**: having a child with an emotional or behavioral disorder does not automatically mean that the family is dysfunctional; however, there are family factors that create or contribute to the development of behavior disorders and emotional disturbance:
- Abuse and neglect.
- Lack of appropriate supervision.
- Lax, punitive, and/or lack of discipline.
- High rates of negative types of interaction among family members.
- Lack of parental concern and interest.
- Negative adult role models.
- Lack of proper health care and/or nutrition.
- Disruption in the family.

Children with Mild Learning, Intellectual and Behavioral Disabilities

Some characteristics of students with mild learning and behavioral disabilities are the following:

- Achieve in accordance with teacher expectations.
- Have areas of talent or ability often overlooked by teachers.
- Higher dropout rate than regular education students.
- Lack of interest in schoolwork.
- Low achievement; limited verbal and/or writing skills.
- Possess weak listening skills.
- Prefer concrete rather than abstract lessons.
- Prefer to receive special help in regular classroom.
- Require modification in classroom instruction and are easily distracted.
- Respond better to active rather than passive learning tasks.

Identify characteristic of students who have a learning disability:

- Academic problems in reading, math, writing or spelling; significant discrepancies in ability levels.
- Disorders of memory and thinking: memory deficits, trouble with problem-solving, concept formation and association, poor awareness of own met cognitive skills (learning strategies).
- Hyperactivity: a rate of motor activity higher than normal.
- Impulsiveness: acts before considering consequences, poor impulse control, often followed by remorselessness.
- Perceptual difficulties: visual, auditory and perceptual problems.

- Perceptual-motor impairments: poor integration of visual and motor systems, often affecting fine motor coordination.

Identify characteristics of individuals with mental retardation or intellectual Disabilities:
- Deficits in memory which often relate to poor initial perception, or inability to apply stored information to relevant situations
- Difficulty in attending to relevant aspects of stimuli: slowness in reaction time or in employing alternate strategies.
- Impaired formulation of learning strategies
- IQ of 70 or below
- Limited cognitive ability; delayed academic achievement, particularly in language-related subjects

Identify characteristics of individuals with Autism

This exceptionality appears very early in childhood. Six common features of autism are:

- **Apparent sensory deficit** - the child may appear not to see or hear or react to a stimulus, then react in an extreme fashion to a seemingly insignificant stimulus.
- **Severe affect isolation** - the child does not respond to the usual signs of affection such as smiles and hugs.
- **Self-stimulation** - stereotyped behavior takes the form of repeated or ritualistic actions that make no sense to others, such as hand flapping, rocking, staring at objects, or humming the same sounds for hours at a time.
- **Tantrums and self-injurious behavior (SIB)** - autistic children may bite themselves, pull their hair, bang their heads, or hit themselves. They can throw severe tantrums, and direct aggression and destructive behavior toward others.
- **Echolalia** - also known as "parrot talk." The autistic child may repeat what is played on television, for example, or respond to others by repeating what was said to him. Alternatively, he may simply not speak at all.
- **Severe deficits in behavior and self-care skills** - autistic children may behave like children much younger than themselves.

SUBAREA II. EVALUATION, ASSESSMENT, AND INDIVIDUALIZED EDUCATIONAL PROGRAMS (IEPs)

Skill 2.01 Demonstrate knowledge of types and characteristics of assessment instruments and methods

Types, Characteristics and Methods of Formal and Informal Assessment
Formal assessments include standardized criterion, norm-referenced instruments, and commercially prepared inventories, which are developmentally appropriate for students across the spectrum of disabilities. Criterion-referenced tests compare a student's performance to a previously established criterion rather than to other students from a normative sample. Norm-referenced tests use normative data for scoring which include performance norms by age, gender or ethnic group.

Informal assessment strategies include non-standardized instruments such as checklists, developmental rating scales, observations, error analysis, interviews, teacher reports and performance-based assessments that are developmentally appropriate students across disabilities. Informal evaluation strategies rely upon the knowledge and judgment of the professional and are an integral part of the evaluation. An advantage of using informal assessments is the ease of design and administration, in addition to the usefulness of information the teacher can gain about the student's strength and weaknesses.

Some instruments can be both formal and informal tools. For example, observation may incorporate structured observation instruments as well as other informal observation procedures, including professional judgment. When evaluating a child's developmental level, a professional may use a formal adaptive rating scale while simultaneously using professional judgment to assess the child's motivation and behavior during the evaluation process.

IDEA requires that a variety of assessment tools and strategies are utilized when conducting assessments. Before utilizing a formal or informal tool, the practitioner should make sure that the tool is the most appropriate one that can be used for that particular population group. Many assessment tools can be used across disabilities. Dependent upon the disability in question, such as blindness, autism or hearing impaired some assessment tools will give more information than others.

Some of the informal and formal assessments that can be used across disabilities are curriculum-based assessments, multiple baseline design, norm-referenced test (see definitions of each in skill 3.01) and momentary time sampling.

Momentary time sampling - this is a technique used for measuring behaviors of a group of individuals or several behaviors from the same individual. Time samples are usually brief, and may be conducted at fixed or variable intervals.

The advantage of using variable intervals is increased reliability, as the students will not be able to predict when the time sample will betaken.

Appropriate purposes, uses and limitations of various types of assessment instruments

Types of Assessment
It is useful to consider the types of assessment procedures that are available to the classroom teacher. The types of assessment discussed below represent many of the more common types, but the list is not comprehensive.

Anecdotal records
These are notes recorded by the teacher concerning an area of interest or concern with a particular student. These records should focus on observable behaviors and should be descriptive in nature. They should not include assumptions or speculations regarding effective areas such as motivation or interest. These records are usually compiled over a period of several days to several weeks.

Rating scales and checklists
These assessments are generally self-appraisal instruments completed by the students or observations-based instruments completed by the teacher. The focus of these is frequently on behavior or effective areas such as interest and motivation.

Portfolio assessment
The use of student portfolios for some aspect of assessment has become quite common. The purpose, nature, and policies of portfolio assessment vary greatly from one setting to another. In general, a student's portfolio contains samples of work collected over an extended period of time. The nature of the subject, age of the student and scope of the portfolio, all contribute to the specific mechanics of analyzing, synthesizing, and otherwise evaluating the portfolio contents.

In most cases, the student and teacher make joint decisions as to which work samples go into the student's portfolios. A collection of work compiled over an extended time period allows teacher, student and parents to view the student's progress from a unique perspective. Qualitative changes over time can be readily apparent from work samples. Such changes are difficult to establish with strictly quantitative records typical of the scores recorded in the teacher's grade book.

Questioning

One of the most frequently occurring forms of assessment in the classroom is oral questioning by the teacher. As the teacher questions the students, she collects a great deal of information about the degree of student learning and potential sources of confusing for the students. While questioning is often viewed as a component of instructional methodology, it is also a powerful assessment tool.

Formal/Informal testing

- Please refer to skill 3.02 for definitions and descriptions.

Additional Types of tests

Tests and similar direct assessment methods represent the most easily identified types of assessment. Thorndike (1997) identifies three types of assessment instruments:
1. Standardized achievement tests.
2. Assessment material packaged with curricular materials.
3. Teacher-made assessment instruments.
    - Effective measures.
    - Oral tests.
    - Pencil and paper test.
    - Performance tests.
    - Product evaluations (p 199).

Kellough and Roberts (1991) take a slightly different perspective. They describe "Three avenues for assessing student achievement,
1. what the learner says;
2. what the learner does; and
3. what the learner writes." (p.343)

Purposes for Assessment

There are a number of different classification systems used to identify the various purposes for assessment. A compilation of several lists identifies some common purposes such as the following:

1. Diagnostic assessments are used to determine individual weakness and strengths in specific areas.
2. Readiness assessments measure prerequisite knowledge and skills.
3. Interest and Attitude assessments attempt to identify topics of high interest or areas in which students may need extra motivational activities.
4. Evaluation assessments are generally programmed or teacher focused.
5. Placement assessments are used for purposes of grouping students or determining appropriate beginning levels in leveled materials.
6. Formative assessment provide on-going feedback student progress and the success of instructional methods and materials.
7. Summative assessment define student accomplishment with the intent to determine the degree of student mastery or learning that has taken place.

For most teachers, assessment purposes vary according to the situation. It may be helpful to consult several sources to help formulate an overall assessment plan. Kellough and Roberts (1991) identify six purposes for assessment. These are:

1. To evaluate and improve student learning.
2. To identify student strengths and weaknesses.
3. To assess the effectiveness of a particular instructional strategy.
4. To evaluate and improve program effectiveness.
5. To evaluate and improve teacher effectiveness.
6. To communicate to parents their children's progress (p.341).

Limitations of Various Types of Assessment

The existence of various types of assessment stems from the unique needs of children with disabilities and the environments in which the disabilities are most troublesome. A student who demonstrates difficulty interacting with peers and acts impulsively may not be effectively evaluated with a portfolio. Anecdotal records, questioning and certain checklists may give a better picture of the extent to which such peer interactions are detrimental to the student's (and others') well being and success. Conversely, a student who displays academic difficulty is better assessed with samples of work (portfolio) and carefully chosen formal tests. In short, assessments are as valuable as the appropriate choice and use thereof.

Alternative assessments (e.g., authentic assessment and portfolio assessment)

Test taking is not a pleasant experience for many students with behavioral and/or learning problems. They may lack study skills, may experience anxiety before or during a test, or may have problems understanding and differentiating the task requirements for different tests. The skills necessary to be successful vary with type of test. Certain students have difficulty with writing answers, but may be able to express their knowledge of subject matter verbally. Therefore, modifications of content area material may be extended to methods and modifications for evaluation and assessment of student progress.

Information about the student's achievement is gathered in a variety of ways including assessments such as intelligence test and various achievement test. In addition to those assessments other information is gathered through alternate assessments such as observations, performance-based assessments, interviews and portfolios.

Observations
Observations are the recording of information about the student as the behavior occurs.

Performance-Based Assessments
Performance assessment is a form of testing that requires students to perform a task rather than select an answer from a ready-made list. The teacher then judges the quality of the student's work based on a predetermined set of criteria.

Portfolios
Portfolios are selected collections of a variety of the student's work. It includes work samples that are demonstrative of the students strengths and weaknesses.

Interview
Formal or informal interviews are often conducted of persons who have a close relationship to the student and can offer valuable information about the students progress socially and academically.

Skill 2.02 Demonstrate knowledge of procedures for conducting a comprehensive evaluation

Identifying procedures used for screening, prereferral, referral, classification and declassification

Referral

Referral is the process through which a teacher, a parent or some other person formally requests an evaluation of a student to determine eligibility for special education services. The decision to refer a student may be influenced by: 1) student characteristics, such as the abilities, behaviors or skills that students exhibit (or lack of them); 2) individual differences among teachers, in their beliefs, expectations, or skill in dealing with specific kinds of problems; 3) expectations for assistance with a student who is exhibiting academic or behavioral learning problems; 4) availability of specific kinds of strategies and materials; 5) parents' demand for referral or opposition to referral; and 6) institutional factors that may facilitate or constrain teachers in making referral decisions. Fewer students are referred when school districts have complex procedures for referral, psychological assessments are backlogged for months, special education classes are filled to capacity, or principals and other administrators do not fully recognize the importance of special services.

It is important that referral procedures be clearly understood and coordinated among all school personnel. All educators need to be able to identify characteristics typically exhibited by special needs students.

Evaluation

The evaluation is comprehensive and includes norm and criterion-referenced tests (e.g., IQ and diagnostic tests), curriculum-based assessment, systematic teacher observation (e.g., behavior frequency checklist), samples of student work and parent interviews. The results of the evaluation are twofold:
  a. determined eligibility for special education services, and
  b. identify a student's strengths and weaknesses in order to plan an individual education program.

The wording in federal law is very explicit about the manner in which evaluations must be conducted, and about the existence of due process procedures that protect against bias and discrimination. Provisions in the law include the following as listed.
   a. The testing of children in their native or primary language unless it is clearly not feasible to do so.
   b. The use of evaluation procedures selected and administered to prevent cultural or ethnic discrimination.
   c. The use of assessment tools validated for the purpose for which they are being used (e.g. achievement levels, IQ scores, adaptive skills).
   d. Assessment by a multidisciplinary team utilizing several pieces of information to formulate a placement decision.

Typically an initial evaluation to determine the student's weaknesses must include: for state specific information please go to
http://www.michigan.gov/documents/2002-06-06MichiganADmRulesSpEd_34533_7.pdf
- A physical examination.
- A psychological evaluation (if determined appropriate for school-age students, but mandatory for pre-school children).
- A social history.
- Observation of the child in his or her current education setting.
- Other tests or assessments that are appropriate for your child (such as a speech and language assessment or a functional behavioral assessment).
- Vocational assessments (required at age 12).

Furthermore, parental involvement must occur in the development of the child's educational program. According to the law, parents must:
1. Be notified before initial evaluation or any change in placement by a written notice in their primary language describing the proposed school action, the reasons for it, and the available educational opportunities.
2. Consent, in writing, before the child is initially evaluated.

Parents may:
1. Request an independent educational evaluation if they feel the school's evaluation is inappropriate.
2. Request an evaluation at public expense if a due process hearing decision is that the public agency's evaluation was inappropriate.
3. Participate on the committee that considers the evaluation, placement, and programming of the student.

All students referred for evaluation for special education should have on file the results of a relatively current vision and hearing screening. This will determine the adequacy of sensory acuity and ensure that learning problems are not due to a vision and/or hearing problem.

Eligibility

Eligibility is based on criteria defined in federal law or state regulations, which vary from state to state. Evaluation methods correspond with eligibility criteria for the special education classifications. For example, a multidisciplinary evaluation for a student being evaluated for intellectual disabilities would include the individual's intellectual functioning, adaptive behavior and achievement levels. Other tests are based on developmental characteristics exhibited (e.g., social, language and motor).

A student evaluated for learning disabilities is given reading, math and/or spelling achievement tests, an intelligence test to confirm average or above average cognitive capabilities, and tests of written and oral language ability. Tests need to show a discrepancy between potential and performance. Classroom observations and samples of student work (such as impaired reading ability or impaired writing ability) also provide indicators of possible learning disabilities.

If considered eligible for special education services, the child's disability should be documented in a written report stating specific reasons for the decision. A meeting must be help with Multidisciplinary Evaluation team, in which the parent and other professionals are a part, to discuss the results. The status of the child's eligibility will be revealed during this meeting. If the child does qualify the parent's permission must be received before official placement occurs. If the child does not qualify, the parent will be information revealing why the child does not qualify. The parent will also be informed of any other programs the child may qualify.

Also if the child qualifies, three-year re-evaluations of a student's progress are required by law and serve the purpose of determining the growth and changing needs of the student. During the re-evaluation, continued eligibility for services in special education must be assessed using a range of evaluation tools similar to those used during the initial evaluation. All relevant information about the student is considered when making a decision about continued eligibility or whether the student no longer needs the service and is ready to begin preparing to exit the program. If the latter is transition that is more appropriate, planning must occur.

LEARNING DISABLED

IEP Development

The IEP committee convenes to discuss the child's current functional level along with assessment results and information gathered from the committee. From that information, the Committee agrees on the goals the child should be working toward. The Committee then discusses the supports and services and modifications that the child needs to reach those goals. Finally, the Committee determines where those special education services will be provided (location and placement). The location where services will be provided and the student's placement must be in the student's least restrictive environment.

Special education services occur at a variety of levels, some more restrictive than others. The largest number of students (i.e.: mild disabilities) is served in settings closest to normal educational placements. Service delivery in more restrictive settings is limited to students with severe or profound disabilities, who comprise a smaller population within special education. The exception is correctional facilities, which serve a limited and restricted populace.

Options for placement of special education students are given on what we call a "cascade of services," the term coined by Deno (1970). The multidisciplinary team must be able to match the needs of the student with an appropriate placement in the cascade system of services. According to Polloway, et al. (1994), two assumptions are made when we place students using the cascade of services as a guide. First, a child should be placed in an educational setting as close to the regular classroom as possible and placed only as far away from this least restrictive environment as necessary to provide an appropriate education.

Second, program exit should be a goal. A student's placement may change when the team obtains data suggesting the advisability of an alternative educational setting. As adaptive, social, cognitive, motor and language skills are developed, the student may be placed in a lesser restrictive environment. The multidisciplinary team is responsible for monitoring and recommending placement changes when appropriate.

Cascade System of Special Education Services[2]

- Level 1 regular classroom, including students with disabilities able to learn with regular class accommodations, with or without medical and counseling services.
- Level 2 regular classroom with supportive services (i.e.: consultation and inclusion).
- Level 3 regular class with part-time special class (i.e.: itinerant services and resource room).
- Level 4 full-time special class (i.e.: self-contained).
- Level 5 special stations (i.e.: special schools).
- Level 6 homebound
- Level 7 residential (i.e.: hospital and institution)

Special Education Procedures

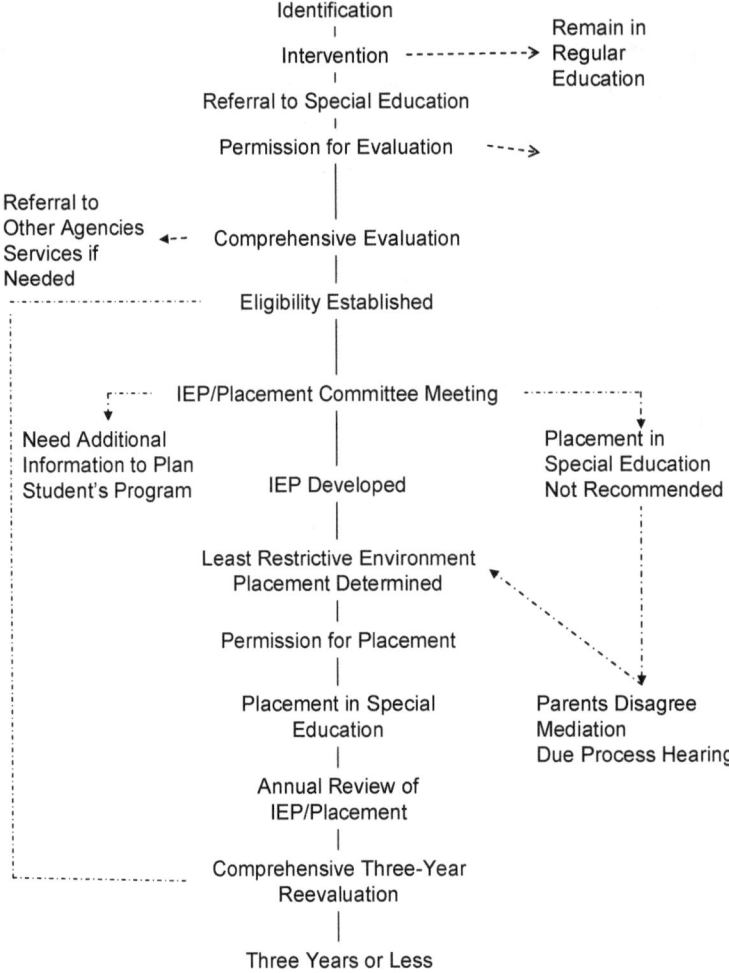

---

[2] Adapted from 1. Deno, "*Special Education as Developmental Capital*." <u>Exceptional Children</u> 1970, 37, 239, 237 Copyright 1970 by The Council for Exceptional Children Reprinted with permission from The Council for Exceptional Children.

Declassification

The student must be evaluated to determine if he or she no longer has a disability. Declassification recommendations should be documented on the student's final IEP.

Skill 2.03 Analyze the uses of ongoing assessment in the education of students with learning disabilities

Use Ongoing Assessment to Evaluate and Modify Instruction

Assessment skills should be an integral part of teacher training, where teachers are able to monitor student learning using pre and post assessments of content areas; analyze assessment data in terms of individualized support for students and instructional practice for teachers; and designing lesson plans that have measurable outcomes and definitive learning standards. Assessment information should be used to provide performance-based criteria and academic expectations for all students in evaluating whether students have learned the expected skills and content of the subject area.

For example in an Algebra I class, teachers can use assessments to see whether students have learned the prior knowledge to engage in the subject area. If the teacher provides students with a pre-assessment on algebraic expression and ascertains whether the lesson plan should be modified to include a pre-algebraic expression lesson unit to refresh student understanding of the content area, then the teacher can create if needed, quantifiable data to support the need of additional resources to support student learning. Once the teacher has taught the unit on algebraic expression, a post assessment test can be used to test student learning and a mastery exam can be used to test how well students understand and can apply the knowledge to the next unit of math content learning.

Teachers can use assessment data to inform and impact instructional practices by making inferences on teaching methods and gathering clues for student performance. By analyzing the various types of assessments, teachers can gather more definitive information on projected student academic performance. Instructional strategies for teachers would provide learning targets for student behavior, cognitive thinking skills and processing skills that can be employed to diversify student learning opportunities.

Skill 2.04 **Demonstrate knowledge of the development and implementation of Individualized Educational Programs (IEPs) for students with learning disabilities**

Analyzing Issues Related to the Preparation and Amendment of an IEP
A considerable amount of preparation and information gathering must be done prior to writing an IEP. Largely, this responsibility lies with the special educator although the school psychologist or psychometrist may be more involved if the IEP is an initial IEP or if it is one written after an evaluation. Other school professionals who may be contributors are nurse, social worker, speech and language therapist, occupational therapist, physical therapist, audiologist and technology consultant. In addition, information from outside sources of the above professions as well as physicians may be included.

Initial IEPs are written only after the student completes an evaluation by a school psychologist or psychometrist and the findings of such are that the student has a disability that adversely affects his school performance. Once eligibility for special services has been determined, the following information should be supplied for the IEP.

Identifying Information includes student's name, address, phone number, Social Security Number (if available), Medicaid number (if applicable), birth date, parents' names, parents' addresses and parents' phone numbers. With whom the student resides (parent, guardian, foster parent) is also included.

Student Eligibility to received special education services is indicated as well as any secondary eligibilities.

Present Level of Functioning (including strengths and weaknesses) for social skills, communication, academic functioning, fine and gross motor skills, independent functioning and vocational skills is recorded.

Current Vision and Hearing Screening Results are included to rule out possible impairment and the need for further assessment in these areas.

State Standards Based Goals with Measurable Objectives should be included in areas where the student is expected to need the greatest concentration of special education.

Program Services Times will outline the amount of time that the student may receive services from various therapists (speech and language, occupational therapy, physical therapy, social work, technology, nurse, vision and hearing), the amount of time that the student will receive special education services in the regular and special education classroom, and the amount of time the student will participate in the regular education curriculum (including time in "specials" classes such as music, PE, library, computers and art). Times are often listed in minutes per week or minutes per month.

Accommodations and Modifications (if any) that will be made to the student's educational program (special equipment needed, reduction in amount of work, assistance needed and extended time).

Student Participation in State and Local Assessments IEP will indicate if the student will participate in these assessments (strongly encouraged due to NCLB, No Child Left Behind) and if accommodations will be made. Accommodations may include things such as testing in a separate setting, untimed testing sessions, use of a calculator and having tests (other than a reading test) read or instructions rephrased. Use of specific assistive technology such as an auditory trainer must be documented. Note: if it is determined that the student cannot participate in "regular" state and local testing, then *Alternative Testing* must be marked on the IEP.

Extended School Year is considered for each student and determination is made based on whether or not the student will have difficulty regaining skills that may be lost during the summer months if extended school year is not attended.

Transportation is considered for the student including the need for special transportation and any special equipment or personnel that may be needed.

Overall Percentage of Time in Special/Regular Education is determined as well as the rationale of why other percentages of time (greater or lesser) were not chosen.

Parental Consent and Notification of an IEP Meeting parents should be notified in writing ten days prior to an IEP meeting. A total of three contacts should be made with the parent prior to the meeting. Parents should also be provided with a document outlining parents' rights in the special education process. Although parental consent is required for initial testing and subsequent consent is not needed unless a change in placement is being considered.

Reconvening of an IEP (Amendment) may be requested by school personnel or parents at any time that the program is considered to not be meeting the needs of the student. However, according to the IDEA 2004, changes may be made in the IEP as deemed necessary by the CPSE (Committee on Pre-school Special Education) / CSE (Committee on Special Education) committee, and as with regular IEP meetings, a Parent Member is not mandatory.

Multi-year IEP Meetings are now being used in some school districts when the existing program seems appropriate for the student. This is an effort to minimize paperwork and meeting times.

Three-year Re-evaluation Meetings determine the appropriateness of the student's program and the possible need for additional testing.

Recognizing the rights, roles and functions of IEP team members (e.g., special education teacher, student, parents/guardians, general education teacher, speech language therapist, occupational therapist and school administrator)

According to IDEA 2004, the IEP team includes:
- Parents of a child with a disability; not less than one regular education teacher of such child (if the child is, or may be, participating in the regular education environment).
- Not less than one special education teacher, or where appropriate, not less than one special education provider of such child.
- A representative of the local educational agency; an individual who can interpret the instructional implications of evaluation results.
- At the discretion of the parent of the agency, other individuals who have knowledge or special expertise regarding the child, including related services personnel as appropriate whenever appropriate, the child with a disability.

The role of the representative of the local education agency is to provide or supervise the provision of specifically designed instruction to meet the unique needs of the child. This is usually the school principal if this is the first time the child has been evaluated. If the representative is not an expert on evaluations, then one of the people who participated in the actual testing of the child must be present.

The role of the teacher is to identify the short and long term goals for the student and to give the student's current progress including strengths and weaknesses. The school must allow any other individual whom the parent wants to invite to attend the meeting. This may be a caseworker involved with the student's family, people involved with the day-to-day care of the student or any person whom the parent feels can contribute vital information to the meeting.

The parent or guardian can also bring someone to help them understand the IEP or the IEP process, such as a lawyer experienced with educational advocacy or parent advocate.

There are lists of related services that may be considered during an IEP meeting. The related services are developmental, corrective, and other supportive services that are required to help a child with special needs benefit from special education. These related services can include speech pathology and audiology, psychological services, physical and occupational therapy, recreation and extracurricular activities, counseling services and medical services for diagnostic or evaluation purposes.

The IEP should specify the services to be provided, the extent to which they are necessary, and who will provide the services. If a specialist such as a speech teacher or occupational therapist will provide specific services, they should be included in the IEP team so they can give input on the types of services required, available, and what may be beneficial to the student in question. Information on how they are doing in particular specialist areas will also be included with an evaluation of student process with speech therapy and occupational therapy.

Identifying information that must be specified in an IEP

It is important to understand how much the law effects the required components of the IEP. Educators must keep themselves apprised of the changes and amendments to laws such as IDEA and the required manner that it must be completed. At present the following elements are required of an IEP:

1. The student's present level of academic performance and functional performance.
2. A statement of how the disability affects the student's involvement and progress in the general education curriculum. Preschool children must have a statement explaining how the disability effects the child's participation in appropriate activities.
3. A statement of annual goals or anticipated attainments.
4. Short-term objectives are no longer required on every IEP. Students with severe disabilities or those taking an alternate assessment may need short term objectives, which lead to the obtainment of annual goals.
5. A statement of when the parent will be notified of their child's progress which must be at least as often as the regular education student.
6. Modifications or accommodations for participation in statewide or citywide assessments; or if it is determined that the child cannot participate, why the assessment is inappropriate for the child and how the child will be assessed.
7. Specific educational services, assistive technology, and related services, to be provided, and those who will provide them.
8. Evaluate criteria and timeliness for determining whether instructional objectives have been achieved.
9. Projected dates for initiating services with their anticipated frequency, location and, duration.
10. The extent to which the child will not participate in the regular education program.

Transition - beginning when a student is 14, and annually thereafter, the student's IEP must contain a statement of his or her transition service needs under the various components of that IEP that focus upon the student's courses of study (e.g., vocational education or advanced placement); and when appropriate include interagency responsibilities and links for possible future assistance beginning at least one year before the student reaches the age of majority under State law, the IEP must contain a statement that the student has been informed of the rights under the law that will transfer to him or her upon reaching the age of majority.

TEACHER CERTIFICATION STUDY GUIDE

Skill 2.05 **Demonstrate knowledge of a continuum of options for program and service delivery for students with learning disabilities**

Supports and Accommodations Needed for Integrating Students with Disabilities into Various Program Placements

The special educator is trained to work in a team approach. This occurs from the initial identification of students who appear o deviate from what is considered to be normal performance or behavior for particular age- and grade-level students. The special education teacher serves as a consultant (or as a team member, depending on the school district) to the student support team. If the student is referred, the special education teacher may be asked to collect assessment data for the forthcoming comprehensive evaluation. This professional then generally serves on the multidisciplinary eligibility, individualized educational planning and placement committees. If the student is placed in a special education setting, the special educator continues to coordinate and collaborate with regular classroom teachers and support personnel at the school-based level.

Support professionals are available at both the district- and school-based levels, and they contribute valuable services and expertise in their respective areas. A team approach between district ancillary services and local school-based staff is essential.

- **School psychologist**. The school psychologist participates in the referral, identification, and program planning processes. She contributes to the multidisciplinary team by adding important observations, data and inferences about the student's performance. As she conducts an evaluation, she observes the student in the classroom environment, takes a case history and administers a battery of formal and informal individual tests. The psychologist is involved as a member of a professional team throughout the stages of referral, assessment, placement and program planning.

- **Physical therapist**. This person works with disorders of bones, joints, muscles, and nerves following medical assessment. Under the prescription of a physician, the therapist applies treatment to the students in the form of heat, light, massage and exercise to prevent further disability or deformity. Physical therapy includes the use of adaptive equipment, and prosthetic and orthotic devices to facilitate independent movement. This type of therapy helps individuals with disabilities to develop or recover their physical strength and endurance.

- **Occupational therapist**. This specialist is trained in helping students develop self-help skills (e.g., self-care, motor, perceptual and vocational skills). The students are actively involved in the treatment process to quicken recovery and rehabilitation.

LEARNING DISABLED

- **Speech and language pathologist**. This specialist assists in the identification and diagnosis of children with speech or language disorders. In addition, she makes referrals for medical or habilitation needs, counsels family members and teachers, and works with the prevention of communicative disorders. The speech and language therapist concentrates on rehabilitative service delivery and continuing diagnosis.

- **Administrators**. Building principals and special education directors (or coordinators) provide logistical as well as emotional support. Principals implement building policy procedures and control designation of facilities, equipment, and materials. Their support is crucial to the success of the program within the parameters of the base school. Special education directors provide information about federal, state, and local policy which is vital to the operation of a special education unit. In some districts the special education director may actually control certain services and materials. Role clarification, preferably in writing, should be accomplished to ensure effectiveness of program services.

- **Guidance counselors, psychometrists and diagnosticians**. These persons often lead individual and group counseling sessions, and are trained in assessment, diagnostic and observation skills, as well as personality development and functioning abilities. They can apply knowledge and skills to multidisciplinary teams, and assist in the assessment, diagnosis, placement and program planning process.

- **Social worker**. The social worker is trained in interviewing and counseling skills. This person possesses knowledge of available community and school services, and makes these known to parents. She often visits homes of students, conducts intake and assessment interviews, counsels individuals and small groups, and assists in district enforcement policies.

- **School nurse**. This person offers valuable information about diagnostic and treatment services. She is knowledgeable about diets, medications, therapeutic services, health-related services and care needed for specific medical conditions. Reports of communicable diseases are filed with the health department to which a health professional has access. A medical professional can sometimes obtain cooperation with the families of children with disabilities in ways that are difficult for the special education teacher to achieve.

- **Regular teachers and subject matter specialists**. These professionals are trained in general and specific instructional areas, teaching techniques, and overall child growth and development. They serve as a vital component to the referral process, as well as in the subsequent treatment program, if the student is determined eligible. They work with the students with special needs for the majority of the school day and function as a link to the children's special education and medical programs.

- **Paraprofessional**. This staff member assists the special educator and often works in the classroom with the special needs students. She helps prepare specialized materials, tutor individual students, lead small groups and provide feedback to students about their work.

Modifying materials is a great accommodation to use in order to include students in the general education classroom. Materials, usually textbooks, are usually modified because of reading level. The goal of modification is to present the material in manner that the student can more understand while preserving the basic ideas and content. Modifications of course material may take the form of:

Simplifying Texts
- Using a highlighter to mark key terms, main ideas and concepts. In some cases, a marker may be used to delete nonessential content.
- Cut and paste. The main ideas and specific content are cut and pasted on separate sheets of paper. Additional headings or other graphic aids can be inserted to help the student understand and organize material.
- Supplement with graphic aids or tables.
- Supplement with study guides, questions and directed preview.
- Use self-correcting materials.
- Allow additional time or break content material into smaller, more manageable units.

Taped Textbooks
Textbooks can be taped by the teacher or aide for students to follow along. In some cases, the students may qualify for recordings of textbooks from agencies such as Recordings for the Blind.

Parallel Curriculum
Projects such as Parallel Alternative Curriculum (PAC) or Parallel Alternative Strategies for Students (PASS), which present the content at a lower grade reading level and come with tests, study guides, vocabulary activities and tests.

Supplementary Texts
Book publishers such as Steck-Vaughn publish series of content-area texts that have been modified for reading level, amount of content presented on pages, highlighted key items, and visual aids.

Accommodations in Test-Taking Situations

Test taking is not a pleasant experience for many students with behavioral and/or learning problems. They may lack study skills, may experience anxiety before or during a test, or may have problems understanding and differentiating the task requirements for different tests. The skills necessary to be successful vary with type of test. Certain students have difficulty with writing answers, but may be able to express their knowledge of subject matter verbally. Therefore, modifications of content area material may be extended to methods and modifications for evaluation and assessment of student progress.

Some of the ways that teachers can modify assessment for individual needs include:

- Help students to get used to timed tests with timed practice tests.
- Provide study guides before tests.
- Make tests easier to read by leaving ample space between the questions.
- Modify multiple choice tests by reducing the number of choices, reforming questions to yes-no or using matching items.
- Modify short-answer tests with cloze (fill-in) statements or provide a list of facts or choices that the student can choose from.
- Essay tests can be modified by using partial outlines for the student to complete, allowing additional time or test items that do not require extensive writing.

- Please refer to skill 2.02 for more information about continuum of services

| SUBAREA III. | METHODOLOGY AND INSTRUCTION |

Skill 3.01 Apply principles and methods involved in individualizing instruction for students with learning disabilities.

Instructional planning for a variety of inclusive models (e.g., co-teaching, push-in, consultant teaching [CT])

According to IDEA 2004, students with disabilities are to participate in the general education program to the extent that it is beneficial for them. As these students are included into a variety of general education activities and classes, the need for collaboration among teachers grows.

Co-teaching one model that is used for general education and special education teachers to collaborate is co-teaching. In this model, both teachers actively teach in the general education classroom. Perhaps both teachers will conduct a small science experiment group at the same time, switching groups at some point in the lesson. Perhaps in social studies, one teacher will lecture while the other teacher writes notes on the board or points out information on a map.

In the co-teaching model, the general education teacher and special educator often switch roles back and forth within a class period or perhaps at the end of a chapter or unit.

Push-in Teaching in the push-in teaching model, the special educator is teaching parallel material in the general education classroom. When the regular education teacher is teaching word problems in math, for example, the special educator may be working with some students on setting up the initial problems and then having them complete the computation. Another example would be in science when the general education teacher is asking review questions for a test, and the special educator is working with a student who has a review study sheet to show the answer from a group of choices.

In the push-in teaching model, it may appear that two versions of the same lesson are being taught or two types of student responses / activities are being monitored on the same material. The push-in teaching model would be considered one type of differentiated instruction in which two teachers are teaching simultaneously.

Consultant Teaching in the consultant teaching model, the general education teacher conducts the class after planning with the special educator about how to differentiate activities so that the needs of the student with a disability are met.

In a social studies classroom using the consultant teaching model, both teachers may discuss what the expectations will be for a student with a learning disability and fine motor difficulty when the class does reports on states. They may decide that doing a state report is appropriate for the student; however, he may use the computer to write his report so that he can utilize the spell check feature and so that is his work is legible.

Instructional Methods, Techniques and Curricula Including Assistive and Instructional Technologies Used with Students to Accommodate Specific Disabilities.

No two students are alike. It follows, then, that no students *learn* alike. To apply a one dimensional instructional approach and a strict tunnel vision perspective of testing is to impose learning limits on students. All students have the right to an education, but there cannot be a singular path to that education. A teacher must acknowledge the variety of learning styles and abilities among students within a class (and, indeed, the varieties from class to class) and apply multiple instructional and assessment processes to ensure that every child has appropriate opportunities to master the subject matter, demonstrate such mastery, and improve and enhance learning skills with each lesson.

It has been traditionally assumed that a teacher will use direct instruction in the classroom. The amount of time devoted to it will vary according to the age of the class as well as other factors. Lecturing can be very valuable because it's the quickest way for transferring knowledge to students and they can also learn note-taking and information-organizing skills in this way. However, having said that, there are many cautions to using an excessive amount of lecturing in a class of any age. In the first place, attention span even of senior high-school students is short when they are using only one sense—the sense of hearing. Teachers should limit how much lecture they do as compared to other methods and how long the lectures last.

Most teachers find students enjoy the learning process when lecturing is limited and the students themselves become active in and responsible for their own learning. Students' attitudes and perceptions about learning are the most powerful factors influencing academic focus and success. When instructional objectives center on students' interests and are relevant to their lives, effective learning occurs. Learners must believe that the tasks that they are asked to perform have some value and that they have the ability and resources to perform them. If a student thinks a task is unimportant, he/she will not put forth much effort. If a student thinks he lacks the ability or resources to successfully complete a task, even attempting the task becomes too great a risk. Not only must the teacher understand the students' abilities and interests, she must also help students develop positive attitudes and perceptions about tasks and learning. Below are a few examples of instructional styles that actively involve the students.

Differentiated instruction

The effective teacher will seek to connect all students to the subject matter through multiple techniques, with the goal that each student, through their own abilities, will relate to one or more techniques and excel in the learning process. Differentiated instruction encompasses several areas:

- **Content**: what is the teacher going to teach? Or, perhaps better put, what does the teacher want the students to learn? Differentiating content means that students will have access to content that piques their interest about a topic, with a complexity that provides an appropriate challenge to their intellectual development.

- **Process**: a classroom management technique where instructional organization and delivery is maximized for the diverse student group. These techniques should include dynamic, flexible grouping activities, where instruction and learning occurs both as whole-class, teacher-led activities, as well peer learning and teaching (while teacher observes and coaches) within small groups or pairs.

- **Product**: the expectations and requirements placed on students to demonstrate their knowledge or understanding. The type of product expected from each student should reflect each student's own capabilities.

Alternative assessments

Alternative assessment is an assessment where students create an answer or a response to a question or task, as opposed to traditional, inflexible assessments where students choose a prepared response from among a selection of responses, such as matching, multiple-choice or true/false.

When implemented effectively, an alternative assessment approach will exhibit these characteristics, among others:

- Requires higher-order thinking and problem-solving.
- Provides opportunities for student self-reflection and self-assessment.
- Uses real world applications to connect students to the subject.
- Provides opportunities for students to learn and examine subjects on their own, as well as to collaborate with their peers.
- Encourages students to continuing learning beyond the requirements of the assignment.
- Clearly defines objective and performance goals.

Teachers are learning the value of giving assignments that meet the individual abilities and needs of students. After instruction, discussion, questioning and practice have been provided, rather than assigning one task to all students - teachers are asking students to generate tasks that will show their knowledge of the information presented. Students are given choices and thereby have the opportunity to demonstrate more effectively the skills, concepts or topics that they as individuals have learned. It has been established that student choice increases student originality, intrinsic motivation, and higher mental processes.

Five basic types of grouping arrangements are typically used in the classroom.

A. Large Group with Teacher

Examples of appropriate activities include show and tell, discussions, watching plays or movies, brainstorming ideas and playing games. Science, social studies and most other subjects, except for reading and math are taught in large groups.

The advantage of large-group instruction is that it is time-efficient and prepares students for higher levels of secondary and post-secondary education settings; however, with large groups, instruction cannot be as easily tailored to high or low levels of students, who may become bored or frustrated. Mercer and Mercer recommend guidelines for effective large-group instruction:

- Keep instruction short, ranging from 5 to 15 minutes for first grade to seventh grade; 5 to 40 minutes, for grades 8 to 12.
- Use questions to involve all students, use lecture-pause routines, and encourage active participation among the lower-performing students.
- Incorporate visual aids to promote understanding, and maintain a lively pace.
- Break up the presentation with different rates of speaking, giving students a "stretch break," varying voice volume and etc.
- Establish rules of conduct for large groups and praise students who follow the rules.

B. Small Group Instruction

Small group instruction usually includes 5 to 7 students and is recommended for teaching basic academic skills such as math facts or reading. This model is especially effective for students with learning problems. Composition of the groups should be flexible to accommodate different rates of progress through instruction. The advantages of teaching in small groups is that the teacher is better able to provide feedback, monitor student progress and give more instruction, praise and feedback. With small groups the teacher will need make sure to provide a steady pace for the lesson, provide questions and activities that allow all to participate, and include lots of positive praise.

C. One Student with Teacher

One-to-one tutorial teaching can be used to provide extra assistance to individual students. Such tutoring may be scheduled at set times during the day or provided as the need arises. The tutoring model is typically found more in elementary and resource classrooms than secondary settings.

D. Peer Tutoring

In an effective peer tutoring arrangement, the teacher trains the peer tutors and matches them with students who need extra practice and assistance. In addition to academic skills, the arrangement can help both students work on social skills such as cooperation and self-esteem. Both students may be working on the same material or the tutee may be working to strengthen areas of weakness. The teacher determines the target goals, selects the material, sets up the guidelines, trains the student tutors, in the rules and methods of the sessions, and monitors and evaluates the sessions.

E. Cooperative Learning

Cooperative learning differs from peer tutoring in that students are grouped in teams or small groups and the methods are based on teamwork, individual accountability and team reward. Individual students are responsible for their own learning and share of the work, as well as the group's success. As with peer tutoring, the goals, target skills, materials and guidelines, are developed by the teacher. Teamwork skills may also need to be taught, too. By focusing on team goals, all members of the team are encouraged to help each other as well as improve their individual performance.

Curriculum Design

Effective curriculum design assists the teacher from teacher demonstration to independent practice. Components of curriculum design include:

- Quizzes or reviews of the previous lesson.
- Step-by-step presentations with multiple examples.
- Guided practice and feedback.
- Independent practice that requires the student to produce faster responses.

The chosen curriculum should introduce information in a cumulative sequence and not introduce too much new information at a time. Review difficult material and practice to aid retention. New vocabulary and symbols should be introduced one at a time, and the relationships of components to the whole should be stressed. Students' background information should be recalled to connect new information to the old. Finally, teach strategies or algorithms first and then move on to tasks that are more difficult.

Course objectives may be obtained from the department head at the local school. The ESE coordinator may have copies of objectives for functional courses or applied ESE courses. District program specialists also have lists of objectives for each course provided in the local school system. Additionally, publishers of textbooks will have scope and sequence lists in the teacher's manual.

Addressing students' needs

There are a number of procedures teachers can use to address the varying need of the students. Some of the more common procedures are:

1. **Vary assignments** - a variety of assignments on the same content allows students to match learning styles and preferences with the assignment. If all assignments are writing assignments, for example, students who are hands-on or visual learners are at a disadvantage unrelated to the content base itself.

2. **Cooperative learning** - cooperative learning activities allow students to share ideas, expertise, and insight with a non-threatening setting. The focus tends to remain on positive learning rather than on competition.

3. **Structure environment** - some students need and benefit from clear structure that defines the expectation and goals of the teacher. The student knows what is expected and when and can work and plan accordingly.

4. **Clearly stated assignments** - assignments should be clearly stated along with the expectation and criteria for completion. Reinforcement and practice activities should not be a guessing game for the students. The exception to this is, of course, those situations in which a discovery method is used.

5. **Independent practice** - independent practice involving application and repetition is necessary for thorough learning. Students learn to be independent learners through practicing independent learning. These activities should always be within the student's abilities to perform successfully without assistance.

6. **Repetition** - very little learning is successful with a single exposure. Learners generally require multiple exposures to the same information for learning to take place. However, this repetition does not have to be dull and monotonous. In conjunction with #1 above, varied assignments can provide repetition of content or skill practiced without repetition of specific activities. This helps keep learning fresh and exciting for the student.

7. **Overlearning** - as a principle of effective learning, overlearning recommends that students continue to study and review after they have achieved initial mastery. The use of repetition in the context of varied assignments and offers the means to help students pursue and achieve overlearning.

Skill 3.02   Demonstrate knowledge of various instructional approaches used with students with learning disabilities.

Cognitive techniques assist the student in processing and manipulating information. Some examples include taking notes, asking questions, or filling out information. Cognitive strategies can be very task-specific. This means that certain cognitive strategies are helpful when learning or doing certain tasks. Metacognitive strategies are the strategies that a student utilizes when planning, examining and assessing learning or strategy performance.

The use of metacognitive strategies indicates that the student is aware of learning as a process and of what will aid in the learning process. Taking the time to plan before writing; for example, shows that the student knows what is involved in writing a good essay. Similarly, he or she might monitor comprehension while reading and take action when something does not make sense; for example, look back in the text for clarification or consciously hold the question in mind while continuing to read. Evaluating one's work, learning or even strategy use is also highly metacognitive in nature, because it shows that a learner is aware of and thinking about how learning takes place.

Metacognitive strategies are at the core of self-regulated learning, which, in turn, is at the core of successful and lifelong learning. Self-regulation involves such strategies as goal setting, self-instruction, self-monitoring and self-reinforcement.

The key to teaching students to use metacognitive strategies entail having students set goals for learning, talk to themselves in positive ways about learning and use self-instruction to guide themselves through a learning problem, monitor their comprehension or progress, and reward themselves for success.

Instructional strategies have also been categorized by their function for the learner. Strategies that help the student initially learn new information are called acquisition strategies. Strategies that help the student manipulate information so that it can be stored in memory are called storage strategies. Strategies that are utilized to help the student remember or demonstrate what they have learned are called demonstration and expression of knowledge strategies.

Multisensory instruction is any learning activity that involves the use of two or more sensory modalities (visual, auditory, tactile/kinesthetic or articulatory) at the same time to express information. An example of multisensory instruction would be when a student is taught the alphabet by feeling, naming, and matching forms or tracing on rough surfaces. Learning is experienced through all senses including the kinesthetic sense, so the multisensory approach focuses on numerous senses at the same time to help reinforce long-term memory.

A number of instructional strategies have been used to help students with learning disabilities. One strategy called reciprocal teaching involves students interacting thoroughly with the text via strategies of summarizing, asking, and predicting. The lesson is organized in the form of a discussion with an assigned leader who can be the teacher or the student. The leader asks a question about a text that has been read and the group responds. Other group members then asks questions and the leader than gives a summary of the main points of the text.

Another instructional strategy is called questioning to find the main idea. This strategy was developed by Wong and Jones and involves finding and questioning the main idea or summary of a paragraph. Students with learning disabilities who were trained in a self-questioning strategy showed higher comprehensive levels then students without this training.

Skill 3.03 Demonstrate knowledge of approaches and techniques used to improve students' receptive language skills

Over the years, theories regarding language development have been very vocal and disagreed at many levels. The major disagreement can be tracked back to the 1950's where two predominant theories emerged.

Behaviorism developed and believed that language was the direct result of the situations surrounding the child. Behaviorists believed that the environment controlled all language and solely these outside forces influenced its development.

On the other hand, nativism theorists believed that all language was similar to genetic traits. They believed that language was determined before birth and developed in a similar manner to other innate characteristics. They ruled out that any outside factors could influence the development process.

Currently, these two opposing viewpoints have been combined to form the interactionist theories. This term indicates that children's language skills are a direct result of inherent predetermined skills and the surrounding environment.

Children who struggle in language developmental will almost certainly have difficulty obtaining a solid foundation in reading skills. As language develops, students begin to understand how sounds blend together to form words, how words go together to form sentences, and how sentences go together to form stories. It is through these stories and sentences that meaning is conveyed from one party to another. If a student is unable to draw conclusions from the message that someone else is sending, they miss a key component of language development. It is in this receptive language breakdown that a learning disability in this area may be identified.

Receptive language begins from birth. Infants react to sounds and respond to their primary care giver's voices. Research indicates that in some cases this recognition of voices begins in the womb. Throughout their first year, children make the connection between words and meaning. Receptive language skills are generally more developed than expressive. In this same way, listening is usually a higher functioning skill in most children than speaking or reading.

Beginning roughly at their second birthday, toddlers begin to understand and follow simple commands, usually beginning with one step directions or simple requests then progressing to more and more complex items. Children who have difficulties following one-step directions beyond their third birthday may be in need of evaluation by a professional.

Although students don't have a lot of problems with speaking in class, listening is something that has to be nurtured and taught. Good listeners will respond emotionally, imaginatively and intellectually to what they hear. Students need to be taught how to respond to presentations by their classmates in ways that are not harmful or derogatory in any way. There are also different types of listening that the teacher can develop in the students. For example: Appreciative listening to enjoy an experience, attentive listening to gain knowledge and critical listening to evaluate arguments and ideas.

Children understand words that are not a common part of their speaking vocabulary and most certainly words they are unable to read. It is because of this, that listening comprehension is a more developed skill in students and why teachers are able to read stories to students they would be unable to read themselves. Even though the text is more difficult, the students are able to understand due to their receptive language skills.

Receptive language skills can be developed and increased thereby improving listening, comprehension and nonverbal communication. Some things to keep in mind include:

- It is important to teach students to ask for clarification if they do not understand.
- Teaching the children that it is allowed to not understand everything.
- Looking at the speaker.
- Active listening.
- Providing a summary or brief recap after a conversation can help to make sure what was presented was understood accurately.
- Watching facial expressions and other nonverbal gestures can help to clarify understanding.
- Asking questions periodically.
- Visualization helps with understanding.

Skill 3.04   Demonstrate knowledge of approaches and techniques used to improve students' reading skills

Beginning Reading Approaches
Methods of teaching beginning reading skills may be divided into two major approaches—code emphasis and meaning emphasis. Both approaches have their supporters and their critics. Advocates of code emphasis instruction point out that reading fluency depends on accurate and automatic decoding skills, while advocates of meaning emphasis favor this approach for reading comprehension. Teachers may decide to blend aspects of both approaches to meet the individual needs of their students.

Bottom-up or Code-Emphasis Approach
- Letter-sound regularity is stressed.
- Reading instruction begins with words that consist of letter or letter combinations that have the same sound in different words. Component letter-sound relationships are taught and mastered before introducing new words.
- Examples—phonics, linguistic, modified alphabet, and programmed reading series such as the Merrill Linguistic Reading Program and DISTAR Reading.

Top-down or Meaning Emphasis Model
- Reading for meaning is emphasized from the first stages of instruction.
- Programs begin with words that appear frequently, which are assumed to be familiar and easy to learn. Words are identified by examining meaning and position in context and are decoded by techniques such as context, pictures, initial letters and word configurations. Thus, a letter may not necessarily have the same sound in different words throughout the passage.
- Examples: whole language, language experience and individualized reading programs.

Other approaches that follow beginning reading instruction are available to help teachers design reading programs. Choice of approach will depend on the student's strengths and weaknesses. No matter what approach or combination of approaches is used, the teacher should encourage independent reading and build activities into the reading program that stimulate students to practice their skills through independent reading.

Developmental Reading Approaches
Developmental reading programs emphasize daily, sequential instruction. Instructional materials usually feature a series of books, often basal readers, as the core of the program.
Basal Reading

Basal reader series form the core of many widely used reading programs from preprimers to eighth grade. Depending on the series, basal readers may be meaning-emphasis or code-emphasis. Teacher manuals provide a highly structured and comprehensive scope and sequence, lesson plans and objectives. Vocabulary is controlled from level to level and reading skills cover word recognition, word attack and comprehension.

Advantages of basal readers are the structured, sequential manner in which reading is taught. The teacher manuals have teaching strategies, controlled vocabulary, assessment materials and objectives. Reading instruction is in a systematic, sequential, and comprehension-oriented manner.

Many basal reading programs recommend the <u>directed reading activity procedure</u>, for lesson presentation. Students proceed through the steps of motivation preparation for the new concepts and vocabulary, guided reading and answering questions that give a purpose or goal for the reading, development of strengths through drills or workbook, application of skills and evaluation.

A variation of the directed reading method is <u>direct reading-thinking</u>, where the student must generate the purposes for reading the selection, form questions and read the selection. After reading, the teacher asks questions designed to get the group to think of answers and justify their answers.

Disadvantages of basal readers are the emphasis on teaching to a group rather than the individual. Critics of basal readers claim that the structure may limit creativity and not provide enough instruction on organizational skills and reading for secondary content levels. Basal readers, however, offer the advantage of a prepared comprehensive program, and may be supplemented with other materials to meet individual needs.

Phonics Approach
Word recognition is taught through grapheme-phoneme associations, with the goal of teaching the student to independently apply these skills to new words. Phonics instruction may be synthetic or analytic. In the synthetic method, letter sounds are learned before the student goes on to blend the sounds to form words. The analytic method teaches letter sounds letter sounds as integral parts of words.

The sounds are usually taught in the sequence: vowels, consonants, consonant blends at the beginning of words (e.g., bl and dr) and consonant blends at the end of words (e.g. ld and mp), consonant and vowel digraphs (e.g., ch and sh) and diphthongs (e.g., au and oy).

Critics of the phonics approach point out that the emphasis on pronunciation may lead to the student focusing more on decoding than comprehension. Some students may have trouble blending sounds to form words and others may become confused with words that do not conform to the phonetic "rules." However, advocates of phonics say that the programs are useful with remedial reading and developmental reading. Examples of phonics series are *Science Research Associates, Merrill Phonics* and DML's *Cove School Reading Program*.

Linguistics Approach
In many programs, the whole-word approach is used. This means that words are taught in families as a whole (e.g., cat, hat, pat and rat). The focus is on words instead of isolated sounds. Words are chosen on the basis of similar spelling patterns and irregular spelling words are taught as sight words. Examples of programs using this approach are *SRA Basic Reading Series* and *Miami Linguistic Readers* by D.C. Heath.

Some advantages of this approach are that the student learns that reading is talk written down, and develops a sense of sentence structure. The consistent visual patterns of the lessons guide students from familiar words to less familiar words to irregular words. Reading is taught by associating with the student's natural knowledge of his own language. Disadvantages are extremely controlled vocabulary, in which word-by-word reading is encouraged. Others criticize the programs for the emphasis on auditory memory skills and the use of nonsense words in the practice exercises.

Whole language Approach
In the whole language approach, reading is taught as a holistic, meaning-oriented activity and is not broken down into a collection of skills. This approach relies heavily on literature or printed matter selected for a particular purpose. Reading is taught as part of a total language arts program and the curriculum seeks to develop instruction in real problems and ideas. Two examples of whole language programs are *Learning through Literature* (Dodds and Goodfellow) and *Victory!* (Brigance). Phonics is not taught in a structured, systematic way. Students are assumed to develop their phonetic awareness through exposure to print. Writing is taught as a complement to reading. Writing centers are often part of this program as students learn to write their own stories and read them back or follow along an audiotape of a book while reading along with it.

While the integration of reading with writing is an advantage of the whole language approach, the approach has been criticized for the lack of direct instruction in specific skill strategies. When working with students with learning problems, instruction that is more direct may be needed to learn the word-recognition skills necessary for achieving comprehension of the text.

Language Experience Approach

The language experience approach is similar to the whole language in that reading is considered as a personal ac, literature is emphasized, and students are encouraged to write about their own life experiences. The major difference is that written language is considered a secondary system. to oral language, while whole language treats the two as parts of the same structure. The language experience approach is used primarily with beginner readers, but can also be used with older elementary and with other older students for corrective instruction. Reading skills are developed along with listening, speaking and writing skills. The materials consist, for the most part, of the student's skills. The philosophy of language experience includes:

- What students think about, they can talk about.
- What students say, they can write, or have someone write.
- What students write or have someone write for them, they can read.

Students dictate a story to a teacher as a group activity. Ideas for stories can originate from student artwork, news items, personal experiences or they may be creative. Topic lists, word cards or idea lists can also be used to generate topics or ideas for a class story. The teacher writes down the story in a first draft and the students read them back. The language patterns come from the students and they read their own written thoughts. The teacher provides guidance on word choice, sentence structure and the sounds of the letters and words. The students edit and revise the story on an experience chart. The teacher provides specific instruction in grammar, sentence structure and spelling, if the need arises, rather than using a specified schedule. As the students progress, they create their individual storybooks, adding illustrations if they wish. The storybooks are placed in folders to share with others. Progress is evaluated in terms of the changes in the oral and written expression as well as in mechanics. There is no set method of evaluating student progress. That is one disadvantage of the language experience approach; however, the emphasis on student experience and creativity stimulates interest and motivates the students.

Individualized Reading Approach

Students select their own reading materials from a variety, according to interest and ability, and they are more able to progress at their own individual rates. Word recognition and comprehension are taught, as the student needs them. The teacher's role is to diagnose errors and prescribe materials, although the final choice is made by the students. Individual work may be supplemented by group activities with basal readers and workbooks for specific reading skills. The lack of systematic check and developmental skills and emphasis on self-learning may be a disadvantage for students with learning problems.

Principles of and Methods for Assessing and Developing Students' Reading and Other Language Arts Skills

Most reading programs conceptually separate the reading process into three major categories: sight word vocabulary, word attack skills and comprehension. These three areas constitute the basic questions that should be asked by a teacher when assessing a student's current level of functioning. From answers obtained, the pertinent questions are:
1. How large is the student's sight word vocabulary?
2. What kinds of word attack skills does the student employ?
3. How well developed are the student's comprehension skills?

Sight words are printed words that are easily identified by the learner. The selection of words to be learned will rely to some extent on the age and abilities of the student. Primary age students will use word lists composed of high-frequency words like basal readers Dolch Word List.

Word attack skills are those techniques that enable a student to decode an unknown word so he can pronounce and understand it in the right context. Word attack skills are included in the areas of phonics, structural analysis, contextual and configuration clues, and decoding.

Comprehension skills are categorized into levels of difficulty. The teacher should consider the following factors when analyzing a student's reading comprehension level (Schloss & Sedlak, 1986):
1. The past experience of the reader.
2. The content of the written passage.
3. The syntax of the written passage.
4. The vocabulary used in the written passage.
5. The oral language comprehension of the student.
6. The questions being asked to assess comprehension.

The major categories of reading skills, basic reading skills within these categories and strategies for the development of each are listed. Suggestions for assisting the reader in improving silent and oral reading skills are given. Some skills overlap categories.

Comprehension involves understanding what is read regardless of purpose or thinking skills employed. Comprehension can be delineated into categories of differentiated skills. Benjamin Bloom's taxonomy includes knowledge, comprehension, application, analysis, synthesis and evaluation. Thomas Barrett suggests that comprehension categories be classified as: literal meaning, reorganization, inference, evaluation and appreciation. An overview of comprehension skills is presented in Skill 4, in this section. Strategies that might prove beneficial in strengthening a student's comprehension involve:

1. Asking questions of the student before he reads a passage. This type of directed reading activity assists the student in focusing attention on the information in the text that will help him to answer the questions.
2. Using teacher questions to assist the student in developing self-questioning skills covering all levels of comprehension.

Silent and Oral Reading Skills

Silent reading refers to the inaudible reading of words or passages. Since the reading act id one on a covert basis, the accuracy of the reading process can only be inferred through questions or activities required of the student following his reading. What may be observed is attention given to the printed material, the eye movements an indication relative pace, and body language signifying frustration, or ease of reading. Strategies that might assist the child in reading silently are:

1. Preparing activities or questions pertaining to the printed passage. Vary the activities so that some are asking specific comprehension questions and other are geared toward creative expression like art, written composition.
2. Allowing time for pleasurable reading, such as through an activity like sustained silent reading.

Skill 3.05   Demonstrate knowledge of approaches and techniques used to improve students' oral expressive language skills

Speaking and listening may be viewed as separate from reading and writing, but all four form the main communication system of the English language. They are interdependent and all other forms of communication depend on the ability to speak and listen. They are also the foundation for many other language skills, which is why teachers should provide ample opportunities for students to speak and listen in class as part of the daily routine. Classrooms are places where talk flows freely and by taking advantage of this talk to find out where students are in their thinking about topics, themes and responses to literature teachers can easily assess this component of language arts. When students can express ideas in their own words, it helps them to make meaning of their experiences with reading.

Within the classroom setting, many opportunities will present themselves for students to speak and listen for various purposes and often these may be spontaneous. Activities for speaking and listening should be integrated throughout the language arts program, but there should also be times when speaking and listening are the focus of the instruction.

Some of the ways that speaking and listening can be integrated include:
- Book talks.
- Brainstorming.
- Choral speaking.
- Class debates.
- Conversations.
- Interviewing.
- Listening to guest speakers.
- Oral reading.
- Oral reports.
- Readers' Theatre.
- Role playing.
- Small group discussions.
- Storytelling.

Students develop speaking vocabularies from the time they say their first word. This happens before their first birthday and usually represents a primary care giver (e.g., mama or dada). From here, words build and build until children have a rather large speaking vocabulary. They are then able to put these words together into sentences and hold complete interactive conversations. This acquisition process occurs throughout the life of a person, as vocabulary is something that increases even into adulthood.

Reading vocabularies start as sight words. These are words the students are able to recognize immediately without having to decode. Vocabulary then develops to words with specific meanings, which are critical to understanding the text.

The interrelationship of these three differing vocabularies is of the utmost importance. Normally, words that are part of the listening vocabulary transform into part of the speaking. This can be seen in very young children easily. Their mother says over and over do you want a cookie and at first the child simply gestures to receive the cookie. Then one day, the child says, "cookie." At this juncture, the former listening vocabulary word is now part of the speaking. The same process goes on as words the child uses regularly orally then transfers and become part of the reading vocabulary. This is how reading begins to make sense to children. As they are learning to decode the words, they come across something that doesn't make sense. It is because of the nature of the spoken language patterns, which they are familiar with, that they know it doesn't make sense.

When these speaking vocabularies do not develop as expected a specialist in language may need to be involved to determine if the student has an expressive language based learning disability. Students with this particular format of disability often have tremendous thoughts and complex ideas about issues presented, but are unable to present that information in a manner decipherable by the average person or more commonly they express it at a much more rudimentary level than others of their same age.

COMPONENTS OF LANGUAGE
Language learning is composed of five components. Children progress through developmental stages through each component.

Phonology
Phonology is the system of rules about sounds and sound combinations for a language. A phoneme is the smallest unit of sound that combines with other sounds to make words. A phoneme, by itself, does not have a meaning; it must be combined with other phonemes. Problems in phonology may be manifested as developmental delays in acquiring consonants or reception problems such as misinterpreting words because a different consonant was substituted. Direct phonics instruction using a very explicit model can be of great benefit to improving students with this issue. An example of a program, which may be beneficial for these students, is the Lindamood-Bell Learning Process System©.

Morphology

Morphemes are the smallest units of language that convey meaning. Morphemes are root words, or free morphemes that can stand alone (e.g., walk), and affixes (e.g., ed, s and ing). Content words carry the meaning in a sentence, and functional words join phrases and sentences. Generally, students with problems in this area may not use inflectional endings in their words, may not be consistent in their use of certain morphemes or may be delayed in learning morphemes such as irregular past tenses. Speech therapists generally provide direct therapy for students with this issue. It is important to provide consistent modeling for students in the classroom setting to help the transfer of skills. Grammar instruction is the perfect place to provide the direct explicit teaching of these skills as well.

Syntax

Syntax rules, commonly known as grammar, govern how morphemes and words are correctly combined. The child using sentences that lack length or complexity for a child that age manifests syntactic deficits. The child may have problems understanding or creating complex sentences and embedded sentences. Improvement for syntax comes from reading, listening, and practicing. A fun way that many students enjoy is to complete some reader's theatre scripts with the class. The students are reading and practicing speaking syntactically correct sentences and the more they practice and hear them, the more they will begin to incorporate them into their own speaking vocabulary.

Semantics

Semantics is language content: objects, actions and relations between objects. Semantic difficulties may include limited vocabulary; inability to understand figurative language or idioms; interprets literally; failure to perceive multiple meanings of words, changes in word meaning from changes in context, resulting in incomplete understanding of what is read; difficulty understanding linguistic concepts (e.g. before/after), verbal analogies, and logical relationships such as possessives, spatial, and temporal; and misuse of transitional words such as "although," "regardless." Many students develop appropriate semantics over time. Using visuals and other picture cues can help students to begin to understand and generalize the semantic issues. It is also a good strategy to have the students role play or act out the issues as much as possible.

Pragmatics

Commonly known as the speaker's intent, pragmatics is used to influence or control actions or attitudes of others. Communicative competence depends on how well one understands the rules of language, as well as the social rules of communication such as taking turns and using the correct tone of voice.

Pragmatic deficits are manifested by failures to respond properly to indirect requests after age 8 (e.g., "Can't you turn down the TV"? elicits a response of "No" instead of "Yes" and the child turning down the volume). Children with these deficits have trouble reading cues that indicate the listener does not understand them. Whereas a person would usually notice this and adjust one's speech to the listener's needs the child with pragmatic problems does not do this. Pragmatic deficits are also characterized by inappropriate social behaviors such as interruptions or monopolizing conversations. Children may use immature speech and have trouble sticking to a topic. These problems can persist into adulthood, affecting academic, vocational and social interactions. Problems in language development often require long-term interventions and can persist into adulthood. Certain problems are associated with different grade levels:

Preschool and Kindergarten: the child's speech may sound immature, the child may not be able to follow simple directions, and often cannot name things such as the days of the week and colors. The child may not be able to discriminate between sounds and the letters associated with the sounds. The child might substitute sounds and have trouble responding accurately to certain types of questions. The child may play less with his peers or participate in non-play or parallel play.

Elementary School: problems with sound discrimination persist and the child may have problems with temporal and spatial concepts (e.g., before/after). As the child progresses through school, he may have problems making the transition from narrative to expository writing. Word retrieval problems may not be very evident because the child begins to devise strategies such as talking around the word he cannot remember, or using fillers, and descriptors. The child might speak more slowly, have problems sounding out words, and get confused with multiple-meaning words. Pragmatic problems show up in social situations such as failure to correctly interpret social cues and adjust to appropriate language, inability to predict consequences and inability to formulate requests to obtain new information.

Secondary School: at this level, difficulties become more subtle. The child lacks the ability to use and understand higher-level syntax, semantics and pragmatics. If the child has problems with auditory language, he may also have problems with short-term memory. Receptive and/or expressive language delays impair the child's ability to learn effectively. The child often lacks the ability to organize/ categorize the information received in school. Problems associated with pragmatic deficiencies persist but because the child is aware of them, he becomes inattentive, withdrawn or frustrated.

Pragmatic skills can be improved through role-playing and other situations, which occur within the school or real-life environment. The guidance counselor may be a colleague whose expertise can be utilized to help students begin to understand how to address social situations appropriately.

Fluency

Speaking fluency is most often thought about in terms of the more common term stuttering. Children, who stutter, have difficulty communicating their thoughts orally and may require additional support to control this issue from a speech therapist. However, less frequently is it referenced the difficulties students who cannot organize their thoughts themselves in a fluent manner have in school. These children sometimes require additional wait time in order to successfully complete assignments, particularly when asked to present their information orally.

This type of fluent factor as well as the more traditional factor of stuttering, can affect students, particularly in the domain of reading. Before the National Reading Panel report, in many schools fluency was not discussed a great deal. Now, since that report, fluency has gained more attention and is discussed in more details.

Research gathered and reviewed by the National Reading Panel indicated over and over that fluency and comprehension could be correlated. The correlation basically indicated that if a student was a fluent reader, they were more than likely to comprehend what they read. It is not a guarantee, but it is a better shot. On the other hand, students who are not fluent, hardly ever are able to demonstrate all the levels of comprehension. The research is more solid on the fact that student with poor fluency will have significant comprehension deficits.

While there is a body of evidence as related to fluency and comprehension, it in of itself is not the only factor. In order for students to have adequate comprehension development there must be other factors involved in addition to fluency.

Skill 3.06 Demonstrate knowledge of approaches and techniques used to improve students' written expression skills.

Identify the Sequence of Development of Written Expression Skills
Composition should be taught as a process rather than a product. The first step in learning composition is having access to literature and writing materials. When adults read aloud to children, the children learn about styles of literature and the function of print and pictures in a book. Having access to paper and writing materials give children opportunities to experiment with drawing and writing.

When children enter school, they can learn to write notes, label pictures and keep journals. Most of the writing children do at school is business related or transactional writing. Transactional writing includes expository (explaining subjects or procedures), descriptive (helps the reader visualize the topic) or persuasive (explaining a point of view). Students may also do expressive writing or poetic writing, which requires knowledge of formal literary style. Initially, students may be resistant to writing, especially expressive writing, because they may be afraid to show their feelings or make mistakes. Journals are especially helpful to encourage students to practice expressive writing.

Writing should be taught as a process, not a product. Free writing will help reduce writing anxiety. Having children participate in journals and free writing will help build confidence. Writing should be integrated in all subject areas, and the atmosphere should be positive. Writing should be fun and include a variety of types of writing. Children's writing should be shared with others for feedback and enjoyment.

Each phase of the writing process has strategies that help the student develop metacognitive skills and proficiency. Instruction should not just focus on the mechanics (e.g., grammar, punctuation and spelling) of writing, but also on developing fluency and positive feelings about the process.

Prewriting: the planning phase. During preplanning, the student must decide on a purpose, find a topic, establish an audience, decide how the paper will be organized, and experiment with ideas. Strategies for generating ideas can be done individually or as a group activity and include:

- Listing.
- Brainstorming—gathering ideas about the topic.
- Interest inventories.
- Free writing.

Organizing content: includes graphic approaches that represent the relationships of ideas visually
- Mapping.
- Webbing.
- Clustering.

Drafting: in this phase, ideas are developed and the writer makes connections between the ideas. During this phase, mechanics should not be considered, and the student should not spend too much time in this phase. Learner activities include:
- Focus on the ideas, not the content
- Consult the teacher or peer about the content
- Read the piece or a portion to defocus and generate new ideas

Revising: After the drafts have been written, the student may reorganize ideas, select ideas for further development, and edit the paper for mistakes in grammar and spelling. Sections of the paper may be removed or reorganized. Strategies include:
- Putting the paper aside for a day or two.
- Asking the teacher or a peer for feedback.
- Use scissors and tape to reorganize sections of the paper.
- Use the computer to aid in revision.

Final Draft: The write gives the paper a final editing, reads the paper to see that everything makes sense, and makes last corrections before turning the paper in. Some of the things that a student can do to prepare the final draft are:
- Use a checklist to check the final copy for errors.
- Read the story into a tape-recorder and play it back with a written copy to listen for grammatical errors and pauses where punctuation marks should be.
- Read the paper one sentence at a time to identify sentence fragments.

Types and Characteristics of Language Arts Difficulties Associated With Various Disabilities

Written expression is one of the highest forms of communication. It reflects a person's level of comprehension, concept development and abstraction (Mercer & Mercer, 1993). Handwriting is primarily a visual-motor process that includes the writing or copying of word forms, whereas written expression reflects a person's cognitive abilities.

Prerequisite to developing skills in written expression is the need for experiences in listening, reading, spelling, handwriting and oral expression. Activities in written expression should begin as early as kindergarten and first grade, with skills developed concurrently with prerequisite experiences. Typically, problems in written expression are not identified until the upper elementary grade levels when the student is required to use language arts skills in written composition.

Problems in written expression can be diagnosed by the teacher through formal and informal means. Written expression produces a tangible product that may be evaluated by the teacher using a criterion-referenced tool.

Students with deficits in reading and spelling typically exhibit difficulties in written expression. Particular areas of difficulty include limited vocabulary, immature topic selections, spelling errors, inaccurate syntax, poor organization of thoughts and obvious stylistic errors. Inadequate cognitive abilities and grammatical inaccuracies may be detected. Children who are lacking in the development of comprehension skills may be unable to reflect upon the subject and use reasoning skills in the development of content. Likewise, children with hyperactive or impulsive traits are often unable to focus upon details of content and subdivide materials. Deficits may be identified at any point where visual, motor, and cognitive abilities come into play in the production of written expression.

Instruction in written expression should culminate in independently written prose by students. Teacher prompting and feedback will vary, based on the degree of dependency individual students exhibit. For example, the language experience approach, largely a teacher directed group - sometimes individual - activity, is typically used as a form of initial instruction in written expression. The benefit of this activity is in the development of a topic of high interest, the use of students' thoughts and the students' speaking vocabulary and, of course, the immediate prompting and feedback of an encouraging and motivating nature from the teacher.

Skill 3.07 Demonstrate knowledge of approaches and techniques used to improve students' mathematical skills

Types and Characteristics of Reasoning and Calculation Difficulties Typically Observed in Students With Disabilities.

Reid, 1985, describes four processes that are directly related to an understanding of numbers. Children typically begin learning these processes in early childhood through the opportunities provided by their caretakers. Children who do not get these opportunities have difficulties when they enter school.

1. Describing characterizing objects, sets or events in terms of their attributes such as calling all cats "kitties" whether they are tigers or house cats.
2. Classifying: sorting objects, sets or events in terms of one or more criterion such as color, size or shape – black cats versus white cats versus tabby cats.
3. Comparing: determining whether two objects, sets or events are similar or different on the basis of a specified attribute, such as differentiating quadrilaterals from triangles on the basis of the number of sides.
4. Ordering: comparing two or more objects, sets or events, such as ordering children in a family on the basis of age or on the basis of height.

Children usually begin learning these concepts during early childhood:

- **Equalizing** - making two or more objects or sets alike on an attribute, such as putting more milk into a glass so that it matches the amount of milk in another glass.
- **Joining** - putting together two or more sets with a common attribute to make one set, such as buying packets of X-Men trading cards to create a complete series.
- **Separating** - dividing an object or set into two or more sets, such as passing out cookies from a bag to a group of children so that each child gets three cookies.
- **Measuring** - attaching a number to an attribute, such as three cups of flour, or ten gallons of gas.
- **Patterns** - recognizing, developing and repeating patterns, such as secret code messages, designs in a carpet or tile floor.

However, most children are not developmentally ready to understand these concepts before they enter school:

- **Understanding and working with numbers larger than ten**: they may be able to recite larger numbers, but are not able to compare or add them, for example.
- **Part-whole concept**: the idea of one number as being a part of another number.
- **Numerical notation**: place value, additive system and zero symbol.

Children with learning problems often have difficulty with these concepts after they enter public school. They have either had not had many experiences with developing these concepts or they are not developmentally ready to understand such concepts as part-whole for example.

Sequence of Mathematics understanding

The understanding of mathematical concepts proceeds in a developmental context from concrete to semi-concrete to abstract. Children with learning difficulties may still be at the semi-concrete level when their peers are ready to work at the abstract level. This developmental sequence has implication for instruction because the teacher will need to incorporate concrete and/or semi-concrete into lessons for students who did not master these stages of development in their mathematics background. These levels may be explained as follows:

- **Concrete**: an example of this would be demonstrating 3 + 4 = 7 by counting out three buttons and four buttons to equal seven buttons.
- **Semi-concrete**: an example would be using pictures of three buttons and four buttons to illustrate 3 + 4 = 7.
- **Abstract**: the student solves 3 + 4 = 7 without using manipulatives or pictures.

In summary, the levels of mathematics content involve:

- Concepts such as the understanding of numbers and terms.
- Development of mathematical relationships.
- Development of mathematical skills such as computation and measuring.

Development of problem-solving ability not only in books, but also in the environment.

Knowledge of Principles and Methods for Improving Students' Computation and Reasoning Skills

The National Council of Teachers of Mathematics, in its *Principles and Standards for School Mathematics* (2000) notes that math is a "highly interconnected and cumulative subject." Accordingly, teachers should begin by steeping classrooms in mathematics awareness, examining their own attitudes and aptitudes in math and preparing themselves to be the best help they can to students. The teacher's deep understanding of math at the concrete, representational and abstract levels is important to helping students to perceive the presence of math across the curriculum and in everyday activities.

David Allsopp, Ph.D., associate professor at University of South Florida has done substantive research on best classroom practices for special needs mathematics students. He suggests that for special needs students:

- Direct instruction with significant guided practice, repetition, and support from teachers is actually more effective than student-centered instruction.

- Teaching problem-solving strategies is more effective than exclusively using rote practice.

- Concrete instruction, persistently applied throughout the levels of mathematics curriculum, is more effective in helping students develop computation and problem solving skills and to prepare for abstract mathematics work.

- Ongoing assessment of students' performance, sharing and discussing with them their progress and successes, improves learning outcomes.

- Engaging students as active participants in their learning by encouraging and teaching metacognitive behaviors like goal setting, self-monitoring, and self-talk, and showing them how to apply these skills not only to their mathematics work but to general problem solving, boosts math proficiency.

- Well-planned cooperative learning activities, such as peer tutoring and work groups, can offer students opportunities for meaningful practice and skill enhancement.

Skilled teachers can apply these special needs principles to a variety of engaging approaches to instruction, which may include instructional games, use of technology, daily living activities, journaling, integration with science or literature and cross-curricular applications in subjects such as physical education and art.

Skill 3.08 **Demonstrate knowledge of approaches and techniques used to improve students' self-esteem and personal and social skills and to facilitate transition into adult life-roles**

Instructional Techniques that Promote the Student's Self-Awareness, Self-Control, Self-Reliance, Self-Esteem and Personal Empowerment.

Self Concept

Self-concept may be defined as the collective attitudes or feelings that one holds about oneself. Children with disabilities perceive, early in life, that they are deficient in skills that seem easier for their peers without disabilities. The also receive expressions of surprise or even disgust from both adults and children in response to their differing appearance and actions, again resulting in damage to the self-concept. The special education teacher, for these reasons, will want to direct special and continuing effort to bettering each child's own perception of himself.

1. The poor self-concept of a child with disabilities causes that student at times to exhibit aggression or rage over inappropriate things. The teacher can ignore this behavior unless it is dangerous to others or too distracting to the total group, thereby reducing the amount of negative conditioning in the child's life. Further, the teacher can praise this child, quickly and frequently, for the correct responses he makes, remembering that these responses may require special effort on the student's part to produce. Further, correction, when needed, can be done tactfully, in private.

2. The child whose poor self-concept manifests itself in withdrawn behavior should be pulled gently into as many social situations as possible by the teacher. This child must be encouraged to share experiences with the class, to serve as teacher helper for projects, and to be part of small groups for tasks. Again, praise for performing these group and public acts is most effective if done immediately.

3. The teacher can plan, in advance, to structure the classroom experiences so that aversive situations will be avoided. Thus, settings that stimulate the aggressive child to act out can be redesigned and situations that stimulate group participation can be set up in advance for the child who acts in a withdrawn manner.

Frequent, positive and immediate are the best terms to describe the teacher feedback required by children with disabilities. Praise for very small correct acts should be given immediately, and repeated when each correct act is repeated. Criticism or outright scolding should be done, whenever possible, in private. The teacher should first check the total day's interactions with students to ensure that the number and qualitative content of verbal stimuli is heavily on the positive side. While this trait is desirable in all good teaching, it is fundamental and utterly necessary to build the fragile self-concept of youngsters with disabilities.

The teacher must have a strategy for use with the child who persists in negative behavior outbursts. One system is to intervene immediately and break the situation down in to three components. First, the teacher requires the child to identify the worst possible outcome from the situation, the thing that he fears. To do this task, the child must be required to state the situation in the most factual way he can. Second, he is required to state what would really happen if this worst possible outcome happened, and to evaluate the likelihood of it happening. Third, he is asked to state an action or attitude that he can take, after examining the consequences in a new light. This process has been termed <u>rational emotive therapy</u>.

Affective and Social Skills transcend to all areas of life. When an individual is unable to acquire information on expectations and reactions of others or misinterprets those cues, he is missing an important element needed for success as an adult in the workplace and community in general.

Special education should incorporate a level of instruction in the affective/social area as many students will not develop these skills without instruction, modeling, practice and feedback.

Affective and social skills taught throughout the school setting might include: social greetings; eye contact with a speaker; interpretation of facial expression, body language and personal space; ability to put feelings and questions into words; and use of words to acquire additional information as needed.

Strategies for Linking Life Skills Instruction to Employment and Independent, Community and Personal Living.
Adaptive life skills refer to the skills that people need to function independently at home, school and in the community. Adaptive behavior skills include communication and social skills (e.g., intermingling and communicating with other people); independent living skills (e.g., shopping, budgeting and cleaning); personal care skills (e.g., eating, dressing and grooming); employment/work skills (following directions, completing assignments and being punctual for work); and functional academics (e.g., reading, solving math problems and telling time).

Teaching adaptive behavior skills is part of the special education program for students with disabilities. Parent input is a critical part of the adaptive behavior assessment process since there are many daily living skills that are observed primarily at home and are not prevalent in the educational setting.

The measurement of adaptive behavior should consist of surveys of the child's behavior and skills in a diverse number of settings including his class, school, home, neighborhood or community. Since it is not possible for one person to observe a child in all of the primary environments, measurement of adaptive behavior depends on the feedback from a number of people. Because parents have many opportunities to observe their child in an assortment of settings, they are normally the best source of information about adaptive behavior. The most prevalent method for collecting information about a child's adaptive behavior skills in the home environment is to have a school social worker, school psychologist or guidance counselor interview the parents using a formal adaptive behavior assessment rating scale. These individuals may interview the parents at home or hold a meeting at the school to talk with the parent about their child's behavior. Adaptive behavior information is also procured from school personnel who work with the student, in order to understand how the child functions in the school environment.

There are a variety of strategies for teaching adaptive life skills including incorporating choice, which entails allowing students to select the assignment, and allowing students to select the order that they complete tasks. In addition, priming or pre-practice is an effective classroom intervention for students with disabilities. Priming entails previewing information or activities that a student is likely to have problems with before they begin working on that activity. Partial participation or multi-level instruction is another strategy and it entails allowing a student with a disability to take part in the same projects as the rest of their class, with specific adaptations to the activity so that it suits a student's specific abilities and requirements. Additional instructional practices include self-management, which entails teaching the student to function independently without relying on a teacher or a one-on-one aid. This strategy allows the student to become more involved in the intervention process and it improves autonomy.

Cooperative groups are an effective instructional technique for teaching social skills. It has been known to result in increased frequency, duration and quality of social interactions. Peer tutoring entails two students working together on an activity with one student giving assistance, instruction and feedback to the other.

Skill 3.09 Demonstrate knowledge of the development and implementation of individual behavior management approaches

Classroom management plans should be in place when the school year begins. Developing a management plan takes a proactive approach, that is, decide what behaviors will be expected of the class as a whole, anticipate possible problems, and teach the behaviors early in the school year.

Behavior management techniques should focus on positive procedures that can be used at home as well as at school. Involving the students in the development of the classroom rules lets the students know the rationale for the rules and allows them to assume responsibility in the rules because they had a part in developing them. When students get involved in helping establish the rules, they will be more likely to assume responsibility for following them. Once the rules are established, enforcement and reinforcement for following the rules should begin right away.

Consequences should be introduced when the rules are introduced, clearly stated, and understood by all of the students. The severity of the consequence should match the severity of the offense and must be enforceable. The teacher must apply the consequence consistently and fairly; so the students will know what to expect when they choose to break a rule.

Like consequences, students should understand what rewards to expect for following the rules. The teacher should never promise a reward that cannot be delivered, and follow through with the reward as soon as possible. Consistency and fairness is also necessary for rewards to be effective. Students will become frustrated and give up if they see that rewards and consequences are not delivered timely and fairly.

About four to six classroom rules should be posted where students can easily see and read them. These rules should be stated positively, and describe specific behaviors so they are easy to understand. Certain rules may also be tailored to meet target goals and IEP requirements of individual students. (For example, a new student who has had problems with leaving the classroom may need an individual behavior contract to assist him or her with adjusting to the class rule about remaining in the assigned area.) As the students demonstrate the behaviors, the teacher should provide reinforcement and corrective feedback. Periodic "refresher" practice can be done as needed, for example, after a long holiday or if students begin to "slack off." A copy of the classroom plan should be readily available for substitute use, and the classroom aide should also be familiar with the plan and procedures.

The teacher should clarify and model the expected behavior for the students. In addition to the classroom management plan, a management plan should be developed for special situations (i.e.: fire drills) and transitions (i.e.: going to and from the cafeteria). Periodic review of the rules, as well as modeling and practice, may be conducted as needed, such as after an extended school holiday.

Procedures that use social humiliation, withholding of basic needs, pain, or extreme discomfort should never be used in a behavior management plan. Emergency intervention procedures used when the student is a danger to himself or others are not considered behavior management procedures. Throughout the year, the teacher should periodically review the types of interventions being used, assess the effectiveness of the interventions used in the management plan, and make revisions as needed for the best interests of the child.

Motivation

Before the teacher begins instruction, he or she should choose activities that are at the appropriate level of student difficulty, are meaningful, and relevant. Teacher behaviors that motivate students include:

- Maintain success expectations through teaching, goal setting and establishing connections between effort and outcome and self-appraisal and reinforcement.

- Have a supply of intrinsic incentives such as rewards, appropriate competition between students, and the value of the academic activities.

- Focus on students' intrinsic motivation through adapting the tasks to students' interests, providing opportunities for active response, including a variety of tasks, providing rapid feedback, incorporating games into the lesson, allowing students the opportunity to make choices, create and interact with peers.

- Stimulate students' learning by modeling positive expectations and attributions. Project enthusiasm and personalize abstract concepts. Students will be better motivated if they know what they will be learning about. The teacher should also model problem-solving and task-related thinking so students can see how the process is done.

For adolescents, motivation strategies are usually aimed at getting the student actively involved in the learning process. Since the adolescent has the opportunity to get involved in a wider range of activities outside the classroom (e.g., job, car and being with friends), stimulating motivation may be the focus even more than academics.

Motivation may be achieved through extrinsic reinforcers or intrinsic reinforcers. This is accomplished by allowing the student a degree of choice in what is being taught or how it will be taught. The teacher will, if possible, obtain a commitment either through a verbal or written contract between the student and the teacher.

Adolescents also respond to regular feedback, especially when that feedback shows that they are making progress.

Rewards for adolescents often include free time for listening to music, recreation or games. They may like extra time for a break or exemption from a homework assignment. They may receive rewards at home for satisfactory performance at school. Other rewards include self-charting progress and tangible reinforcers. In summary, motivational activities may be used for goal setting, self-recording of academic progress, self-evaluation and self-reinforcement.

Classroom interventions
Classroom interventions anticipate student disruptions and nullify potential discipline problems. Every student is different and each situation is unique; therefore, student behavior cannot be matched to specific interventions. Good classroom management requires the ability to select appropriate interventions strategies from an array of alternatives. The following non-verbal and verbal interventions were explained in Henley, Ramsey and Algonzzine (1993).

- Nonverbal Intervention - the use of nonverbal interventions allows classroom activities to proceed without interruption. These interventions also enable students to avoid "power struggles" with students.

- Body Language - teachers can convey authority and command respect through body language. Posture, eye contact, facial expressions and gestures are examples of body components that signal leadership to students.

- Planned Ignoring - many minor classroom disturbances are best handled through planned ignoring. When teachers ignore attention-seeking behaviors, often students do likewise.

- Signal Interference - there are numerous non-verbal signals that teachers can use to quiet a class. Some of these are eye contact, snapping fingers, a frown, shaking the head or making a quieting gesture with the hand. A few teachers present signs like flicking the lights, putting her finger over her lips or wink at a selective student.

- Proximity Control - teachers who move around the room merely need to stand near a student or small group of students or gently place a hand on a student's shoulder to stop a disturbing behavior. Teachers who stand or sit as if rooted are compelled to issue verbal directions in order to deal with student disruptions.

- Removal of Seductive Objects - some students become distracted by objects. Removing seductive objects eliminates the need some students have to handle, grab or touch objects that distract their attention.

- Verbal Interventions - because non-verbal interventions are the least intrusive, they are generally preferred. Verbal Interventions are useful after it is clear that non-verbal interventions have been unsuccessful in preventing or stopping disruptive behavior.

- Humor - some teachers have been successful in dispelling discipline problems with a quip or an easy comment that produces smiles or gentle laughter from students. This does not include sarcasm, cynicism or teasing, which increase tension and often creates resentment.

- Sane Messages - sane messages are descriptive and model appropriate behavior. They help students understand how their behavior affects others. "Karol, when you talk during silent reading, you disturb everyone in your group," is an example of a sane message.

- Restructuring - when confronted with student disinterest, the teacher makes the decision to change activities. This is an example of an occasion when restructuring could be used by the teacher to regenerate student interest.

- Hypodermic Affection - sometimes students get frustrated, discouraged and anxious in school. Hypodermic affection lets students know they are valued. Saying a kind word, giving a smile or just showing interest in a child give the encouragement that is needed.

- Praise and Encouragement - effective praise is directed at student behavior rather than at the student personally. "*Catching a child being good*," is an example of an effective use of praise that reinforces positive classroom behavior. Comments like, "*you are really trying hard*," encourages student effort.

- Alerting - making abrupt changes from one activity to another can bring on behavior problems. Alerting helps students to make smooth transitioning by giving them time to make emotional adjustments to change.

- Accepting Student Feelings - providing opportunities for students to express their feelings, even those that are distressful, helps them to learn to do so in appropriate ways. Role playing, class meetings or discussions, life space interviews, journal writings and other creative modes help students to channel difficult feelings into constructive outlets.

Transfer between classes and subjects

Effective teachers use class time efficiently. This results in higher student subject engagement and will likely result in more subject matter retention. One way teachers use class time efficiently is through a smooth transition from one activity to another; this activity is also known as "management transition." Management transition is defined as "teacher shifts from one activity to another in a systemic, academically oriented way." One factor that contributes to efficient management transition is the teacher's management of instructional material. Effective teachers gather their materials during the planning stage of instruction. Doing this, a teacher avoids flipping through things looking for the items necessary for the current lesson. Momentum is lost and student concentration is broken when this occurs.

Additionally, teachers who keep students informed of the sequencing of instructional activities maintain systematic transitions, because the students are prepared to move on to the next activity. For example, the teacher says, "When we finish with this guided practice together, we will turn to page twenty-three and each student will do the exercises. I will then circulate throughout the classroom helping on an individual basis. Okay, let's begin." Following an example such as this will lead to systematic smooth transitions between activities because the students will be turning to page twenty-three when the class finishes the practice without a break in concentration.

Another method that leads to smooth transitions is to move students in groups and clusters rather than one by one. This is called *"group fragmentation."* For example, if some students do seat work while other students gather for a reading group, the teacher moves the students in pre-determined groups. Instead of calling the individual names of the reading group, which would be time consuming and laborious, the teacher simply says, *"Will the blue reading group please assemble at the reading station. The red and yellow groups will quietly do the vocabulary assignment I am now passing out."* As a result of this activity, the classroom is ready to move on in a matter of seconds rather than minutes. Additionally, the teacher may employ academic transition signals, defined as academic transition signals - "teacher utterance that indicate[s] movement of the lesson from one topic or activity to another by indicating where the lesson is and where it is going." For example, the teacher may say, *"That completes our description of clouds, now we will examine weather fronts."* Like the sequencing of instructional materials, this keeps the student informed on what is coming next so they will move to the next activity with little or no break in concentration.

Therefore, effective teachers manage transitions from one activity to another in a systematically oriented way through efficient management of instructional matter, sequencing of instructional activities, moving students in groups and by employing academic transition signals. Through an efficient use of class time, achievement is increased, because students spend more class time engaged in on-task behavior.

Transition refers to changes in class activities that involve movement. Examples are:
1. Breaking up from large group instruction into small groups for learning centers and small-group instructions.
2. Classroom to lunch, to the playground, or to elective classes.
3. Finishing reading at the end of one period and getting ready for math the next period.
4. Emergency situations such as fire drills.

Successful transitions are achieved by using proactive strategies. Early in the year, the teacher pinpoints the transition periods in the day and anticipates possible behavior problems, such as students habitually returning late from lunch. After identifying possible problems with the environment or the schedule, the teacher plans proactive strategies to minimize or eliminate those problems. Proactive planning also gives the teacher the advantage of being prepared, addressing behaviors before they become problems, and incorporating strategies into the classroom management plan right away. Transition plans can be developed for each type of transition and the expected behaviors for each situation taught directly to the students.

Skill 3.10 Apply techniques for promoting career awareness and initiating transition services for students with learning disabilities.

Career development is the complex process of acquiring the knowledge, skill, and attitudes necessary to create a plan of choosing and being successful in a particular career field. Career development typically has four different stages. The stages of career development are awareness, exploration, preparation and placement.

A. Career Awareness
Career Awareness activities focus on introducing students to the broad range of career options. First, students must be provided with current, in-depth information about careers, which includes job-related skills, necessary education and training, and a description of typical duties, responsibilities and tasks. Students must be instructed on how to access the variety of available resources, such as Internet, professional magazines, newspapers and periodicals. Guest speakers and career fairs are provided for students to speak with and interview workers with first hand experiences.

B. Career Exploration

Career exploration focuses on learning about careers through direct, hands on activities. This stage is also important to gain insight into the characteristics of these occupations as well as personal interests and strengths. These activities can be provided through in-school and work-based experiences. In-school activities include contextual learning activities, simulated work experiences and career fairs. Work-based experiences range from non-paid to paid activities. These activities include job shadowing, mentors, company tours, internship, service learning, cooperative education and independent study.

C. Career Preparation

Career preparation provides students with the specific academic and technical knowledge and skills needed in order to be successful at a particular occupation. This may include Career and Technical Education programs or postsecondary education. They include the core activities of career assessments (formal and informal) and work-readiness skills (soft-skills development, computer competency and job search skills). Community organizations, employers and professional organizations are also available to provide trainings and insight on accommodations that may be provided for students with special needs.

D. Career Placement

Students transitioning from high school need to work collaboratively with involved parents, teachers and guidance counselors to successfully enter either the workplace or post-secondary education. Placement should depend on the student's aptitude, skills, experiences and interest.

Transitional planning

Transition planning is mandated in the Individuals with Disabilities Education Act (IDEA). The transition planning requirements ensure that planning is begun at age 14 and continued through high school. Transition planning and services focus on a coordinated set of student-centered activities designed to facilitate the student's progression from school to post-school activities. Transition planning should be flexible and focus on the developmental and educational requirements of the student at different grades and times.

Transition planning is a student-centered event that necessitates a collaborative endeavor. In reference to secondary students, the responsibilities are shared by the student, parents, secondary personnel and postsecondary personnel, who are all members of the transition team.

In most cases when transition is mentioned, it is referring to a child 14 or over, but in some cases children younger than 14 may need transition planning and assistance. Depending on the child's disability and its severity, a child may need assistance with transitioning to school from home, or to school from a hospital or institution or any other setting. In those cases the members of the transition team may also include doctors or nurses, social workers, speech therapist and physical therapists.

It is important that the student play a key role in transition planning. This will entail asking the student to identify preferences and interests and to attend meetings on transition planning. The degree of success experienced by the student in postsecondary educational settings depends on the student's degree of motivation, independence, self-direction, self-advocacy and academic abilities developed in high school. Student participation in transition activities should be implemented as early as possible, and no later than age 16.

In order to contribute to the transition planning process, the student should:
- Understand his learning disability and the impact it has on learning and work.
- Implement achievable goals; present a positive self-image by emphasizing strengths, while understanding the impact of the learning disability.
- Know how and when to discuss and ask for needed accommodations; be able to seek instructors and learning environments that are supportive and establish an ongoing personal file that consists of school and medical records, individualized education program (IEP), resume and samples of academic work.

The primary function of parents during transition planning is to encourage and assist students in planning and achieving their educational goals. Parents also should encourage students to cultivate independent decision-making and self-advocacy skills.

Transition planning involves input from four groups: the student, parents, secondary education professionals, and postsecondary education professionals. The result of effective transition from a secondary to a postsecondary education program is a student with a learning disability who is confident, independent, self motivated, and striving to achieve career goals. This effective transition can be achieved if the team consisting of the student, parents, and professional personnel work as a group to create and implement effective transition plans.

TEACHER CERTIFICATION STUDY GUIDE

The transition team of a student entering the workforce may also include community members, organizations, company representatives, vocational education instructor and job coaches. Transition services will be different for each student. Transition services must take into account the student's interests and preferences. Evaluation of career interests, aptitudes, skills and training may be considered.

Transition Services

Transition services will be different for each student. Transition services must take into account the student's interests and preferences. Evaluation of career interests, aptitudes, skills and training may be considered.

The transition activities that have to be addressed, unless the IEP team finds it uncalled for, are: a) instruction; b) community experiences; and c) the development of objectives related to employment and other post-school areas.

a) a) **Instruction** – the instruction part of the transition plan deals with school instruction. The student should have a portfolio completed upon graduation. They should research and plan for further education and/or training after high school. Education can be in a college setting, technical school, or vocational center. Goals and objectives created for this transition domain depend upon the nature and severity of the student's disability, the students interests in further education, plans made for accommodations needed in future education and training, identification of post-secondary institutions that offer the requested training or education.

b) **Community experiences** – this part of the transition plan investigates how the student utilizes community resources. Resources entail places for recreation, transportation services, agencies and advocacy services. It is essential for students to deal with the following areas:

- **Recreation and Leisure** - examples: movies, YMCA and religious activities.
- **Personal and Social Skills** - examples: calling friends, religious groups and going out to eat.
- **Mobility and Transportation** - examples: passing a driver's license test or utilizing Dial-A-Ride.
- **Agency Access** - examples: utilizing a phone book and making calls.
- **System Advocacy** - example: have a list of advocacy groups to contact.
- **Citizenship and Legal Issues** - example: registering to vote.

c. **Development of Employment** - this segment of the transition plan investigates becoming employed. Students should complete a career interest inventory. They should have chances to investigate different careers. Many work skill activities can take place within the classroom, home, and community. Classroom activities may concentrate on employability skills, community skills, mobility and vocational training. Home and neighborhood activities may concentrate on personal responsibility and daily chores. Community based activities may focus on part-time work after school and in the summer, cooperative education or work-study, individualized vocational training and volunteer work.

d) **Daily Living Skills** - this segment of the transition plan is also important although not essential to the IEP. Living away from home can be an enormous undertaking for people with disabilities. Numerous skills are needed to live and function as an adult. In order to live as independently as possible, a person should have an income, know how to cook, clean, shop, pay bills, get to a job and have a social life. Some living situations may entail independent living, shared living with a roommate, supported living or group homes. Areas that may need to be looked into include personal and social skills, living options, income and finances, medical needs, community resources and transportation.

TEACHER CERTIFICATION STUDY GUIDE

SUBAREA IV.   PROGRAM AND SERVICE DELIVERY

Skill 4.01   Apply knowledge of state regulations and historical trends in the delivery of special education and related services

Includes major historical trends and concepts in the education of students with learning disabilities, ways in which approaches in the field have changed over time, resources for ongoing professional development, and the application of Michigan regulations to various situations involving special education.

PARTIAL VOID – Need information on application of Michigan regulations; Also need to modify text to apply more to learning disabilities.

Legal Mandates and Historical Aspects
Special education is precisely what the term denotes: education of a special nature for students who have special needs. The academic and behavioral techniques that are used today in special education are a culmination of "best practices" and evolved from a number of disciplines (e.g., medicine, psychology, sociology, language, ophthalmology and otology) to include education. Each of these disciplines contributed uniquely to their field so that the needs of special students might be better met in the educational arena.

Unfortunately, during the earlier part of the 1900s and mid-1950s, too many educators placed in positions of responsibility, refused to recognize their professional obligation for assuring all children a free, appropriate, public education. Today, door can no longer be shut, eyes cannot be closed, and heads cannot be turned since due process rights have established for special needs students and their caregivers. Specific mandates are now stated in national laws, state regulations, and local policies. These mandates are the result of many years of successful litigation and politically advocacy, and they govern the delivery of special education.

What special educators do is one thing; how services are delivered is yet another. The concept if **inclusion** stresses the need for educators to rethink the continuum of services, which was designed by Evelyn Deno and has been in existence since the early 1970s. Many school districts developed educational placement sites, which contain options listed on this continuum. These traditional options extend from the least restrictive to the most restrictive special education settings. The least restrictive environment is the regular education classroom. The present trend is to team special education and regular classroom teachers in regular classrooms. This avoids pulling out students for resource room services and provides services by specialists for students who may be showing difficulties similar to those of special education students.

LEARNING DISABLED

The competencies in this section include the mandates (i.e.: laws, regulations and policies) that apply to or have a bearing upon the respective states and local districts, as well as the major provisions of federal laws implemented twenty or more years ago, such as Public Laws 94-142 (1975), 93-112 (1973) and 101-476 (1990). These laws culminated into the comprehensive statute, IDEA, which requires the states to offer comprehensive special education service programs to students with disabilities and to plan for their transition into the work world. Most local districts have elaborately articulated delivery systems, which are an extension of national or state.

Department of Education of Department of Public Instruction. Any inquires should be directed to the unit that administers programs for exceptional children.

The Major Developments in the History Of Special Education
Although the origin of special education services for youngsters with disabilities is relatively recent, the history of public attitude toward people with disabling conditions was recorded as early as 1552. The Spartans practiced infanticide, the killing of abandonment of malformed or sickly babies. The ancient Greeks and Romans thought people with disabilities were cursed and forced them to beg for food and shelter. Those who could who could not fend for themselves were allowed to perish. Some with mental disabilities were employed as fools for the entertainment of the Roman royalty.

In the time of Christ, people with disabilities were thought to be suffering the punishment of God. Those with emotional disturbances were considered to be possessed by the devil and although early Christianity advocated humane treatment of those who were not normal physically or mentally, many remained outcasts of society, sometimes pitied and sometimes scorned.

During the Middle Ages, persons with disabilities were viewed within the aura of the unknown, and were treated with a mixture of fear and reverence. Some were wandering beggars, while others were used as jesters in the courts. The Reformation brought about a change of attitude, however. Individuals with disabilities were accused of being possessed by the devil and exorcism flourished. Many innocent people were put in chains and cast into dungeons.

The early seventeenth century was marked by a softening of public attitude toward persons with disabilities. Hospitals began to provide treatment for those with emotional disturbances and mental retardation. A manual alphabet for those with deafness was developed and John Locke became the first person differentiate between persons who were mentally retarded and those who were emotionally disturbed.

In America the colonists treated people with severe mental disorders as criminals, while those who were harmless were left to beg or were treated as paupers. At one time, it was common practice to sell them to the person who would provide for them at the least cost to the public. When this practice was stopped, persons with mental retardation were put into poorhouses, where conditions were often extremely filthy.

The Nineteenth Century: The Beginning of Training
In 1799, Jean Marc Itard, a French physician, found a 12-year old boy who had been abandoned in the woods of Averyron, France. His attempts to civilize and educate the boy, Victor, established many of the educational principles presently in use in the field of special education, including developmental and multisensory approaches, sequencing of tasks, individualized instruction and a curriculum geared toward functional life skills.

Itard's work had an enormous impact upon public attitude toward individuals with disabilities. They began to be seen as educable. During the late 1700s, rudimentary procedures were devised by which those with sensory impairments (i.e.: deaf or blind) could be taught, closely followed in the early 1800s by attempts to teach students with mild intellectual disabilities and emotional disorders (i.e.: at that time to as the "idiotic" and "insane"). Throughout Europe, schools for students with visual and hearing impairments were erected, paralleled by the founding of similar institutions in the United States. In 1817, Thomas Hopkins Galludet founded the first American school for students who were deaf, known today as Galludet College in Washington, D.C., one of the world's best institutions of higher learning for those with deafness. Galludet's work was followed closely by that of Samuel Gridley However, who was instrumental in the founding of the Perkins Institute for students who were blind in 1829.

The mid-1800s saw the further development of Itard's philosophy of education of students with mental disabilities. Around that time, his student, Edward Seguin, immigrated to the United States, where he established his philosophy of education for persons with mental retardation in a publication entitled *Idiocy and Its Treatment by the Physiological Method in 1866*. Seguin was instrumental in the establishment of the first residential school for individuals with retardation in the United States.

State legislatures began to assume the responsibility for housing people with physical and mental disabilities - the institutional care was largely custodial. Institutions were often referred to as warehouses due to the deplorable conditions of many. Humanitarians like Dorothea Dix helped to relieve anguish and suffering to institutions for persons with mental illnesses.

1900 - 1919: Specific Programs

The early twentieth century saw the publication of the first standardized test of intelligence by Alfred Binet of France. The test was designed to identify educationally sub-standard children, but by 1916, the test was revised by an American Louis Terman and the concept of the intelligence quotient (IQ) was introduced. Since then the IQ test has come to be used as a predictor of both retarded (delayed) and advanced intellectual development.

At approximately the same time, Italian physician Maria Montessori was concerned with the development of effective techniques for early childhood education. Although she is known primarily for her contributions to this field, her work included methods of education for children with mental retardation as well, and the approach she developed is used in preschool programs today.

Ironically, it was the advancement of science and the scientific method that led special education to its worst setback in modern times. In 1912, psychologist Henry Goddard published a study based on the Kallikak family, in which he traced five generations of the descendants of a man who had one legitimate child and one illegitimate child. Among the descendants of the legitimate child were numerous mental defectives and social deviates. This led Goddard to conclude that mental retardation and social deviation were inherited traits, and therefore that mental and social deviates were a threat to society, an observation that he called the **Eugenics** Science Movement Ethics **Theory**. Reinforcing the concept of retardation as hereditary deviance was a popular philosophy called positivism, under which these unscientific conclusions were believed to be fixed, mechanical laws that were carrying mankind to inevitable improvement. Falling by the wayside was seen as the natural, scientific outcome for the defective person in society. Consequently, during this time mass institutionalization and sterilization of person with mental retardation and criminals were practiced.

Nevertheless, public school programs for persons with retardation gradually increased during this same period. Furthermore, the first college programs for the preparation of special education teachers were established between 1900 and 1920.

1919 - 1949: Professional and Expansion of Services

As awareness of the need for medical and mental health treatment in the community, was evidenced during the 1920s. Halfway houses became a means for monitoring the transition from institution to community living; outpatient clinics were established to provide increased medical care. Social workers and other support personnel were dispensed into the community to coordinate services for the needy. The thrust toward humane treatment within the community came to an abrupt halt during the 1930s and 1940s, primarily due to economic depression and widespread dissatisfaction toward the recently enacted social programs.

Two factors related to the Word Wars I and II helped to improve public opinion toward persons with disabilities. First, the intensive screening of the population of young men with physical and mental disabilities that were in the United States. Second, patriotism caused people to regard the enormous number of young men who returned from the wars with physical and emotional disabilities in a different light than they would have been regarded before that time. People became more sensitive to the problems of the veterans with disabilities, and this acceptance generalized to other groups in the special needs population.

With increased public concern for people with disabilities came new research. John B. Watson introduced behaviorism, which shifted the treatment emphasis from psychoanalysis to learned behavior. He demonstrated in 1920 that maladaptive (or abnormal) behavior was learned by Albert, an 11-month old boy, through conditioning. B.F. Skinner followed with a book entitled the *Behavior of Organisms*, which outlined principles of operant behavior (i.e.: voluntary) behavior.

In 1922, the Council for Exceptional Children (first called the International Council for Exceptional Children) was founded. During the 1920s, many comprehensive statewide programs were initiated. The number of special education programs in public schools increased at a rapid rate until the 1930s, when the push for humane and effective treatment of people with disabilities began to diminish once again. The period of the Depression was marked by large-scale institutionalization and lack of treatment. Part of the cause was inadequately planned programs and poorly trained teachers. WW II did much to swing the pendulum back in the other direction, however, and inaugurated the most active period in the history of the development of special education.

1950 - 1969: The Parents, the Legislators and the Courts Become Involved
The first two decades of the second half of this century was characterized by increased federal involvement in general education, gradually extending to special education. In 1950, came the establishment of the National Association of Retarded Children, later renamed the National Association of Retarded Citizens (NARC). It was the result of the efforts among concerned parents who felt the need of an appropriated public education. Increased media coverage exposed the miserable conditions in some of the institutions devoted to caring for people with disabilities, especially those with intellectual and emotional disabilities, and treatment consequently became more humane.

It was at about this time that parents of children with disabilities discovered the federal courts as a powerful agent on behalf of their children. The 1954 decision in the Brown v. Board of Education of Topeka case guaranteed equal opportunity rights to a free public education for all citizens. The parents of children and youth with disabilities insisted that their children be included in that decision. From this point on, the court cases and public laws enacted[3] as a result of court decisions, are too numerous to include in their entirety. Only those few, which had the greatest impact on the development of special education, as we know it today, are listed. Collectively, they are part of a movement in U.S. Supreme Court history known as the Doctrine of Selective Incorporation, under which the states are compelled to honor various substantive rights under procedural authority of the 14th Amendment.

- 1954: The Cooperative Research Act was passed, the first designation of general funds for the use of students with disabilities.

- **1958**: Public Law 85-926 provided grants to intuitions of higher learning and to state education agencies for training professional personnel who would, in turn, train teachers of students with mental retardation..

- **1963**: Public Law 88-164 (Amendment to Public Law 85-926) extended support to the training of personnel for teaching those with other disabling conditions (i.e.: hard of hearing, speech impaired, visually impaired, seriously emotionally disturbed, crippled and other health impaired).

- **1965**: Elementary and Secondary Education Act provided funds for the education of children who were disadvantaged and disabled (Public Law 89-10).

- **1965**: Public Law 89-313 (Educational Consolidation and Improvement Act -State Operated Programs) provided funds for children with disabilities who are or have been in state-operated or state-supported schools.

- **1966**: Public Law 89-750 authorized the establishment of the Bureau Education for the Handicapped (BEH) and a National Advisory Committee on the Handicapped.

- **1967**: Hanson v. Hobson ruled that ability grouping (tracking) based on student performance on standardized tests is unconstitutional.

- **1968**: Public Law 80-538 (Handicapped Children's Early Education Assistance Act) funded model demonstration programs for preschool students with disabilities.

---

[3] The first cluster of two digits of each public law represents the congressional session during which the law, numbered by the last three digits, was passed. Congressional sessions begin every two years on the odd numbered year. The first biennial session sat in 1787-88. Bills may be passed and signed into law during either of the two years during which the congressional session is being held. For example, Public Law 94-142 was the 142nd law passed by the Ninety-fourth Congress, which was in session in 1975-76 and was passed and signed in 1975.

LEARNING DISABLED

- **1968**: Public law 90-247 included provisions for deaf-blind centers, resource centers and expansion of media services for students with disabilities.
- **1968**: Public Law 90-576 specified that 10 percent of vocational education funds be earmarked for youth with disabilities.
- **1969**: Public Law 91-230 (Amendments to Public Law 89-10), previous enactment relating to children with disabilities was consolidated into one act: Education of the Handicapped.

1970 - Present: Federal Involvement in the Education of Children and Youth with Disabilities

During early involvement of the government in the education of individuals with disabilities, states were encouraged to establish programs, and they were rewarded with monetary assistance for compliance. Unfortunately, this assistance as often abused by those in control of services and funds. Therefore, a more dogmatic attitude arose, and the states were mandated to provide education for those with disabilities, or else experience the cutoff of education funds from the federal government. Federal legal authority for this action was the 14th Amendment due process denial, paralleling enforcement of the 1954 Brown v. Board of Education of Topeka desegregation decision. High proportions of minority students in programs for mental retardation resulted in a mandatory reexamination of placement procedures, which in turn brought about a rigid legal framework for the provision of educational services for students with disabilities.

- **1970**: Diana v. the State Board of Education resulted in the decision that all children must be tested in their native language.
- **1971**: Wyatt v. Stickney established the right to adequate treatment (education) for institutionalized persons with mental retardation.
- **1971**: the decision in Pennsylvania Association for Retarded Children (PARC) v. the Commonwealth of Pennsylvania prohibited the exclusion of students with mental retardation from educational treatment at state schools.
- **1972**: Mills v. the Board of Education of the District of Columbia asserted the right of children and youth with disabilities to a constructive education, which includes appropriate specialized instruction.
- **1973**: Public Law 93-112 (Rehabilitation Amendments of 1973) was the first comprehensive federal statute to address specifically the rights of disabled youth. It prohibited illegal discrimination in education, employment or housing on the basis of a disability.
- **1974**: Public Law 93-380 (Education Amendments of 1974. Public Law 94-142 is the funding portion of this act). It requires the states to provide full educational opportunities for children with disabilities. It addressed identification, fair evaluation, alternative placements, due process procedures and free appropriate public education.

- **1975**: Public Law 94-142 (Education for all Handicapped Children Act) provided for a free, appropriate public education for all children with disabilities, defined special education and related services and imposed rigid guidelines on the provisions of those services. It paralleled the provision for a free and appropriate public education in Section in 504 of Public Law 94-142 and extended these services to preschool children with disabilities (ages 3-5) through provisions to preschool incentive grants.

- **1975**: Goss v. Lopez ruled that the state could not deny a student: education without following due process. While this decision is not based on a special education issue, the process of school suspension and expulsion is obviously critical in assuring an appropriate public education to children with disabilities.

- **1978**: Public Law 95-56 (Gifted and Talented Children's Education Act) defined the gifted and talented population and focused upon this exceptionally category, which was not included in Public Law 94-142 (Education of All Handicapped Children Act).

- **1979**: Larry P. v. Riles ordered the reevaluation of black students enrolled in classes for educable mental retardation (EMR) and enjoined the California State department of Education from the use of intelligence tests in subsequent EMR placement decisions.

- **1980**: Parents in Action on Special Education (PASE) v. Hannon ruled that IQ tests are necessarily biased against ethnic and racial subcultures.

- **1982**: the appeal for services of an interpreter during the school day for a deaf girl was denied by the Supreme Court in Hendrick Hudson Board of Education v. Rowley. Established that an "appropriate" education does not mean the "best" education has to be provided. What is required is that individuals benefit and those due process procedures are followed in developing the educational program.

- **1983**: Public Law 98-199 (Education of the Handicapped Act Amendments). Public Law 94-142 was amended to provide added emphasis on parental education and preschool, secondary and post-secondary programs for children and youth with disabilities.

- **1984**: Irving Independent School District v. Tatro (468 U.S. 883) established that catheterization and similar health-type services are "related services" when they are relatively simple to provide and medical assistance is not needed in providing them.

- **1985**: Public Law 99-457, Infant and Toddlers Act: 20 U.S.C. §1471 mandated service systems for infants and young children.

- **1986**: Public Law 99-372, Handicapped Children's Protection Act of 1986. This law allowed parents who are unsuccessful in due process hearings or reviews to seek recovery of attorney's fees.

- **1986**: Public Law 99-457, Education of the Handicapped Act Amendments of 1986. It re-authorized existing EHA, amended Public Law 94-142 to include financial incentives for states to educate children 3 to 5 years old by the 1990-1991 school years and established incentive grants to promote programs serving infants with disabilities (birth to 2 years of age).

- **1986**: Public Law 99-506, the Rehabilitation Act Amendments of 1986. It authorized formula grant funds for the development of supported employment demonstration projects.

- **1987**: School Board Of Nassau County, Florida, Et Al. V. Arline established that contagious diseases are a disability under Section 504 of the Rehabilitation Act and that people with them are protected from discrimination, if otherwise qualified (actual risk to health and safety to others may persons unqualified).

- **1988**: Honig vs. Doe. 484 U.S. 305 (1988) established that expulsion from school programs for more than ten days constitutes a change in placement for which all due process provisions must be met; temporary removals permitted in emergencies.

- **1990**: Public Law 101-336 (American with Disabilities Act [ADA]) provides civil rights protection to individuals with disabilities in private sector employment, all public services, public accommodations, transportation, and telecommunications. Patterned after Section 504 of the Rehabilitation Act of 1973.

- **1990**: The U.S. House of Representatives opened for citizen comment the issue of a separate exceptionality category for students with attention deficit disorders. The issue was tabled without legislative action.

- **1990**: Public Law 101-476, the Individuals with Disabilities Education Act (IDEA) reauthorized and renamed existing EHA. This amendment to EHA changed the term "handicapped" to "disability," expanded related services, and required individual education programs (IEPs) to contain transitional goals and objectives for adolescents (ages 16 and above special situations)..

- **1993** Florence County Sch. Dist. Four v. Carter (91-1523), 510 U.S. 7 (1993) established that when a school district does not provide FAPE for a student with disability, the parents may seek reimbursement for private schooling. This decision has encouraged districts to be more inclusive of students with autism who receive ABA/Lovaas method therapy.

- **1994** Goals 2000: Educate America Act, Pub. L. 103-227, established national education goals to help guide state and local education systems

- **1997** Reauthorization of IDEA—required involvement of a regular education teacher as part of the IEP team. Provided additional strength to school administrators for the discipline of students with special needs.

- **2002** Public Law 107-110 No Child Left Behind Act of 2001 (Public Law 107-110), commonly known as **NCLB**, reauthorizes a number of federal programs aiming to improve the performance of U.S. primary and secondary schools by increasing the standards of accountability for states, school districts and schools, as well as providing parents more flexibility in choosing which schools their children will attend..
- **2004** M.L. v. Federal Way School District (WA) in the Ninth Circuit Court of Appeals ruled that absence of a regular education teacher on an IEP team was a serious procedural error.
- **2004** Reauthorization of IDEA, requires all Special Education Teachers on a Secondary Level to be no less qualified than other teachers of the subject areas.

Present and Future Perspectives

What is the state of special education today? What can we anticipate as far as changes that might occur in the near future? It has been two decades since the passage of the initial Individuals with Disabilities Education Act as Public Law 93-142 in 1975. So far, mandates stand with funding intact. The clients are still here and in greater numbers to improved identification procedures and to medical advances that has left many, who might have died in the past, with conditions considered disabling. Among the disabling conditions afflicting the population with recently discovered lifesaving techniques are blindness, deafness, amputation, central nervous system or neurological impairments, brain dysfunction and mental retardation from environmental, genetic, traumatic, infectious and unknown etiologies.

Despite challenges to the principles underlying PL 94-142 in the early 1980s, total federal funding for the concept increased as new amendments were passed throughout the decade. These amendments expanded services to infants, preschoolers, and secondary students. (Rothstein, 1995).

Following public hearings, Congress voted in 1990 not to include Attention Deficit Disorders (ADD) as a new exceptionality area. Determining factors included the alleged ambiguity of the definition and eligibility criteria for students with ADD, the large number of students who might be identified if it became a service delivery area, the subsequent cost of serving such a large population, and the fact that many of these students are already served in the exceptionality areas of learning disabilities and behavior disorders.

The revision of the original law that we now call IDEA included some other changes. These changes were primarily in language (terminology), procedures (especially transition), and addition of new categories (autism and traumatic brain injury). (Read Objective 4 in this section for these specific changes.)

Thus, we can see that despite challenges to federal services and mandates in special education as an extension of the Fourteenth Amendment since 1980, there has actually been growth in mandated categories and net funding. The Doctrine of Selective Incorporation is the name for one major set of challenges to this process. While the 1994 conservative turnover in the Congress might seem to undercut the force of PL 94-132, two decades of recent history show strong bi-partisan support for special education, and consequently, IDEA, or a joint federal-state replacement, will most likely remain strong. Lobbyists and activists representing coalition and advocacy groups for those with disabilities have combined with bi-partisan congressional support to avert the proposed changes, which would have meant drastic setbacks in services for persons with disabilities.

Nevertheless, there remain several philosophical controversies in special education for the late 1990s. The need for labels for categories continues to be questioned. Many states are serving special needs students by severity level rather than by the exceptionality category.

Presently, special educators are faced with possible changes in what is considered to be the least restrictive environment for educating students with special needs. Following upon the heels of the Regular Education Initiative, the concept of inclusion has come to the forefront. Both of these movements were, and are, an attempt to educate special needs students in the mainstream of the regular classroom. Both would eliminate pulling out students from regular classroom instructional activities, and both would incorporate the services of special education teachers in the regular classroom in collaboration with general classroom teachers.

Michigan Regulations
The Michigan state Board of Education has a set of regulations pertaining to Special Education in the Michigan Administrative Code. The most recent revision was amended on May 20, 2005.

The Special Education regulations give guidelines on the types of programs that should be made available for students with disabilities. It lists information on the number of students that are allowed in each class depending on the type of disability that the class is for. For example, the regulations state that students with severe language impairments must be in a program for students with severe language impairment. The class cannot have more than ten students with severe language impairment in the class at a time, and the teacher cannot teach more than fifteen total.

The Administrative code also gives guidance to teachers and other personnel on qualifications that they have to hold to teach Special Education students.

Skill 4.02　Apply consultation, collaboration and coordination procedures

The Individuals with Disabilities Education Act (1997) requires the collaboration of educational professionals in order to provide equitable opportunities for students with disabilities.

Collaboration in a school environment can take place between a variety of advocates for the students, including general educators, special education teachers, school psychologists, speech and language pathologists, interpreters, administrators, parents and other professionals serving students with special needs. Sporadic communication between mainstream educators and other educational professionals damages the educational experience given to students.

Students with disabilities developed greater self-images and recognized their own academic and social strengths when included in the mainstream classroom and serviced by teams of educational professionals. The staff reported professional growth, personal support, and enhanced teaching motivation. The frequent practice of creating teacher assistance teams in order to provide intervention support to the general educator, often fail due to time constraints and the lack of commitment given to collaboration.

Every member of a collaborative team has precise knowledge of his or her discipline, and transdisciplinary teams integrate these areas. For example, an ESL teacher can provide knowledge regarding the development of language skills and language instruction methodology. Counselors and psychologists can impart knowledge as human development specialists and show their expertise in conducting small-group counseling and large-group interventions. School staff and instructors can benefit from what mainstream teachers can add in the area of performance information and knowledge of measures and benchmarks. Special education teachers can provide insight into designing and implementing behavior management programs and strategies for effective instruction to students with special needs. Speech pathologists can contribute their knowledge of speech and language development and provide insight into the identification of learning disabilities in language- minority students. Transdisciplinary teaming requires team members to build on the strengths and the needs of their particular populations. Therefore each professional can contribute when it comes to developing and implementing appropriate curricula.

Effective Collaboration Among Teachers and Other Professionals to Identify Appropriate Modifications to the Learning Environment (i.e.: Schedule and Physical Arrangement) to Manage Inappropriate Behaviors. Teachers of exceptional students are expected to manage many roles and responsibilities, not only concerning their students, but also with respect to students' caregivers and other involved educational, medical, therapeutic and administrative professionals. Because the needs of exceptional students are by definition multidisciplinary, a teacher of exceptional children often serves as the hub of a many-pronged wheel while communicating, consulting and collaborating with the various stakeholders in a child's educational life. Managing these relationships effectively can be a challenge, but is central to successful work in exceptional education.

Collaboration

- Special educators are part of the instructional or planning team.
- Teaming approaches are used for problem solving and program implementation.
- Regular teachers, special education teachers and other specialists collaborate (e.g., co-teach, team teach and work together on teacher assistance teams).

To ensure the greatest possibility of the child's educational success, all concerned parties must collaborate to discuss appropriate modifications to the learning environment. Each professional will bring forth information from their area of expertise and share it with the remainder of the team. Members should also share their knowledge of the child from previous interactions with the child. For example, the child's previous teacher maybe able to offer some suggestions about modifications that were previously successful. The team discusses the best accommodations for the child depending on the child's exceptionality and strengths and weaknesses. The team should communicate often to verify the success or failure of the modifications and adjust or add modifications as needed.

Skill 4.03   Demonstrate knowledge of methods of communicating with and providing information for the families of students with learning disabilities

Communicating Assessment Results to Parents
The special educator must be able to communicate assessment results into understandable language for a variety of individuals. These individuals may include parents or guardians, paraprofessionals and professionals in general education, administration and (in the case of older students) even the student himself.

A review of assessment and evaluation results may be done during an IEP meeting in which the formal test lingo is used but paired with an interpretation in layman's terms. Results may also be done in the form of a written report.

Ability to Represent Test Results and Educational Implications in Written Format.
Although the school psychologist often completes student evaluations and writes a report, this may be the task of the special educator when assessment is done in the classroom in preparation for the student's annual review. In this case, the special education teacher will be asked to write a report summarizing assessment findings and educational implications. The teacher should be able to organize the data in a concise, readable format. Some components of such a report include:

- Identifying information (e.g., student name, age, date of birth, address and gender).
- Reason for Assessment.
- Test administration information (e.g., date, time, duration of test and response of student).
- Test results.
- Summary of Educational Recommendations.

Knowledge of the Level of Functioning of the Student's Typically Developing Peers
Standardized test results without comparison to what typically developing students of the same age are doing are of little value. IEP programming and implementation depend on the areas where the student show significant delay. For example, a student may show progress in the area of reading and yet still be several grade levels behind his peers. In that case, goals and objectives for reading would be warranted.

Often students with disabilities show peaks and valleys in their abilities. A student may be progressing at a similar rate and at a similar level as his peers in language arts, but may have delays in math. Again, IEP goals and objectives in the area of delay (in this case math) would be needed.

Sometimes students demonstrate splinter skills. For example, a young deaf child may be able to rote count by tens to five hundred. This does not mean that that student has comparable math skills to those of a first grader. Knowledge of typical range and sequence of developmental skills is needed and should be communicated to those involved in IEP meetings.

Knowledge of the Various Program Options Within the School District and Probable Appropriate Placement.

An overall picture of the student with a disability (including his assessment results) and knowledge of the cascade of services provided is important to communicate to the CSE team.

Special Educators Must be Culturally Sensitive to Communicate with Parents

Hispanic children represent the fastest-growing minority and approximately ¾ of the children designated as limited English proficiency (LEP). Additionally, culturally diverse students may speak a dialect of a language such as Spanish, which has its own system of pronunciation and rules. It should be stressed that speaking a dialect does not in itself mean that the child has a language problem. Certain English sounds and grammar structures may not have equivalents in some languages, and failure to produce these elements may be a function of inexperience with English, rather than a language delay.

When minority or culturally diverse children are being screened for language problems, learning disabilities, or other exceptional student programs, the tests and assessment procedures must be non-discriminatory. Furthermore, testing should be done in the child's native language; however, if school instruction has not been in the native language, there may appear to be a problem because assessments typically measure school language. Even with native English-speaking children, there are differences between the language that functional at home and community and the language requirements of school.

Normality in child behavior is influenced by society's attitudes and cultural beliefs about what is normal for children (e.g., the motto for the Victorian era was "Children should be seen and not heard"). Cultural and societal attitudes towards gender change over time. While attitudes towards younger boys playing with dolls or girls preferring sports to dolls have relaxed, children eventually are expected as adults to conform to the expected behaviors for males and females. Other factors that influence students with disabilities and their families include abuse, neglect, and substance abuse.

- **Abuse** - whether abuse to the child or to a parent, the effect transcends the immediate situation to interaction with others in the home, school and community. If the child with a disability is the one who is abused, he will be distrustful of others. He may also continue the cycle of behavior by acting out in abusive ways towards others.

  If a parent of the child with a disability is being abused, the child may feel responsible. He may be actively trying to protect the abused parent. At the least, he will carry emotional and possibly psychological effects of living in a home where abuse happens.

  A parent who is being abused will be less likely to be able to attend to the needs of the child with a disability. She may be secretive about the fact that the abuse even occurs.

  Unfortunately, having a child with a disability puts excessive strain on a marriage. Abusive tendencies may be exaggerated.

- **Neglect** – if a child with a disability is neglected physically or emotionally, he may exhibit a number of behaviors. He will most likely be distrustful of adults in general. He may horde classroom materials, snacks, etc. At the very least he will be unfocused on school work.

  In the instances of abuse and neglect (or suspected instances), the special educator (as all educators) is a mandated reporter to the appropriate agency (such as DCFS – Division of Child and Family Services).

- **Substance Abuse** - if a child with a disability or a parent is involved in substance abuse, that abuse will have a negative effect in the areas of finances, health, productivity and safety. It is important for the special education teacher to be aware of signs of substance abuse. She should be proactive in teaching drug awareness. She should also know the appropriate school channels for getting help for the student as well as community agencies that can help parents involved in substance abuse.

Parents and Families

Families know students better than almost anyone, and are a valuable resource for teachers of exceptional students. Often, an insight or observation from a family member, or his or her reinforcement of school standards or activities, mean the difference between success and frustration in a teacher's work with children. Suggestions for relationship building and collaboration with parents and families include:

- Using laypersons' terms when communicating with families, and make the communication available in the language of the home.
- Searching out and engage family members' knowledge and skills in providing services, educational and therapeutic, to student.
- Exploring and discussing the concerns of families and helping them find tactics for addressing those concerns.
- Planning collaborative meetings with children and their families and assisting them to become active contributors to their educational team.
- Ensuring that communications with and about families is confidential and conducted with respect for their privacy.
- Offering parents accurate and professionally presented information about the pedagogical and therapeutic work being done with their child.
- Keeping parents abreast of their rights, of the kinds of practices that might violate them, and of available recourse if needed.
- Acknowledging and respect cultural differences.

Skill 4.04   Analyze procedures for communicating with and promoting self-advocacy in students with learning disabilities

Communication

Finding a way to accurately communicate with students who have been identified with learning disabilities can be a difficult task to complete. It can be most challenging for the students whose basis for the learning disability relates to language. Finding other ways to communicate so accurate messages are received and sent is important for all personnel working with the student. In some cases it may be necessary to use pictures or other nonverbal ways to communicate effectively.

For other students, it is imperative they understand the nature of their disability in age appropriate terms. There are many resources for students. Henry Winkler has written several children's books (e.g., Niagara Falls or Does it?) using fictional characters to portray his own personal struggles with being learning disabled. There are also workbooks and other materials available to teachers to work through helping to explain the challenges and successes of having a disability.

Self-advocacy

Learning about one's self involves the identification of learning styles, strengths and weakness, interests and preferences. For students with mild disabilities, developing an awareness of the accommodations they need will help them ask for necessary accommodations on a job and in postsecondary education. Students can also help identify alternative ways they can learn. Self-advocacy involves the ability to effectively communicate one's own rights, needs, and desires and to take responsibility for making decisions that impact one's life.

There are many elements in developing self-advocacy skills in students who are involved in the transition process. Helping the student to identify future goals or desired outcomes in transition planning areas is a good place to start. Self-knowledge is critical for the student in determining the direction that transition planning will take.

The role of the teacher in promoting self-advocacy should include encouraging the student to participate in the IEP process as well as other key parts of their educational development. Self-advocacy issues and lessons are effective when they are incorporated into the student's daily life. Teachers should listen to the student's problems and ask the student for input on possible changes that he may need. The teacher should talk with the student about possible solutions, discussing the pros and cons of doing something. A student who self-advocates should feel supported and encouraged. Good self-advocates know how to ask questions and get help from other people. They do not let other people do everything for them.

Students need to practice newly acquired self-advocacy skills. Teachers should have student's role play various situations, such as setting up a class schedule, moving out of the home, and asking for accommodations needed for a course.

The impact of transition planning on a student with a disability is very great. The student should be an active member of the transition team, as well as the focus of all activities. Students often think that being passive and relying on others to take care of them is the way to get things done. Students should be encouraged to express their opinions throughout the transition process. They need to learn how to express themselves so that others listen and take them seriously. These skills should be practiced within a supportive and caring environment.

POST-TEST

1. One technique that has proven especially effective in reducing self-stimulation and repetitive movements in autistic or severely retarded children is:

A. Shaping
B. Overcorrection
C. Fading
D. Response cost

2. In math class, Mary talked out without raising her hand. Her teacher gave her a warning and asked her to state the rule for being recognized to speak. However, Mary was soon talking out again and lost a point from her daily point sheet. This is an example of:

A. Shaping
B. Overcorrection
C. Fading
D. Response cost

3. Which body language would not likely be interpreted as a sign of defensiveness, aggression, or hostility?

A. Pointing
B. Direct eye contact
C. Hands on hips
D. Arms crossed

4. The minimum number of IEP meetings required per year is:

A. As many as necessary
B. One
C. Two
D. Three

5. Satisfaction of the LRE requirement means that:

A. A school is providing the best services it can offer there.
B. The school is providing the best services the district has to offer.
C. The student is being educated in the least restrictive setting that meets his or her needs.
D. The student is being educated with the fewest special education services necessary.

6. A review of a student's eligibility for an exceptional student program must be done:

A. At least once every 3 years.
B. At least once a year.
C. Only if a major change occurs in academic or behavioral performance.
D. When a student transfers to a new school.

7. Crisis intervention methods are above all concerned with:

A. Safety and well-being of the staff and students.
B. Stopping the inappropriate behavior.
C. Preventing the behavior from occurring again.
D. The student learning that outbursts are inappropriate.

8. Ricky, a third grade student, runs out of the classroom and onto the roof of the school. He paces around the roof, looks around to see who is watching, and laughs at the people on the ground. He appears to be in control of his behavior. What should the teacher do?

A. Go back inside and leave him up there until he decides he is ready to come down.
B. Climb up to get Ricky so he doesn't fall off and get hurt.
C. Notify the crisis teacher and arrange to have someone monitor Ricky.
D. Call the police.

9. Judy, a fourth grader, is often looking around the room or out of the window. She does not disturb anyone but has to ask for directions to be repeated and does not finish her work. Her teacher decides to reinforce Judy when she is on task. This would be an example of which method of reinforcement?

A. Fading
B. DRO
C. DRI
D. Shaping

10. An appropriate time out for a ten-year-old would be:

A. Ten minutes
B. Twenty minutes
C. No more than one-half hour.
D. Whatever time it takes for the disruptive behavior to stop.

11. During the science lesson Rudy makes remarks from time to time, but his classmates are not attending to them. The teacher reinforces the students who are raising their hands to speak, but ignores Rudy. The teacher reinforces Rudy when he raises his hand. This technique is an example of:

A. Fading
B. Response Cost
C. Extinction
D. Differential Reinforcement of Incompatible behavior

12. Mike was caught marking graffiti on the walls of the bathroom. His consequence was to clean all the walls of the bathroom. This type of overcorrection would be:

A. Response cost
B. Restitution
C. Positive Practice
D. Negative Practice

13. Which of these would probably not be a result of implementing an extinction strategy?

A. Maladaptive behavior gets worse before it gets better.
B. Maladaptive behavior stops, then starts up again for a brief time.
C. Aggression may occur for a brief period following implementation of extinction.
D. The length of time and patience involved to implement the strategy might tempt the teacher to give up.

14. Withholding or removing a stimulus that reinforces a maladaptive behavior is:

A. Extinction
B. Overcorrection
C. Punishment
D. Reinforcing an incompatible Behavior

15. Which of these would not be used to strengthen a desired behavior?

A. Contingency contracting
B. Tokens
C. Chaining
D. Overcorrection

16. If the arrangement in a fixed-ratio schedule of reinforcement is 3, when will the student receive the reinforcer?

A. After every third correct response.
B. After every third correct response in a row.
C. After the third correct response in the time interval of the behavior sample.
D. After the third correct response even if the undesired behavior occurs in between correct responses.

17. Wesley is having trouble ignoring distractions. At first you have him seated at a carrel that is located in a corner of the room. He does well, so you eventually move him out of the carrel for increasing portions of the day. Eventually, he is able to sit in a seat with the rest of his classmates. This is an example of:

A. Shaping
B. Extinction
C. Fading
D. Chaining

18. Laura is beginning to raise her hand first instead of talking out. An effective schedule of reinforcement would be:

A. Continuous
B. Variable
C. Intermittent
D. Fixed

19. As Laura continues to raise her hand to speak, the teacher would want to change this schedule of reinforcement in order to wean her from reinforcement:

A. Continuous
B. Variable
C. Intermittent
D. Fixed

20. Laura has demonstrated that she has mastered the goal of raising her hand to speak; reinforcement during the maintenance phase should be:

A. Continuous
B. Variable
C. Intermittent
D. Fixed

21. An integral part of ecological interventions are consequences that:

A. Are natural and logical.
B. Include extinction and overcorrection.
C. Are immediate and consistent.
D. Involve fading and shaping.

22. Examples of behaviors that are appropriate to be measured for their duration include all EXCEPT:

A. Thumb-sucking
B. Hitting
C. Temper tantrums
D. Maintaining eye contact

23. Examples of behaviors that are appropriate to be monitored by measuring frequency include all EXCEPT:

A. Teasing
B. Talking out
C. Being on time for class
D. Daydreaming

24. Criteria for choosing behaviors to measure by frequency include all but those that:

A. Have an observable beginning.
B. Last a long time.
C. Last a short time.
D. Occur often.

25. Criteria for choosing behaviors to measure by duration include all but those that:

A. Last a short time.
B. Last a long time.
C. Have no readily observable beginning or end.
D. Do not happen often.

26. Data on quiet behaviors (e.g., nail biting or daydreaming) are best measured using a:

A. Interval or time sample.
B. Continuous sample.
C. Variable sample.
D. Fixed-ratio sample.

27. Mr. Jones wants to design an intervention for reducing Jason's sarcastic remarks. He wants to find out who or what is reinforcing Jason's remarks, so he records data on Jason's behavior, as well as the attending behavior of his peers. This is an example of collecting data on:

A. Reciprocal behaviors
B. Multiple behaviors for single subjects
C. Single behaviors for multiple subjects
D. Qualitative data on Jason

28. Ms. Beekman has a class of students who frequently talk out. She wishes to begin interventions with the students who are talking out the most. She monitors the talking behavior of the entire class for 1-minute samples every half hour. This is an example of collecting data on:

A. Multiple behaviors for single subjects
B. Reciprocal behaviors
C. Single behaviors for multiple subjects
D. Continuous behaviors for fixed intervals

29. Mark got a B on his social studies test. Mr. Wilner praised him for his good grade, but Mark replies, "I was lucky this time. It must have been an easy test." Mark's statement is an example of:

A. External locus of control
B. Internal locus of control
C. Rationalization of his performance
D. Modesty

30. Mr. Smith is on a field trip with a group of high school EH students. On the way, they stop at a fast food restaurant for lunch, and Warren and Raul get into a disagreement. After some heated words, Warren stalks out of the restaurant and refuses to return to the group. He leaves the parking lot, continues walking away from the group, and ignores Mr. Smith's directions to come back. What would be the best course of action for Mr. Smith?

A. Leave the group with the class aide and follow Warren to try to talk him into coming back.
B. Wait a little while and see if Warren cools off and returns.
C. Telephone the school and let the crisis teacher notify the police in accordance with school policy.
D. Call the police himself.

31. Which is the least effective of reinforcers in programs for mildly to moderately handicapped learners?

A. Tokens
B. Social
C. Food
D. Activity

32. Tyrone likes to throw paper towards the trash can instead of getting up to throw it away. After several attempts of positive interventions, Tyrone has to serve a detention and continue to throw balls of paper at the trash can for the entire detention period. This would be an example of:

A. Negative practice
B. Overcorrection
C. Extinction
D. Response cost

33. A student may have great difficulty in meeting a target goal if the teacher has not first considered:

A. If the student has external or internal locus of control.
B. If the student is motivated to attain the goal.
C. If the student has the essential prerequisite skills to perform the goal.
D. If the student has had previous success or failure meeting the goal in other classes.

34. The Premack principle of increasing the performance of a less-preferred activity by immediately following it with a highly-preferred activity is the basis of:

A. Response cost
B. Token systems
C. Contingency contracting
D. Self-recording management

35. Mr. Brown finds that his chosen consequence does not seem to be having the desired effect of reducing the target misbehavior. Which of these would LEAST LIKELY account for Mr. Brown's lack of success with the consequence?

A. The consequence was aversive in Mr. Brown's opinion, but not the students'.
B. The students were not developmentally ready to understand the connection between the behavior and the consequence.
C. Mr. Brown was inconsistent in applying the consequence.
D. The intervention had not previously been shown to be effective in studies.

36. Teaching techniques that stimulate active participation and understanding in the mathematics class include all but which of the following?

A. Having students copy computation facts for a set number of times.
B. Asking students to find the error in an algorithm.
C. Giving immediate feedback to Students.
D. Having students chart their Progress.

37. Justin, a second grader, is reinforced if he is on task at the end of each 10-minute block of time that the teacher observes him. This is an example of what type of reinforcement schedule?

A. Continuous
B. Fixed interval
C. Fixed ratio
D. Variable ratio

38. Addressing a student's maladaptive behavior right away with a "time out" should be reserved for situations where:

A. The student has engaged in the behavior continuously throughout the day.
B. Harm might come to the student or others.
C. Lesser interventions have not been effective.
D. The student displayed the behavior the day before.

39. At the beginning of the school year, Annette had a problem with being late to class. Her teacher reinforced her each time she was in her seat when the bell rang. In October, her teacher decided to reward her every other day when she was not tardy to class. The reinforcement schedule appropriate for making the transition to the maintenance phase would be:

A. Continuous
B. Fixed interval
C. Variable ratio
D. Fixed ratio

40. By November, Annette's teacher is satisfied with her record of being on time and decides to change the schedule of reinforcement. The best type of reinforcement schedule for maintenance of behavior is:

A Continuous
B. Fixed interval
C. Variable ratio
D. Fixed Ratio

41. Which of these groups is not comprehensively covered by IDEA?

A. Gifted and talented
B. Mentally retarded
C. Specific learning disabilities
D. Speech and language impaired

42. Organizing ideas by use of a web or outline is an example of which writing activity?

A. Revision
B. Drafting
C. Prewriting
D. Final Draft

43. When a teacher is choosing behaviors to modify, the issue of social validity must be considered. Social validity refers to:

A. The need for the behavior to be performed in public.
B. Whether the new behavior will be considered significant by those who deal with the child.
C. Whether there will be opportunities to practice the new behavior in public.
D. Society's standards of behavior.

44. Dena, a second grader, is a messy eater who leaves her lunch area messy as well. Dena's teacher models correct use of eating utensils and napkins for her. As Dena approximates the target behavior of eating neatly and leaving her area clean, she receives praise and a token. Finally, Dena reaches her target behavior goal and redeems her tokens. Dena's teacher used the strategy of:

A. Chaining
B. Extinction
C. Overcorrection
D. Shaping

45. Educators who advocate educating all children in their neighborhood classrooms and schools, propose the end of labeling and segregation of special needs students in special classes, and call for the delivery of special supports and services directly in the classroom may be said to support the:

A. Full Service Model
B. Regular Education Initiative
C. Full Inclusion Model
D. Mainstream Model

46. In Ellis's ABC model, maladaptive behavior in response to a situation results from:

A. Antecedent events
B. Stimulus events
C. Thinking about the consequences
D. Irrational beliefs about the event

47. Section 504 differs from the scope of IDEA because its main focus is on:

A. Prohibition of discrimination on the basis of disability.
B. A basis for additional support services and accommodations in a special education setting.
C. Procedural rights and safeguards for the individual.
D. Federal funding for educational services.

48. Public Law 99-457 amended the IDEA to make provisions for:

A. Education services for "uneducable" children.
B. Educational services for children in jail settings.
C. Procedural rights and safeguards for the individual.
D. Federal funding for educational services.

49. A holistic approach to stress management should include all of the following EXCEPT:

A. Teaching a variety of coping methods.
B. Cognitive modification of feelings.
C. Teaching the flight or fight response.
D. Cognitive modification of behaviors.

50. Marisol has been mainstreamed into a ninth grade language arts class. Although her behavior is satisfactory and she likes the class, Marisol's reading level is about two years below grade level. The class has been assigned to read *Great Expectations* and write a report. What intervention would be LEAST successful in helping Marisol complete this assignment?

A. Having Marisol listen to a taped recording while following the story in the regular text.
B. Giving her a modified version of the story.
C. Telling her a modified version of the story.
D. Showing a film to the entire class and comparing and contrasting it to the book.

51. Fractions may be thought of in each of these ways EXCEPT:

A. Part of a whole
B. Part of a parent set
C. Ratio
D. An exponent

52. Many special education students may have trouble with the skills necessary to be successful in algebra and geometry for all but one of these reasons:

A. Prior instruction focused on computation rather than understanding.
B. Unwillingness to problem solve.
C. Lack of instruction in prerequisite skills.
D. Large amount of new vocabulary.

53. Which of these processes is NOT directly related to the meaningful development of number concepts in young children:

A. Describing
B. Classifying
C. Grouping
D. Ordering

54. Mr. Ward wants to assess Jennifer's problem-solving skills in mathematics. Which question would not address her use of strategies?

A. Does Jennifer check for mistakes in computation?
B. Does Jennifer use trial and error to solve problems?
C. Does Jennifer have an alternative strategy if the first one fails?
D. Does Jennifer become easily frustrated if she doesn't immediately get an answer?

55. Ryan is working on a report about dogs. He uses scissors and tape to cut and rearrange sections and paragraphs and then photocopies the paper so he can continue writing. Ryan is in which stage of the writing process?

A. Final Draft
B. Prewriting
C. Revision
D. Drafting

56. Talking into a tape reorder is an example of which writing activity?

A. Prewriting
B. Drafting
C. Final Draft
D. Revision

57. Publishing a class newsletter, looking through catalogues and filling out order forms, and playing the role of secretaries and executives are activities designed to teach:

A. Expressive writing
B. Transactional writing
C. Poetic writing
D. Creative writing

58. Under the provisions of IDEA, the student is entitled to all of these EXCEPT:

A. Placement in the best Environment.
B. Placement in the least restrictive environment.
C. Provision of educational needs at no cost.
D. Provision of individualized, appropriate educational program.

59. Teacher modeling, student-teacher dialogues, and peer interactions are part of which teaching technique designed to provide support during the initial phases of instruction?

A. Reciprocal teaching
B. Scaffolding
C. Peer tutoring
D. Cooperative learning

60. Modeling of a behavior by an adult who verbalizes the thinking process, overt self-instruction, and covert self-instruction are components of:

A. Rational-Emotive Therapy
B. Reality Therapy
C. Cognitive Behavior Modification
D. Reciprocal Teaching

61. Standards of accuracy for a student's spelling should be based on the student's:

A. Grade level spelling list
B. Present reading book level
C. Level of spelling development
D. Performance on an informal assessment

62. Which of these techniques is least effective in helping children correct spelling problems?

A. The teacher models the correct spelling in a context.
B. Student sees the incorrect and the correct spelling together in order to visualize the correct spelling.
C. Positive reinforcement as the child tests the rules and tries to approximate the correct spelling.
D. Copying the correct word 5 times.

63. The single most important activity for eventual reading success of young children is:

A. Giving them books.
B. Watching animated stories.
C. Reading aloud to them.
D. Talking about pictures in books.

64. Skilled readers use all but which one of these knowledge sources to construct meanings beyond the literal text:

A. Text Knowledge
B. Syntactic Knowledge
C. Morphological Knowledge
D. Semantic Knowledge

LEARNING DISABLED

65. The cooperative nature of Glasser's Reality Therapy, in which the problem-solving approach is used to correct misbehavior, is best signified by:

A. Minimal punishment.
B. Its similar approach to methods that teach students how to deal with academic mistakes.
C. Students' promises to use the alternative behavior plan to help them reach their goals.
D. Procedure sheets used during conflict situations.

66. Diaphragmatic breathing, progressive relaxation training, and exercises are examples of which type of stress coping skills?

A. Rational-emotive
B. Cognitive-psychological
C. Somatic-physiological
D. Stress inoculation

67. The stress that we experience when we win a race or accomplish a difficult task is called:

A. Stressor
B. Stresses
C. Eustress
D. Distress

68. Jane is so intimidated by a classmate's teasing that she breaks down in tears and cannot stand up for herself. The feeling(s) she is experiencing is/are:

A. Stressors
B. Stresses
C. Eustress
D. Distress

69. The movement towards serving as many children with disabilities as possible in the regular classroom with supports and services is known as:

A. Full service Model
B. Regular Education Initiative
C. Full Inclusion Model
D. Mainstream Model

70. Which of the following is NOT a feature of effective classroom rules?

A. They are about 4 to 6 in number.
B. They are negatively stated.
C. Consequences for infractions are consistent and immediate.
D. They can be tailored to individual classroom goals and teaching styles.

71. A suggested amount of time for a large-group instruction lesson for a sixth or seventh grade group would be:

A. 5 to 40 minutes
B. 5 to 50 minutes
C. 5 to 30 minutes
D. 5 to 15 minutes

LEARNING DISABLED

72. Sam is working to earn half an hour of basketball time with his favorite P.E. teacher. At the end of each half hour, Sam marks his point sheet with an X if he reached his goal of no call-outs. When he has received 25 marks, he will receive his basketball free time. This behavior management strategy is an example of:

A. Self-recording
B. Self-evaluation
C. Self-reinforcement
D. Self-regulation

73. Mark has been working on his target goal of completing his mathematics class work. Each day he records, on a scale of 0 to 3, how well he has done his work, and his teacher provides feedback. This self-management technique is an example of:

A. Self-recording
B. Self-reinforcement
C. Self-regulation
D. Self-evaluation

74. When Barbara reached her target goal, she chose her reinforcer and softly said to herself, "I worked hard, and I deserve this reward." This self-management technique is an example of:

A. Self-reinforcement
B. Self-recording
C. Self-regulation
D. Self-evaluation

75. Grading should be based on all of the following EXCEPT:

A. Clearly-defined mastery of course objectives
B. A variety of evaluation methods
C. Performance of the student in relation to other students
D. Assigning points for activities and basing grades on a point total

76. The following words describe an IEP objective EXCEPT:

A. Specific
B. Observable
C. Measurable
D. Criterion-referenced

77. Teacher feedback, task completion, and a sense of pride over mastery or accomplishment of a skill are examples of:

A. Extrinsic reinforcers
B. Behavior modifiers
C. Intrinsic reinforcers
D. Positive feedback

78. Social approval, token reinforcers, and rewards, such as pencils or stickers, are examples of:

A. Extrinsic reinforcers
B. Behavior modifiers
C. Intrinsic reinforcers
D. Positive feedback

79. Aggression, escape, and avoidance are unpleasant side effects that can be avoided by using:

A. Time out
B. Response cost
C. Overcorrection
D. Negative practice

80. Josie forgot that it was school picture day and did not dress up for the pictures. In the media center, Josie notices some girls in the line waiting to have their pictures taken. They appear to be looking over at her and whispering. Josie feels certain that they are making fun of the way her hair and clothes look and gets so upset that she leaves the line and hides out in the bathroom. Josie did not think to ask when the makeup day for pictures would be. According to Ellis's ABC Model, Jodie's source of stress is:

A. Her forgetting to dress appropriately for picture day.
B. The girls in the library who appear to be whispering about her.
C. Her belief that they are making fun of her appearance.
D. The girls' insensitive behavior.

81. Token systems are popular for all of these advantages EXCEPT:

A. The number needed for rewards may be adjusted as needed.
B. Rewards are easy to maintain.
C. They are effective for students who generally do not respond to social reinforcers.
D. Tokens reinforce the relationship of desirable behavior and reinforcement.

82. Which would not be an advantage of using a criterion-referenced test?

A. Information about an individual's ability level is too specific for the purposes of the assessment.
B. It can pinpoint exact areas of weaknesses and strengths.
C. You can design them yourself.
D. You do not get comparative information.

83. Which is NOT an example of a standard score?

A. T Score
B. Z Score
C. Standard deviation
D. Stanine

84. The most direct method of obtaining assessment data, and perhaps the most objective, is:

A. Testing
B. Self-recording
C. Observation
D. Experimenting

85. The basic tools necessary to observe and record behavior include all BUT:

A. Cameras
B. Timers
C. Counters
D. Graphs or charts

86. Which of these characteristics is NOT included in the P.L. 94-142 definition of emotional disturbance:

A. General pervasive mood of unhappiness or depression
B. Social maladjustment manifested in a number of settings
C. Tendency to develop physical symptoms, pains, or fear associated with school or personal problems
D. Inability to learn which is not attributed to intellectual, sensory, or health factors

87. Of the various factors that contribute to delinquency and antisocial behavior, which has been found to be the weakest?

A. Criminal behavior and/or alcoholism in the father
B. Lax mother and punishing father
C. Socioeconomic disadvantage
D. Long history of broken home or marital discord among parents

88. Poor moral development, lack of empathy, and behavioral excesses, such as aggression, are the most obvious characteristics of which behavioral disorder?

A. Autism
B. ADD-H
C. Conduct disorder
D. Pervasive development disorder

89. School refusal, obsessive-compulsive disorders, psychosis, and separation anxiety are also frequently accompanied by:

A. Conduct disorder
B. ADD-H
C. Depression
D. Autism

90. Signs of depression do not typically include:

A. Hyperactivity
B. Changes in sleep patterns
C. Recurring thoughts of death or suicide
D. Significant changes in weight or appetite

91. Children who are characterized by impulsivity generally:

A. Do not feel sorry for their actions.
B. Blame others for their actions.
C. Do not weigh alternatives before Acting.
D. Do not outgrow their problem.

LEARNING DISABLED

92. Which of these is listed as only a minor scale on the Behavior Problem Checklist?

A. Motor Excess
B. Conduct Disorder
C. Socialized Aggression
D. Anxiety Withdrawal

93. The extent that a test measures what it claims to measure is called:

A. Reliability
B. Validity
C. Factor Analysis
D. Chi Square

94. Which is not a goal of collaborative consultation?

A. Prevent learning and behavior problems with mainstreamed students.
B. Coordinate the instructional programs between mainstream and ESE classes.
C. Facilitate solutions to learning and behavior problems.
D. Function as an ESE service Model.

95. An important goal of collaborative consultation is:

A. Mainstream as many ESE students as possible
B. Guidance on how to handle ESE students from the ESE teacher
C. Mutual empowerment of both the mainstream and the ESE teacher.
D. Document progress of mainstreamed students.

96. Knowledge of evaluation strategies, program interventions, and types of data are examples of which variable for a successful consultation program?

A. People
B. Process
C. Procedural implementation
D. Academic preparation

97. Skills as an administrator and background in client, consulter, and consultation skills are examples of which variable in a successful consultation program?

A. People
B. Process
C. Procedural implementation
D. Academic preparation

98. The ability to identify problems, generate solutions, and knowledge of theoretical perspectives of consultation are examples of which variable in a successful consultation program?

A. People
B. Process
C. Procedural implementation
D. Academic preparation

99. A serious hindrance to successful mainstreaming is:

A. Lack of adapted materials
B. Lack of funding
C. Lack of communication among teachers
D. Lack of support from administration

LEARNING DISABLED

100. Which of the following statements was not offered as a rationale for the REI?

A. Special education students are not usually identified until their learning problems have become severe.
B. Lack of funding will mean that support for the special needs children will not be available in the regular classroom.
C. Putting children in segregated special education placements is stigmatizing.
D. There are students with learning or behavior problems who do not meet special education requirements but who still need special services.

101. The key to success for the exceptional student placed in a regular classroom is:

A. Access to the special aids and materials.
B. Support from the ESE teacher.
C. Modifications in the curriculum.
D The mainstream teacher's belief that the student will profit from the placement.

102. Lack of regular follow-up, difficulty in transporting materials, and lack of consistent support for students who need more assistance are disadvantages of which type of service model?

A. Regular classroom
B. Consultant with Regular Teacher
C. Itinerant
D. Resource Room

103. Ability to supply specific instructional materials, programs, and methods and to influence environmental learning variables are advantages of which service model for exceptional students?

A. Regular Classroom
B. Consultant Teacher
C. Itinerant Teacher
D. Resource Room

104. An emphasis on instructional remediation and individualized instruction in problem areas and a focus on mainstreaming students are characteristics of which model of service delivery?

A. Regular Classroom
B. Consultant Teacher
C. Itinerant Teacher
D. Resource Room

105. Which of these would not be considered a valid attempt to contact a parent for an IEP meeting?

A. Telephone call
B. Copy of correspondence
C. Message left on an answering machine
D. Record of home visits

106. A best practice for evaluating student performance and progress on IEPs is:

A. Formal assessment
B. Curriculum-based assessment
C. Criterion-based assessment
D. Norm-referenced evaluation

107. Guidelines for an Individualized Family Service Plan (IFSP) would be described in which legislation?

A. PL 94-142
B. PL 99-457
C. PL 101-476
D. ADA

108. In a positive classroom environment, errors are viewed as:

A. Symptoms of deficiencies
B. Lack of attention or ability
C. A natural part of the learning process
D. The result of going too fast

109. Recess, attending school social or sporting events, and eating lunch with peers are examples of:

A. Privileges
B. Allowances
C. Rights
D. Entitlements

110. Free time, shopping at the school store, and candy are examples of:

A. Privileges
B. Allowances
C. Rights
D. Entitlements

111. Eating lunch, access to a bathroom, and privacy are examples of:

A. Privileges
B. Allowances
C. Rights
D. Entitlements

112. Cheryl is a 15-year-old student receiving educational services in a full-time EH classroom. The date for her IEP review will take place two months before her 16th birthday. According to the requirements of IDEA, what must ADDITIONALLY be included in this review?

A. Graduation plan
B. Individualized transition plan
C. Individualized Family Service Plan
D. Transportation planning

113. Hector is a 10th grader in a program for the severely emotionally handicapped. After a classmate taunted him about his mother, Hector threw a desk at the other boy and attacked him. As a crisis intervention team attempted to break up the fight, one teacher hurt his knee. The other boy received a concussion. Hector now faces disciplinary measures. How long can he be suspended without the suspension constituting a "change of placement"?

A. 5 days
B. 10 days
C. 10 + 30 days
D. 60 days

114. The concept that a handicapped student cannot be expelled for misconduct which is a manifestation of the handicap itself is not limited to students labeled "seriously emotionally disturbed". Which reason does NOT explain this concept?

A. Emphasis on individualized evaluation.
B. Consideration of the problems and needs of handicapped students.
C. Right to a free and appropriate public education.
D. Putting these students out of school will just leave them on the streets to commit crimes.

115. An effective classroom behavior management plan includes all but which of the following?

A. Transition procedures for changing activities
B. Clear consequences for rule infractions
C. Concise teacher expectations for student behavior
D. Copies of lesson plans

116. Statements like, "Darrien is lazy," are not helpful in describing his behavior for all but which of these reasons?

A. There is no way to determine if any change occurs from the information given.
B. The student and not the behavior becomes labeled.
C. Darrien's behavior will manifest itself clearly enough without any written description.
D. Constructs are open to various interpretations among the people who are asked to define them.

117. Mercie often is not in her seat when the bell rings. She may be found at the pencil sharpener, throwing paper away, or fumbling through her notebook. Which of these descriptions of her behavior can be described as a "pinpoint"?

A. Is tardy a lot
B. Is out of seat
C. Is not in seat when late bell rings
D. Is disorganized

118. When choosing behaviors for change, the teacher should ask if there is any evidence that the behavior is presently or potentially harmful to the student or others. This is an example of which test?

A. Fair-Pair
B. "Stranger" Test
C. Premack Principle
D. "So-What" Test

119. Ms. Taylor takes her students to a special gymnastics presentation that the P.E. coach has arranged in the gym. She has a rule against talk-outs and reminds the students that they will lose 5 points on their daily point sheet for talking out. The students get a chance to perform some of the simple stunts. They all easily go through the movements except for Sam, who is known as the class klutz. Sam does not give up, and he finally completes the stunts. His classmates cheer him on with comments like, "Way to go!" Their teacher, however, reminds them that they broke the no-talking rule and will lose the points. What mistake was made here?

A. The students forgot the no-talking rule.
B. The teacher considered talk-outs to be maladaptive in all school settings.
C. The other students could have distracted Sam with talk-outs and caused him to get hurt.
D. The teacher should have let the P.E. coach handle the discipline in the gym.

120. Which of the following should be avoided when writing objectives for social behavior?

A. Nonspecific adverbs
B. Behaviors stated as verbs
C. Criteria for acceptable performance
D. Conditions where the behavior is expected to be performed

121. Criteria for choosing behaviors that are in the most need of change involve all but the following:

A. Observations across settings to rule out certain interventions.
B. Pinpointing the behavior that is the poorest fit in the child's environment.
C. The teacher's concern about what is the most important behavior to target.
D. Analysis of the environmental reinforcers.

122. Ms. Wright is planning an analysis of Audrey's out-of-seat behavior. Her initial data would be called:

A. Pre-referral phase
B. Intervention phase
C. Baseline phase
D. Observation phase

123. To reinforce Audrey each time she is on-task and in her seat, Ms. Wright decides to deliver specific praise and stickers, which Audrey may collect and redeem for a reward. The data collected during the time Ms. Wright is using this intervention is called:

A. Referral phase
B. Intervention phase
C. Baseline phase
D. Observation phase

LEARNING DISABLED

124. Indirect requests and attempts to influence or control others through one's use of language is an example of:

A. Morphology
B. Syntax
C. Pragmatics
D. Semantics

125. Kenny, a fourth grader, has trouble comprehending analogies, using comparative, spatial, and temporal words, and multiple meanings. Language interventions for Kenny would focus on:

A. Morphology
B. Syntax
C. Pragmatics
D. Semantics

126. Celia, who is in fourth grade, asked, "Where are my ball?" She also has trouble with passive sentences. Language interventions for Celia would target:

A. Morphology
B. Syntax
C. Pragmatics
D. Semantics

127. Scott is in middle school but still says statements like "I gotted new high-tops yesterday," and, "I saw three mans in the front office." Language interventions for Scott would target:

A. Morphology
B. Syntax
C. Pragmatics
D. Semantics

128. Which is not indicative of a handwriting problem?

A. Errors persist over time.
B. Little improvement on simple handwriting tasks.
C. Fatigue after writing for a short time.
D. Occasional letter reversals, word omissions, and poor spacing.

129. All of these are effective in teaching written expression EXCEPT:

A. Exposure to various styles and direct instruction in those styles.
B. Immediate feedback from the teacher with all mistakes clearly marked.
C. Goal setting and peer evaluation of written products according to a set criteria.
D. Incorporating writing with other academic subjects.

130. Mr. Mendez is assessing his students written expression. Which of these is not a component of written expression?

A. Vocabulary
B. Morphology
C. Content
D. Sentence Structure

131. Ms. Tolbert is teaching spelling to her students. The approach stresses phoneme-grapheme relationships within parts of words. Spelling rules, generalizations, and patterns are taught. A typical spelling list for her third graders might include light, bright, night, fright, and slight. Which approach is Ms. Tolbert using?

A. Rule-based instruction
B. Fernald Method
C. Gillingham Method
D. Test-Study-Test

132. At the beginning of the year, Mr. Johnson wants to gain an understanding of his class' social structure in order to help him assess social skills and related problems. The technique that would best help Mr. Johnson accomplish this is:

A. Personal interviews with each student
B. Parent rating form
C. Sociometric techniques
D. Self-reports

133. In assessing a group's social structure, asking a student to list the classmates whom he or she would choose to be his or her best friends, preferred play partners, and preferred work partners is an example of:

A. Peer nomination
B. Peer rating
C. Peer assessment
D. Sociogram

134. Naming classmates who fit certain behavioral descriptions, such as smart, disruptive, or quiet, is an example of which type of sociometric assessment?

A. Peer nomination
B. Peer rating
C. Peer assessment
D. Sociogram

135. Mr. Johnson asks his students to score each of their classmates in areas such as who they would prefer to play with and work with. A Likert-type scale with non-behavioral criteria is used. This is an example of:

A. Peer nomination
B. Peer rating
C. Peer assessment
D. Sociogram

136. Which of these explanations would not likely account for the lack of a clear definition of behavior disorders?

A. Problems with measurement
B. Cultural and/or social influences and views of what is acceptable
C. The numerous types of manifestations of behavior disorders
D. Differing theories that use their own terminology and definitions

137. Ryan is 3, and her temper tantrums last for an hour. Bryan is 8, and he does not stay on task for more than 10 minutes without teacher prompts. These behaviors differ form normal children in terms of their:

A. Rate
B. Topography
C. Duration
D. Magnitude

138. All children cry, hit, fight, and play alone at different times. Children with behavior disorders will perform these behaviors at a higher than normal:

A. Rate
B. Topography
C. Duration
D. Magnitude

139. The exhibition of two or more types of problem behaviors across different areas of functioning is known as:

A. Multiple maladaptive behaviors
B. Clustering
C. Social maladjustment
D. Conduct disorder

140. Children with behavior disorders often do not exhibit stimulus control. This means that they have not learned:

A. The right things to do
B. Where and when certain behaviors are appropriate
C. Right from wrong
D. Listening skills

141. Social withdrawal, anxiety, depression, shyness, and guilt are indicative of:

A. Conduct disorder
B. Personality disorders
C. Immaturity
D. Socialized aggression

142. Short attention span, daydreaming, clumsiness, and preference for younger playmates are associated with:

A. Conduct disorder
B. Personality disorders
C. Immaturity
D. Socialized aggression

143. Truancy, gang membership, and feelings of pride in belonging to a delinquent subculture are indicative of:

A. Conduct disorder
B. Personality disorders
C. Immaturity
D. Socialized aggression

144. Temper tantrums, disruption of class, disobedience, and bossiness are associated with:

A. Conduct disorder
B. Personality disorders
C. Immaturity
D. Socialized aggression

145. Which of these is not true for most children with behavior disorders?

A. Many score in the "slow learner" or "mildly retarded" range on IQ tests.
B. They are frequently behind their classmates in terms of academic achievement.
C. They are bright, but bored with their surroundings.
D. A large amount of time is spent on nonproductive, nonacademic behaviors.

146. Echolalia, repetitive stereotype actions, and a severe disorder of thinking and communication are indicative of:

A. Psychosis
B. Schizophrenia
C. Autism
D. Paranoia

147. Teaching children functional skills that will be useful in their home life and neighborhoods is the basis of:

A. Curriculum-based instruction
B. Community-based instruction
C. Transition planning
D. Functional curriculum

148. Disabilities caused by fetal alcohol syndrome are many times higher for which ethnic group?

A. Native Americans
B. Asian Americans
C. Hispanic Americans
D. African Americans

149. Which of these would be the least effective measure of behavioral disorders?

A. Projective test
B. Ecological assessment
C. Standardized test
D. Psychodynamic analysis

150. Which behavioral disorder is difficult to diagnose in children because the symptoms are manifested quite differently than in adults?

A. Anorexia
B. Schizophrenia
C. Paranoia
D. Depression

Rationale with Sample Questions

1. One technique that has proven especially affective in reducing self-stimulation and repetitive movements in autistic or severely retarded children is:
   a. Shaping
   b. Overcorrection
   c. Fading
   d. Response cost

A Shaping: To change a person's behavior gradually using rewards as the person comes closer to the desired behavior or punishment for moving away from it.
B Overcorrection: a form of punishment, e.g., cleaning of a marked surface.
C Fading: gradual lessening of a reward or punishment.
D Response cost: a form of punishment, e.g., loss of privileges.

b. is correct.
Rationale: All behavior is learned.

2. In math class, Mary talked out without raising her hand. Her teacher gave her a warning and asked her to state the rule for being recognized to speak. However, Mary was soon talking again and lost a point from her daily point sheet. This is an example of:
   a. Shaping
   b. Overcorrection
   c. Fading
   d. Response cost

d. is correct.
Rationale: Mary lost a point in response to the undesirable behavior.

3. Which body language would not likely be interpreted as a sign of defensiveness, aggression, or hostility?
   a. Pointing
   b. Direct eye contact
   c. Hands on hips
   d. Arms

b. is correct.
Rationale: In our culture, A, C, and D are considered nonverbal acts of defiance. Direct eye contact is not considered an act of defiance.

TEACHER CERTIFICATION STUDY GUIDE

4. The minimum number of IEP meetings required per year is:
   a. as many as necessary
   b. one
   c. two
   d. three

b. is correct.
Rationale: P. L. 99-457 (1986) grants an annual IEP.

5. Satisfaction of the LRE requirement means:
   a. The school is providing the best services it can offer.
   b. The school is providing the best services the district has to offer.
   c. The student is being educated with the fewest special education services necessary.
   d. The student is being educated in the least restrictive setting that meets his or her needs.

d. is correct.
Rationale: The legislation mandates **LRE** Least Restrictive Environment.

6. A review of a student's eligibility for an exceptional student program must be done:
   a. At least once every three years
   b. At least once a year
   c. Only if a major change occurs in academic or behavioral performance
   d. When a student transfers to a new school

a. is correct.
Rationale: P. L. 95-56 1978 (Gifted and Talented Children's Act)

7. Crisis intervention methods are above all concerned with:
   a. Safety and well-being of the staff and students
   b. Stopping the inappropriate behavior
   c. Preventing the behavior from occurring again
   d. The student learning that outbursts are inappropriate

a. is correct.
Rationale: It encompasses B, C, and D.

LEARNING DISABLED

8. Ricky, a third grade student, runs out of the classroom and onto the roof of the school. He paces around the roof, looks around to see who is watching, and laughs at the person standing on the ground. He appears to be in control of his behavior. What should the teacher do?
   a. Go back inside and leave him up there until he decides he is ready to come down
   b. Climb up to get Ricky so he does not fall off and get hurt
   c. Notify the crisis teacher and arrange to have someone monitor Ricky
   d. Call the police

c. is correct.
Rationale: The teacher cannot be responsible for both Ricky and his or her class. He must pass the responsibility to the appropriate person.

9. Judy, a fourth grader, is often looking around the room or out the window. She does not disturb anyone but has to ask for directions to be repeated and does not finish her work. Her teacher decides to reinforce Judy when she is on task. Which method of reinforcement is she using?
   a. Fading
   b. DRO
   c. DRI
   d. Shaping

c. is correct.
Rationale: This is an example of Direct Reinforcement (Individual).

10. An appropriate time out for a ten-year old would be:
    a. Ten minutes
    b. Twenty minutes
    c. No more than one half-hour
    d. Whatever time it takes for the disruptive behavior to stop

a. is correct.
Rationale: An appropriate time-out is no more than 10 minutes.

11. During the science lesson, Rudy makes remarks from time to time, but his classmates are not attending to them. The teacher reinforces the students who are raising their hands to speak but ignores Rudy. The teacher reinforces Rudy when he raises his hand. This technique is an example of:
    a. Fading
    b. Response cost
    c. Extinction
    d. Differential reinforcement of incompatible behavior

c. is correct.
Rationale: By ignoring the behavior, the teacher hopes it will become extinct.

12. Mike was caught marking up the walls of the bathroom with graffiti. His consequence was to clean all the walls of the bathroom. This type of overcorrection would be:
    a. Response cost
    b. Restitution
    c. Positive practice
    d. Negative practice

c. is correct.
Rationale: This is a positive form of over correction in which the student is learning another skill.

13. Which of these would probably not be a result of implementing an extinction strategy?
    a. Maladaptive behavior gets worse before it gets better
    b. Maladaptive behavior stops, then starts up again for a brief time
    c. Aggression may occur for a brief period following implementation of extinction
    d. The length of time and patience involved to implement the strategy might tempt the teacher to give up

b. is correct.
Rationale: The student responds in A, B, and C. In B, he ignores the teacher's action.

14. Withholding or removing a stimulus that reinforces a maladaptive behavior is:
    a. Extinction
    b. Overcorrection
    c. Punishment
    d. Reinforcing an incompatible behavior

a. is correct.
Rationale: There is no stimulus involved in this strategy.

15. Which of these would not be used to strengthen a desired behavior?
    a. Contingency contracting
    b. Tokens
    c. Chaining
    d. Overcorrection

d. is correct.
Rationale: A, B, and C are all used to strengthen a desired behavior. D is punishment.

16. If the arrangement in a fixed-ratio schedule of reinforcement is 3, when will the student receive the reinforcer?
    a. After every third correct response
    b. After every third correct response in a row
    c. After the third correct response in the time interval of the behavior sample
    d. After the third correct response even if the undesired behavior occurs in between correct responses

b. is correct.
Rationale: This is the only one that follows a pattern. A fixed ratio is a pattern.

17. Wesley is having difficulty ignoring distractions. At first you have him seated at a carrel which is located in a corner of the room. He does well, so you eventually move him out of the carrel for increasing portions of the day. Eventually, he is able to sit in a seat with the rest of his classmates. This is an example of:
    a. Shaping
    b. Extinction
    c. Fading
    d. Chaining

a. is correct.
Rationale: The teacher is shaping a desired behavior.

18. Laura is beginning to raise her hand first instead of talking out. An effective schedule of reinforcement should be:
    a. Continuous
    b. Variable
    c. Intermittent
    d. Fixed

a. is correct.
Rationale: The pattern of reinforcement should not be variable, intermittent, or fixed. It should be continuous.

19. As Laura continues to raise her hand to speak, the teacher would want to change to this schedule of reinforcement in order to wean her from the reinforcement:
    a. Continuous
    b. Variable
    c. Intermittent
    d. Fixed

d. is correct.
Rationale: The pattern should be in a fixed ratio.

20. Laura has demonstrated that she has mastered the goal of raising her hand to speak; reinforcement during the maintenance phase should be:
    a. Continuous
    b. Variable
    c. Intermittent
    d. Fixed

c. is correct.
Rationale: Reinforcement should be intermittent, as the behavior should occur infrequently.

21. An integral part of ecological interventions are consequences that:
    a. Are natural and logical
    b. Include extinction and overcorrection
    c. Are immediate and consistent
    d. Involve fading and shaping

a. is correct.
Rationale: The student must understand both the behavior and the consequence. The consequence should fit the infraction.

22. Examples of behaviors that are appropriate to be monitored by measuring frequency include all EXCEPT:
    a. Thumb sucking
    b. Hitting
    c. Temper tantrums
    d. Maintaining eye contact

b. is correct.
Rationale: Hitting takes place in an instant. This should be measured by frequency.

23. Examples of behaviors that are appropriate to be monitored by measuring frequency include all EXCEPT:
    a. Teasing
    b. Talking out
    c. Being on time for class
    d. Daydreaming

d. is correct.
Rationale: Daydreaming cannot be measured by frequency. It should be measured by duration.

24. Criteria for choosing behaviors to measure by frequency include all but those that:
    a. Have an observable beginning
    b. Last a long time
    c. Last a short time
    d. Occur often

b. is correct.
Rationale: We use frequency to measure behaviors that do not last a long time.

25. Criteria for choosing behaviors to measure by duration include all but those that:
    a. Last a short time
    b. Last a long time
    c. Have no readily observable beginning or end
    d. Don't happen often

a. is correct.
Rationale: We use duration to measure behaviors that do not last a short time.

26. Data on quiet behaviors e.g., nail biting or daydreaming, are best measured using a (an):
    a. Interval or time sample
    b. Continuous sample
    c. Variable sample
    d. Fixed-ratio sample

a. is correct.
Rationale: An interval or time sample is best to measure the duration of the behavior.

27. Mr. Jones wants to design an intervention for reducing Jason's sarcastic remarks. He wants to find out who or what is reinforcing Jason's remarks, so he records data on Jason's behavior, as well as the attending behavior of his peers. This is an example of collecting data on:
   a. Reciprocal behaviors
   b. Multiple behaviors for single subjects
   c. Single behaviors for multiple subjects
   d. Qualitative data on Jason

a. is correct.
Rationale: Jason's peers' behaviors are in response to Jason's disruptive behaviors.

28. Ms Beekman has a class of students who frequently talk out. She wishes to begin interventions with the students who are talking out the most. She monitors the talking behavior of the entire class for 1-minute samples every half-hour. This is an example of collecting data on:
   a. Multiple behavior for single subjects
   b. Reciprocal behaviors
   c. Single behaviors for multiple subjects
   d. Continuous behaviors for fixed intervals

c. is correct.
Rationale: Talking out is the only behavior being observed.

29. Mark got a B on his social studies test. Mr. Wilner praised him for his good grade, but Mark replies, "I was lucky this time. It must have been an easy test." Mark's statement is an example of:
   a. External locus of control
   b. Internal locus of control
   c. Rationalization of his performance
   d. Modesty

a. is correct.
Rationale: Locus of control refers to the way a person perceives the relation between his or her efforts and the outcome of an event. A person who has an external orientation anticipates no relation between his or her efforts and the outcome of an event.

30. Mr. Smith is on a field trip with a group of high school EH students. On the way, they stop at a fast-food restaurant for lunch, and Warren and Raul get into an argument. After some heated words, Warren stalks out of the restaurant and refuses to return to the group. He leaves the parking lot, continues walking away from the group, and ignores Mr. Smith's directions to come back. What would be the best course of action for Mr. Smith?

    a. Leave the group with the class aide and follow Warren to try to talk him into coming back.
    b. Wait a little while and see if Warren cools off and returns.
    c. Telephone the school and let the crisis teacher notify the police in accordance with school policy.
    d. Call the police himself.

c. is correct.
Rationale: Mr. Smith is still responsible for his class. This is his only option.

31. Which is the least effective of reinforcers in programs for mildly to moderately handicapped learners?
    a. Tokens
    b. Social
    c. Food
    d. Activity

c. is correct.
Rationale: Food is the least effective reinforcer for most handicapped children. Tokens, social interaction, or activity are more desirable. Food may have reached satiation.

32. Tyrone likes to throw paper towards the trashcan instead of getting up to throw it away. After several attempts at positive interventions, Tyrone has to serve a detention and continue to throw balls of paper at the trashcan for the entire detention period. This would be an example of:
    a. Negative practice
    b. Overcorrection
    c. Extinction
    d. Response cost

a. is correct.
Rationale: Tyrone has to continue to practice the negative behavior.

33. A student may have great difficulty in meeting a target goal if the teacher has not first considered:
    a. If the student has external or internal locus of control.
    b. If the student is motivated to attain the goal.
    c. If the student has the essential prerequisite skills to perform the goal.
    d. If the student has had previous success or failure meeting the goal in other classes.

c. is correct.
Rationale: Prerequisite skills are essential in both setting goals and attaining goals.

34. The Premack Principle of increasing the performance of a less-preferred activity by immediately following it with a highly-preferred activity is the basis of:
    a. response cost
    b. token systems
    c. contingency contracting
    d. self-recording management

c. is correct.
Rationale: In an unwritten contract, the student eagerly completes the less desirable activity to obtain the reward of the more desirable activity.

35. Mr. Brown finds that his chosen consequence does not seem to be having the desired effect of reducing the target misbehavior. Which of these would LEAST LIKELY account for Mr. Brown's lack of success with the consequence?
    a. The consequence was aversive in Mr. Brown's opinion but not the students'.
    b. The students were not developmentally ready to understand the connection.
    c. Mr. Brown was inconsistent in applying the consequence.
    d. The intervention had not previously been shown to be effective in studies.

d. is correct.
Rationale: A, B, and C might work if applied in the classroom, but research is the least of Mr. Brown's options.

36. Teaching techniques that stimulate active participation and understanding in the mathematics class include all but which of the following?
    a. Having students copy computation facts for a set number of times.
    b. Asking students to find the error in an algorithm.
    c. Giving immediate feedback to students.
    d. Having students chart their progress.

a. is correct.
Rationale: Copying does not stimulate participation or understanding.

37. Justin, a second grader, is reinforced if he is on task at the end of each 10-minute block of time that the teacher observes him. This is an example of what type of schedule?
    a. Continuous
    b. Fixed interval
    c. Fixed-ratio
    d. Variable ratio

b. is correct.
Rationale: 10 minutes is a fixed interval of time.

38. Addressing a student's maladaptive behavior right away with a "time out" should be reserved for situations where:
    a. The student has engaged in the behavior continuously throughout the day.
    b. Harm might come to the student or others.
    c. Lesser interventions have not been effective.
    d. The student displayed the behavior the day before.

b. is correct.
Rationale: The best intervention is to move the student away from the harmful environment.

39. At the beginning of the school year, Annette had a problem with being late for class. Her teacher reinforced her each time she was in her seat when the bell rang. In October, her teacher decided to reward her every other day when she was not tardy to class. The reinforcement schedule appropriate for making the transition to maintenance phase would be:
    a. Continuous
    b. Fixed interval
    c. Variable ratio
    d. Fixed ratio

b. is correct.
Rationale: Every other day is a fixed interval of time.

TEACHER CERTIFICATION STUDY GUIDE

40. By November, Annette's teacher is satisfied with her record of being on time and decides to change the schedule of reinforcement. The best type of reinforcement schedule for maintenance of behavior is:
    a. Continuous
    b. Fixed interval
    c. Variable ratio
    d. Fixed ratio

c. is correct.
Rationale: The behavior will occur infrequently. Variable Ratio is the best schedule.

41. Which of these groups is not comprehensively covered by IDEA?
    a. Gifted and talented
    b. Mentally retarded
    c. Specific learning disabilities
    d. Speech and language impaired

c. is correct.
Rationale: IDEA: Individuals with Disabilities Education Act 101-476 (1990) did not cover all exceptional children. The Gifted and Talented Children's Act, P. L. 95-56 was passed in 1978.

42. Organizing ideas by use of a web or outline is an example of which writing activity?
    a. Revision
    b. Drafting
    c. Prewriting
    d. Final draft

c. is correct.
Rationale: Organizing ideas come before Drafting, Final Draft, and Revision.

43. When a teacher is choosing behaviors to modify, the issue of social validity must be considered. Social validity refers to:
    a. The need for the behavior to be performed in public.
    b. Whether the new behavior will be considered significant by those who deal with the child.
    c. Whether there will be opportunities to practice the new behavior in public.
    d. Society's standards of behavior.

d. is correct.
Rationale: Validity has to do with the appropriateness of the behavior. Is it age appropriate? Is it culturally appropriate?

LEARNING DISABLED

TEACHER CERTIFICATION STUDY GUIDE

44. Dena, a second grader, is a messy eater who leaves her lunch area messy as well. Dena's teacher models correct use of eating utensils and napkins for her. As Dena approximates the target behavior of eating neatly and leaving her area clean, she receives praise and a token. Finally, Dena reaches her target behavior goal and redeems her tokens. Dena's teacher used the strategy of:
   a. Chaining
   b. Extinction
   c. Overcorrection
   d. Shaping

a. is correct.
Rationale: Chaining is a procedure in which individual responses are reinforced when occurring in sequence to form a complex behavior. Shaping, however, targets single behaviors.

45. Educators who advocate educating all children in their neighborhood classrooms and schools propose the end of labeling and segregation of special needs students in special classes, and who call for the delivery of special supports and services directly in the classroom, may be said to support the:
   a. Full service model
   b. Regular education initiative
   c. Full inclusion model
   d. Mainstream model

c. is correct.
Rationale: All students must be included in the regular classroom.

46. In Ellis' ABC model, maladaptive behavior in response to a situation results from:
   a. Antecedent events
   b. Stimulus events
   c. Thinking about the consequences
   d. Irrational beliefs about the event

d. is correct.
Rationale: All behavior is learned. This behavior is different from the norm. It is different because of something the child has experienced or learned.

47. Section 504 differs from the scope of IDEA because its main focus is on:
    a. Prohibition of discrimination on the basis of disability.
    b. A basis for additional support services and accommodations in a special education setting.
    c. Procedural rights and safeguards for the individual.
    d. Federal funding for educational services.

a. is correct.
Rationale: Section 504 prohibits discrimination on the basis of disability.

48. Public Law 99-457 amended the EHA to make provisions for:
    a. Education services for "uneducable" children
    b. Education services for children in jail settings
    c. Special education benefits for children birth to five years
    d. Education services for medically-fragile children

c. is correct.
Rationale: P.L. 99-457 amended EHA to provide Special Education programs for children 3-5 years, with most states offering outreach programs to identify children with special needs from birth to age 3.

49. A holistic approach to stress management should include all of the following EXCEPT:
    a. Teaching a variety of coping methods
    b. Cognitive modification of feelings
    c. Teaching the fight or flight response
    d. Cognitive modification of behaviors

c. is correct.
Rationale: A, B, and D are coping interventions. C is not.

50. Marisol has been mainstreamed into a ninth grade language arts class. Although her behavior is satisfactory, and she likes the class, Marisol's reading level is about two years below grade level. The class has been assigned to read *Great Expectations* and write a report. What intervention would be LEAST successful in helping Marisol complete this assignment?
    a. Having Marisol listen to a taped recording while following the story in the regular text.
    b. Giving her a modified version of the story.
    c. Telling her to choose a different book that she can read.
    d. Showing a film to the entire class and comparing and contrasting it with the book.

c. is correct.
Rationale: A, B, and D are positive interventions. C is not an intervention.

51. Fractions may be thought of in each of these ways EXCEPT:
    a. Part of a whole
    b. Part of a parent set
    c. Ratio
    d. An exponent

d. is correct.
Rationale: An exponent can never be a fraction.

52. Many special education students may have trouble with the skills necessary to be successful in algebra and geometry for all but one of these reasons:
    a. Prior instruction focused on computation rather than understanding
    b. Unwillingness to problem solve
    c. Lack of instruction in prerequisite skills
    d. Large amount of new vocabulary

a. is correct.
Rationale: In order to build skills in math, students must be able to understand math concepts.

53. Which of these processes is NOT directly related to the meaningful development of number concepts in younger children?
    a. Describing
    b. Classifying
    c. Grouping
    d. Ordering

c. is correct.
Rationale: Grouping does not involve the meaningful development of number concepts.

54. Mr. Ward wants to assess Jennifer's problem-solving skills in mathematics. Which question would not address her use of strategies?
    a. Does Jennifer check for mistakes in computation?
    b. Does Jennifer use trial and error to solve problems?
    c. Does Jennifer have an alternative strategy if the first one fails?
    d. Does Jennifer become easily frustrated if she doesn't get an answer immediately?

d. is correct.
Rationale: A, B, and C are problem-solving skills Jennifer needs to develop.

55. Ryan is working on a report about dogs. He uses scissors and tape to cut and rearrange sections and paragraphs and then photocopies the paper so he can continue writing. In which stage of the writing process is Ryan?
   a. Final draft
   b. Prewriting
   c. Revision
   d. Drafting

c. is correct.
Rationale: Ryan is revising and reordering before final editing.

56. Talking into a tape recorder is an example of which writing activity?
   a. Prewriting
   b. Drafting
   c. Final Draft
   d. Revision

c. is correct.
Rationale: Ryan is preparing his final draft.

57. Publishing a class newsletter, looking through catalogues, filling out order forms and playing the role of secretaries are activities designed to teach:
   a. Expressive writing
   b. Transactional writing
   c. Poetic writing
   d. Creative writing

b. is correct.
Rationale: Transactional writing includes expository writing, descriptive writing, and persuasive writing. It does not include any of the other three types of writing listed.

58. Under the provisions of IDEA, the student is entitled to all of these EXCEPT:
   a. Placement in the best environment
   b. Placement in the least restrictive environment
   c. Provision of educational needs at no cost
   d. Provision of individualized, appropriate educational program

a. is correct.
Rationale: IDEA mandates a **least restrictive environment, an IEP, (individual education plan) and a free public education.**

59. Teacher modeling, student-teacher dialogues, and peer interactions are part of which teaching technique designed to provide support during the initial stages of instruction?
    a. Reciprocal teaching
    b. Scaffolding
    c. Peer tutoring
    d. Cooperative learning

b. is correct.
Rationale: Scaffolding provides support.

60. Modeling of a behavior by an adult who verbalizes the thinking process, overt self-instruction, and covert self-instruction are components of:
    a. Rational-emotive therapy
    b. Reality therapy
    c. Cognitive behavior modification
    d. Reciprocal teaching

c. is correct.
Rationale: Neither A, B, nor D involves modification or change of behavior.

61. Standards of accuracy for a student's spelling should be based on the student's:
    a. Grade level spelling list
    b. Present reading book level
    c. Level of spelling development
    d. Performance on an informal assessment

c. is correct.
Rationale: Spelling instruction should include words misspelled in daily writing, generalizing spelling knowledge, and mastering objectives in progressive stages of development.

62. Which of these techniques is least effective in helping children correct spelling problems?
    a. The teacher models the correct spelling in a context
    b. Student sees the incorrect and the correct spelling together in order to visualize the correct spelling
    c. Positive reinforcement as the child tests the rules and tries to approximate the correct spelling
    d. Copying the correct word five times

d. is correct.
Rationale: Copying the word is least effective.

63. The single most important activity for eventual reading success of young children is:
    a. Giving them books
    b. Watching animated stories
    c. Reading aloud to them
    d. Talking about pictures in books

c. is correct.
Rationale: Reading aloud exposes them to language.

64. Skilled readers use all but which one of these knowledge sources to construct meanings beyond the literal text:
    a. Text knowledge
    b. Syntactic knowledge
    c. Morphological knowledge
    d. Semantic knowledge

c. is correct.
Rationale: The student is already skilled, so morphological knowledge is already in place.

65. The cooperative nature of Glasser's Reality Therapy, in which a problem-solving approach is used to correct misbehavior, is best signified by:
    a. Minimal punishment
    b. It's similar approach to methods that teach students how to deal with academic mistakes
    c. Students' promises to use the alternative behavior plan to help them reach their goals
    d. Procedure sheets used during conflict situations

c. is correct.
Rationale: Glasser's Reality Therapy makes use of an alternative behavior plan, a form of group therapy.

66. Diaphragmatic breathing, progressive relaxation training, and exercises are examples of which type of stress coping skills?
    a. Rational-emotive
    b. Cognitive-psychological
    c. Somatic-physiological
    d. Stress inoculation

c. is correct.
Rationale: When we analyze the expression somatic-physiological, we find, somatic: relating to the body; physiological: relating to nature and natural phenomena.

67. The stress that we experience when we win a race or experience a difficult task is called:
    a. Stressor
    b. Stresses
    c. Eustress
    d. Distress

c. is correct.
Rationale: Eustress is a sort of elation or release of anxiety. It is the opposite of distress.

68. Jane is so intimidated by a classmate's teasing that she breaks down in tears and cannot stand up for herself. The feeling(s) she is experiencing is/are:
    a. Stressors
    b. Stresses
    c. Eustress
    d. Distress

d. is correct.
Rationale: Jane is in a state of distress.

69. The movement towards serving as many children with disabilities as possible in the regular classroom with supports and services is known as:
    a. Full service model
    b. Regular education initiative
    c. Full inclusion model
    d. Mainstream model

c. is correct.
Rationale: It is the movement to include all students in the regular classroom.

70. Which of the following is NOT a feature of effective classroom rules?
    a. They are about 4 to 6 in number
    b. They are negatively stated
    c. Consequences are consistent and immediate
    d. They can be tailored to individual teaching goals and teaching styles

b. is correct.
Rationale: Rules should be positively stated, and they should follow the other three features listed.

71. A suggested amount of time for a large-group instruction lesson for a sixth or seventh grade group would be:
    a. 5 to 40 minutes
    b. 5 to 20 minutes
    c. 5 to 30 minutes
    d. 5 to 15 minutes

c. is correct.
Rationale: The recommended time for large group instruction is 5 - 15 minutes for grades 1-5 and 5 – 40 minutes for grades 8-12.

72. Sam is working to earn half an hour of basketball time with his favorite P.E. teacher. At the end of each half hour, Sam marks his point sheet with an X if he reached his goal of no call-outs. When he has received 25 marks, he will receive his basketball free time. This behavior management strategy is an example of:
    a. Self-recording
    b. Self-evaluation
    c. Self-reinforcement
    d. Self-regulation

Self-Management: This is an important part of social skills training, especially for older students preparing for employment. Components for self-management include:
    1. *self-monitoring:* choosing behaviors and alternatives and monitoring those actions.
    2. *self-evaluation:* deciding the effectiveness of the behavior in solving the problem.
    3. *self-reinforcement:* telling oneself that one is capable of achieving success.

a. is correct.
Rationale: Sam is recording his behavior.

73. Mark has been working on his target goal of completing his mathematics class work. Each day he records, on a scale of 0 to 3, how well he has done his work, and his teacher provides feedback. This self-management technique is an example of:
    a. Self-recording
    b. Self reinforcement
    c. Self-regulation
    d. Self-evaluation

d. is correct.
Rationale: Sam is evaluating his behavior, not merely recording it.

74. When Barbara reached her target goal, she chose her reinforcer and said softly to herself, "I worked hard, and I deserve this reward". This self-management technique is an example of:
   a. Self-reinforcement
   b. Self recording
   c. Self-regulation
   d. Self-evaluation

a. is correct.
Rationale: Barbara is reinforcing her behavior.

75. Grading should be based on all of the following EXCEPT:
   a. Clearly-defined mastery of course objectives
   b. A variety of evaluation methods
   c. Performance of the student in relation to other students
   d. Assigning points for activities and basing grades on a point total

c. is correct.
Rationale: Grading should never be based on the comparison of performance of other students. It should always be based on the student's mastery of course objectives, the methods of evaluation, and the grading rubric (how points are assigned).

76. The following words describe an IEP objective EXCEPT:
   a. Specific
   b. Observable
   c. Measurable
   d. Criterion-referenced

D. is correct.
Rationale: An Individual Education Plan should be specific, observable, and measurable.

77. Teacher feedback, task completion, and a sense of pride over mastery or accomplishment of a skill are examples of:
   a. Extrinsic reinforcers
   b. Behavior modifiers
   c. Intrinsic reinforcers
   d. Positive feedback

Motivation may be achieved through intrinsic reinforcers or extrinsic reinforcers. Intrinsic rieinforcers are usually intangible, and extrinsic reinforcers are usually tangible rewards and from an external source.

c. is correct.
Rationale: These are intangibles.

78. Social approval, token reinforcers, and rewards, such as pencils or stickers, are examples of:
    a. Extrinsic reinforcers
    b. Behavior modifiers
    c. Intrinsic reinforcers
    d. Positive feedback reinforcers

a. is correct.
Rationale: These are rewards from external sources.

79. Aggression, escape, and avoidance are unpleasant side effects, which can be avoided by using:
    a. Time-out
    b. Response cost
    c. Overcorrection
    d. Negative practice

b. is correct.
Rationale: In response cost, students know that there will be consequences for these undesirable behaviors.

80. Josie forgot that it was school picture day and did not dress up for the pictures. In the media center, Josie notices some girls in the line waiting to have their pictures taken. They appear to be looking over at her and whispering. Josie feels certain that they are making fun of the way her hair and clothes look and gets so upset that she leaves the line and hides out in the bathroom. Josie did not think of asking when the make-up day for pictures would be. According to Ellis' ABC model, Josie's source of stress is:
    a. Her forgetting to dress appropriately for picture day
    b. The girls in the library who appear to be whispering about her
    c. Her belief that they are making fun of her appearance
    d. The girls' insensitive behavior

c. is correct.
Rationale: Josie is responding to her belief.

81. Token systems are popular for all of these advantages EXCEPT:
    a. The number needed for rewards may be adjusted as needed
    b. Rewards are easy to maintain
    c. They are effective for students who generally do not respond to social reinforcers
    d. Tokens reinforce the relationship between desirable behavior and reinforcement

b. is correct.
Rationale: The ease of maintenance is not a valid reason for developing a token system.

82. Which would not be an advantage of using a criterion-referenced test?
    a. Information about an individual's ability level is too specific for the purposes of the assessment
    b. It can pinpoint exact areas of weaknesses and strengths
    c. You can design them yourself
    d. You do not get comparative information

d. is correct.
Rationale: Criterion-referenced tests measure mastery of content rather than performance compared to others. Test items are usually prepared from specific educational objectives and may be teacher made or commercially prepared. Scores are measured by the percentage of correct items for a skill (e.g., adding and subtracting fractions with like denominators).

83. Which is NOT an example of a standard score?
    a. T score
    b. Z score
    c. Standard deviation
    d. Stanine

c. is correct.
Rationale: A, B, and D are all standardized scores. Stanines are whole number scores from 1 to 9, each representing a wide range of raw scores. Standard deviation is **not a score**. It measures how widely scores vary from the mean.

84. The most direct method of obtaining assessment data, and perhaps the most objective, is:
   a. Testing
   b. Self-recording
   c. Observation
   d. Experimenting

c. is correct.
Rationale: Observation is often better than testing, due to language, culture, or other factors.

85. The basic tools necessary to observe and record behavior include all BUT:
   a. Cameras
   b. Timers
   c. Counters
   d. Graphs or charts

a. is correct.
Rationale: The camera gives a snapshot. It does not record behavior.

86. Which of these characteristics is NOT included in the P.L. 94-142 definition of emotional disturbance?
   a. General pervasive mood of unhappiness or depression
   b. Social maladjustment manifested in a number of settings
   c. Tendency to develop physical symptoms, pains, or fear associated with school or personal problems
   d. Inability to learn that is not attributed to intellectual, sensory, or health factors

b. is correct.
Rationale: Social maladjustment is not considered a disability.

87. Of the various factors that contribute to delinquency and anti-social behavior, which has been found to be the weakest?
   a. Criminal behavior and/or alcoholism in the father
   b. Lax mother and punishing father
   c. Socioeconomic disadvantage
   d. Long history of broken home and marital discord among parents

c. is correct.
Rationale: There are many examples of A, B, and D where there is socio-economic advantage.

88. Poor moral development, lack of empathy, and behavioral excesses, such as aggression, are the most obvious characteristics of which behavioral disorder?
    a. Autism
    b. ADD-H
    c. Conduct disorder
    d. Pervasive developmental disorder

c. is correct.
Rationale: A student with conduct disorder or social maladjustment displays behaviors/values that are in conflict with the school, home, or community. The characteristics listed are all behavioral/social.

89. School refusal, obsessive-compulsive disorders, psychosis, and separation anxiety are also frequently accompanied by:
    a. Conduct disorder
    b. ADD-H
    c. depression
    d. autism

c. is correct.
Rationale: These behaviors are usually accompanied by depression in ADD-H.

90. Signs of depression do not typically include:
    a. Hyperactivity
    b. Changes in sleep patterns
    c. Recurring thoughts of death or suicide
    d. Significant changes in weight or appetite

a. is correct.
Rationale: Depression is usually characterized by listlessness, brooding, low anxiety, and little activity. Conversely, hyperactivity is over activity.

91. Children who are characterized by impulsivity generally:
    a. Do not feel sorry for their actions
    b. Blame others for their actions
    c. Do not weigh alternatives before acting
    d. Do not outgrow their problem

c. is correct.
Rationale: They act without thinking, so they either cannot think or do not think before they act.

92. Which of these is listed as only a minor scale on the Behavior Problem Checklist?
    a. Motor Excess
    b. Conduct Disorder
    c. Socialized Aggression
    d. Anxiety/Withdrawal

a. is correct.
Rationale: Motor Excess has to do with over activity, or hyperactivity, in physical movement. The other three items are disorders, all of which may be characterized by excessive activity.

93. The extent that a test measures what it claims to measure is called:
    a. Reliability
    b. Validity
    c. Factor analysis
    d. Chi Square

b. is correct.
Rationale: The degree to which a test measures what it claims to measure.

94. Which is not a goal of collaborative consultation?
    a. Prevent learning and behavior problems with mainstreamed students
    b. Coordinate the instructional programs between mainstream and ESE classes
    c. Facilitate solutions to learning and behavior problems
    d. Function as an ESE service model

d. is correct.
Rationale: A, B, and C are goals. Functioning as an Exceptional Student Education model is not a goal. Collaborative consultation is necessary for the classification of students with disabilities and provision of services to satisfy their needs.

95. An important goal of collaborative consultation is:
    a. Mainstream as many ESE students as possible
    b. Guidance on how to handle ESE students from the ESE teacher
    c. Mutual empowerment of both the mainstream and the ESE teacher
    d. Document progress of mainstreamed students

C. is correct.
Rationale: Empowerment of these service providers is extremely important.

96. Knowledge of evaluation strategies, program interventions, and types of data are examples of which variable for a successful consultation program?
    a. People
    b. Process
    c. Procedural implementation
    d. Academic preparation

b. is correct.
Rationale: Consultation programs cannot be successful without knowledge of the process.

97. Skills as an administrator and background in client, consulter, and consultation skills are examples of which variable in a successful consultation program?
    a. People
    b. Process
    c. Procedural implementation
    d. Academic preparation

a. is correct.
Rationale: Consultation programs cannot be successful without people skills.

98. The ability to identify problems, generate solutions, and knowledge of theoretical perspectives of consultation are examples of which variable in a successful consultation program?
    a. People
    b. Process
    c. Procedural implementation
    d. Academic preparation

c. is correct.
Rationale: Consultation programs cannot be successful without implementation skills.

99. A serious hindrance to successful mainstreaming is:
    a. Lack of adapted materials
    b. Lack of funding
    c. Lack of communication among teachers
    d. Lack of support from administration

c. is correct.
Rationale: All 4 choices are hindrances, but lack of communication and consultation between the service providers is serious.

100. Which of the following statements was not offered as a rationale for REI?
    a. Special education students are not usually identified until their learning problems have become severe
    b. Lack of funding will mean that support for the special needs children will not be available in the regular classroom.
    c. Putting children in segregated special education placements is stigmatizing
    d. There are students with learning or behavior problems who do not meet special education requirements but who still need special services

b. is correct.
Rationale: All except lack of funding were offered in support of Regular Education Intervention or Inclusion.

101. The key to success for the exceptional student placed in a regular classroom is:
    a. Access to the special aids and materials
    b. Support from the ESE teacher
    c. Modification in the curriculum
    d. The mainstream teacher's belief that the student will profit from the placement

d. is correct.
Rationale: Without the regular teacher's belief that the student can benefit, no special accommodations will be provided.

102. Lack of regular follow-up, difficulty in transporting materials, and lack of consistent support for students who need more assistance are disadvantages of which type of service model?
a. Regular classroom
b. Consultant with regular teacher
c. Itinerant
d. Resource room

c. is correct.
Rationale: The itinerant model, as the name implies, is not regular.

103. Ability to supply specific instructional materials, programs, and methods and to influence environmental learning variables are advantages of which service model for exceptional students?
a. Regular classroom
b. Consultant teacher
c. Itinerant teacher
d. Resource room

b. is correct.
Rationale: Consultation is usually done by specialists.

104. An emphasis on instructional remediation and individualized instruction in problem areas, and a focus on mainstreaming, are characteristics of which model of service delivery?
a. Regular classroom
b. Consultant teacher
c. Itinerant teacher
d. Resource room

d. is correct.
Rationale: The resource room is usually a bridge to mainstreaming.

105. Which of these would not be considered a valid attempt to contact a parent for an IEP meeting?
a. Telephone call
b. Copy of correspondence
c. Message left on answering machine
d. Record of home visits

c. is correct.
Rationale: A message left on an answering machine is not direct contact.

106. A best practice for evaluating student performance and progress on IEPs is:
a. Formal assessment
b. Curriculum-based assessment
c. Criterion-based assessment
d. Norm-referenced evaluation

b. is correct.
Rationale: This is a teacher-prepared test that measures the student's progress, but at the same time shows the teacher whether or not the accommodations are effective.

107. Guidelines for an Individualized Family Service Plan (IFSP) would be described in which legislation?
   a. P.L. 94-142
   b. P.L. 99 – 457
   c. P.L. 101 – 476
   d. ADA

B. is correct.
Rationale: P.L. 99-457, 1986, provides services for children ages 3-5 and their families; P.L. 101 – 476 is IDEA; P.L. 94 – 142, Education for All Handicapped Children Act, was passed in the Civil Rights era. ADA is the Americans with Disabilities Act.

108. In a positive classroom environment, errors are viewed as:
   a. Symptoms of deficiencies
   b. Lack of attention or ability
   c. A natural part of the learning process
   d. The result of going too fast

c. is correct.
Rationale: We often learn a great deal from our mistakes and shortcomings. It is normal. Where it is not normal, fear develops. This fear of failure inhibits children from working and achieving. Copying and other types of cheating result from this fear of failure.

109. Recess, attending school social or sporting events, and eating lunch with peers are examples of:
   a. Privileges
   b. Allowances
   c. Rights
   d. Entitlements

d. is correct.
Rationale: These are entitlements. They may be used as consequences.

110. Free time, shopping at the school store, and candy are examples of:
   a. Privileges
   b. Allowances
   c. Rights
   d. Entitlements

a. is correct.
Rationale: These are privileges or positive consequences.

111. Eating lunch, access to a bathroom, and privacy are examples of:
    a. Privileges
    b. Allowances
    c. Rights
    d. Entitlements

c. is correct.
Rationale: These are rights. They may not be used as consequences.

112. Cheryl is a 15-year old student receiving educational services in a full-time EH classroom. The date for her IEP review is planned for two months before her 16th birthday. According to the requirements of IDEA, what must ADDITIONALLY be included in this review?
    a. Graduation plan
    b. Individualized transition plan
    c. Individualized family service plan
    d. Transportation planning

b. is correct.
Rationale: This is necessary, as the student should be transitioning from school to work.

113. Hector is a 10th grader in a program for the severely emotionally handicapped. After a classmate taunted him about his mother, Hector threw a desk at the other boy and attacked him. A crisis intervention team tried to break up the fight, and one teacher hurt his knee. The other boy received a concussion. Hector now faces disciplinary measures. How long can he be suspended without the suspension constituting a "change of placement"?
    a. 5 days
    b. 10 days
    c. 10 + 30 days
    d. 60 days

b. is correct.
Rationale: According to *Honig versus Doe,* 1988, *Where the student has presented an immediate threat to others, that student may be temporarily suspended for up to 10 school days to give the school and the parents time to review the IEP and discuss possible alternatives to the current placement*.

TEACHER CERTIFICATION STUDY GUIDE

114. The concept that a handicapped student cannot be expelled for misconduct that is a manifestation of the handicap itself is not limited to students which are labeled "seriously emotionally disturbed". Which reason does not explain this concept?
    a. Emphasis on individualized evaluation
    b. Consideration of the problems and needs of handicapped students
    c. Right to a free and appropriate public education
    d. Putting these students out of school will just leave them on the streets to commit crimes

d. is correct.
Rationale: A, B, and C are tenets of IDEA and should take place in the least restrictive environment. D does not explain this concept.

115. An effective classroom behavior management plan includes all but which of the following?
    a. Transition procedures for changing activities
    b. Clear consequences for rule infractions
    c. Concise teacher expectations for student behavior
    d. Copies of lesson plans

d. is correct.
Rationale: D is not a part of any behavior management plan. A, B, and C are.

116. Statements like, "Darren is lazy," are not helpful in describing his behavior for all but which of these reasons?
    a. There is no way to determine if any change occurs from the information given
    b. The student and not the behavior becomes labeled
    c. Darren's behavior will manifest itself clearly enough without any written description
    d. Constructs are open to various interpretations among the people who are asked to define them

c. is correct.
Rationale: 'Darren is lazy' is a label. It can be interpreted in a variety of ways, and there is no way to measure this description for change. A description should be measurable.

LEARNING DISABLED

117. Often, Marcie is not in her seat when the bell rings. She may be found at the pencil sharpener, throwing paper away, or fumbling through her notebook. Which of these descriptions of her behavior can be described as a pinpoint?
    a. Is tardy a lot
    b. Is out of seat
    c. Is not in seat when late bell rings
    d. Is disorganized

c. is correct.
Rationale: Even though A, B, and D describe the behavior, C is most precise.

118. When choosing behaviors for change, the teacher should ask if there is any evidence that the behavior is presently or potentially harmful to the student or others. This is an example of which test?
    a. Fair-Pair
    b. "Stranger" Test
    c. Premack Principle
    d. "So – What?" Test

d. is correct.

119. Mrs. Taylor takes her students to a special gymnastics presentation that the P.E. coach has arranged in the gym. She has a rule against talk-outs and reminds the students that they will lose 5 points on their daily point sheet for talking out. The students get a chance to perform some of the simple stunts. They all easily go through the movements except for Sam, who is known as the class klutz. Sam does not give up and finally completes the stunts. His classmates cheer him on with comments like, "Way to go". Their teacher, however, reminds them that they broke the no talking rule and will lose the points. What mistake was made here?
    a. The students forgot the no talking rule
    b. The teacher considered talk-outs to be maladaptive in all school settings
    c. The other students could have distracted Sam with talk-outs and caused him to get hurt
    d. The teacher should have let the P.E. coach handle the discipline in the gym

d. is correct.
The gym environment is different from a classroom environment. The gym teacher should have been in control of a possibly hazardous environment.

120. Which of the following should be avoided when writing objectives for social behavior?
    a. Non-specific adverbs
    b. Behaviors stated as verbs
    c. Criteria for acceptable performance
    d. Conditions where the behavior is expected to be performed

a. is correct.
Rationale: Behaviors should be specific. The more clearly the behavior is described, the less the chance for error.

121. Criteria for choosing behaviors that are in the most need of change involve all but the following:
    a. Observations across settings to rule out certain interventions
    b. Pinpointing the behavior that is the poorest fit in the child's environment
    c. The teacher's concern about what is the most important behavior to target
    d. Analysis of the environmental reinforcers

c. is correct.
Rationale: The teacher must take care of the criteria in A, B, and D. Her concerns are of the least importance.

122. Ms. Wright is planning an analysis of Audrey's out-of-seat behavior. Her initial data would be called:
    a. Pre-referral phase
    b. Intervention phase
    c. Baseline phase
    d. Observation phase

c. is correct.
Rationale: Ms Wright is a teacher. She should begin at the baseline phase.

123. To reinforce Audrey each time she is on task and in her seat, Ms. Wright delivers specific praise and stickers, which Audrey may collect and redeem for a reward. The data collected during the time Ms. Wright is using this intervention is called:
    a. Referral phase
    b. Intervention phase
    c. Baseline phase
    d. Observation phase

b. is correct.
Rationale: Ms Wright is involved in behavior modification. This is the intervention phase.

124. Indirect requests and attempts to influence or control others through one's use of language is an example of:
    a. Morphology
    b. Syntax
    c. Pragmatics
    d. Semantics

c. is correct.
Rationale: Pragmatics involves the way that language is used to communicate and interact with others. It is often used to control the actions and attitudes of people.

125. Kenny, a fourth grader, has trouble comprehending analogies, using comparative, spatial, and temporal words, and multiple meanings. Language interventions for Kenny would focus on:
    a. Morphology
    b. Syntax
    c. Pragmatics
    d. Semantics

d. is correct.
Rationale: Semantics has to do with word meanings. Semantic tests measure receptive and expressive vocabulary skills.

126. Celia, who is in first grade, asked, "Where are my ball?" She also has trouble with passive sentences. Language interventions for Celia would target:
    a. Morphology
    b. Syntax
    c. Pragmatics
    d. Semantics

b. is correct.
Rationale: Syntax refers to the rules for arranging words to make sentences.

127. Scott is in middle school but still makes statements like, "I gotted new high-tops yesterday," and "I saw three mans in the front office." Language interventions for Scott would target:
   a. Morphology
   b. Syntax
   c. Pragmatics
   d. Semantics

a. is correct.
Rationale: Morphology is the process of combining phonemes into meaningful words.

128. Which is not indicative of a handwriting problem?
   a. Errors persisting over time
   b. Little improvement on simple handwriting tasks
   c. Fatigue after writing for a short time
   d. Occasional letter reversals, word omissions, and poor spacing

d. is correct.
Rationale: A, B, and C are physical handwriting problems. D, however, is a problem with language development.

129. All of these are effective in teaching written expression EXCEPT:
   a. Exposure to various styles and direct instruction in those styles
   b. Immediate feedback from the teacher with all mistakes clearly marked
   c. Goal setting and peer evaluation of written products according to set criteria
   d. Incorporating writing with other academic subjects

b. is correct.
Rationale: Teacher feedback is not always necessary. The student can have feedback from his peers, or emotional response, or apply skills learned to other subjects.

130. Mr. Mendez is assessing his students' written expression. Which of these is not a component of written expression?
   a. Vocabulary
   b. Morphology
   c. Content
   d. Sentence structure

b. is correct.
Rationale: Morphology is correct. Vocabulary consists of words, content is made up of ideas, which are expressed in words, and sentences are constructed from words. Morphemes, however, are not always words. They may be prefixes or suffixes.

131. Ms. Tolbert is teaching spelling to her students. The approach stresses phoneme-grapheme relationships within parts of words. Spelling rules, generalizations, and patterns are taught. A typical spelling list for her third graders might include light, bright, night, fright, and slight. Which approach is Ms. Tolbert using?
   a. Rule-based Instruction
   b. Fernald Method
   c. Gillingham Method
   d. Test-Study-Test

a. is correct.
Rationale: Rule-based Instruction employs a system of rules and generalizations. It may be taught using the linguistic or phonics approach.

132. At the beginning of the year, Mr. Johnson wants to gain an understanding of his class' social structure in order to help him assess social skills and related problems. The technique that would best help Mr. Johnson accomplish this is:
   a. Personal interviews with each student
   b. Parent rating form
   c. Sociometric techniques
   d. Self-reports

c. is correct.
Rationale: The issue of reliability and validity arises with A, B, and D. C is the best technique.
Sociometric Measures: There are three basic formats. (a) peer nominations based on non-behavioral criteria, such as preferred playmates, (b) peer ratings in which students rate all of their peers on non-behavioral criteria, such as work preferences, and (c) peer assessments, in which peers are rated with respect to specific behaviors.

133. In assessing a group's social structure, asking a student to list the classmates whom he or she would choose to be his or her best friends, preferred play partners, and preferred work partners is an example of:
   a. Peer nomination
   b. Peer rating
   c. Peer assessment
   d. Sociogram

a. is correct.
Rationale: Students are asked to nominate their peers.

134. Naming classmates who fit certain behavioral descriptions, such as smart, disruptive, or quiet, is an example of which type of sociometric assessment?
    a. Peer nomination
    b. Peer rating
    c. Peer assessment
    d. Sociogram

c. is correct.
Rationale: Students are asked to assess their peers' behavior.

135. Mr. Johnson asks his students to score each of their classmates in areas such as who they would prefer to play with and work with. A Likert-type scale with non-behavioral criteria is used. This is an example of:
    a. Peer nomination
    b. Peer rating
    c. Peer assessment
    d. Sociogram

a. is correct.
Rationale: Students are asked for their preferences on non-behavioral criteria.

136. Which of these explanations would not likely account for the lack of a clear definition of behavior disorders?
    a. Problems with measurement
    b. Cultural and/or social influences and views of what is acceptable
    c. The numerous types of manifestations of behavior disorders
    d. Differing theories that use their own terminology and definitions

c. is correct.
Rationale: A, B, and D are factors that account for the lack of a clear definition of some behavioral disorders. C is not a factor.

137. Ryan is 3, and her temper tantrums last for an hour. Bryan is 8, and he does not stay on task for more than 10 minutes without teacher prompts. These behaviors differ from normal children in terms of their:
    a. Rate
    b. Topography
    c. Duration
    d. Magnitude

c. is correct.
Rationale: It is not normal for temper tantrums to last an hour. At age eight, a normal student stays on task much longer than ten minutes without teacher prompts.

138. All children cry, hit, fight, and play alone at different times. Children with behavior disorders will perform these behaviors at a higher than normal:
 a. Rate
 b. Topography
 c. Duration
 d. Magnitude

a. is correct.
Rationale: Children with behavior disorders display them at a much higher rate than normal children.

139. The exhibition of two or more types of problem behaviors across different areas of functioning is known as:
 a. Multiple maladaptive behaviors
 b. Clustering
 c. Social maladjustment
 d. Conduct disorder

b. is correct.
Rationale: Children with behavior disorders do not display a single behavior. They display a range of behaviors. These behaviors are usually clustered together, hence, clustering.

140. Children with behavior disorders often do not exhibit stimulus control. This means they have not learned:
 a. The right things to do
 b. Where and when certain behaviors are appropriate
 c. Right from wrong
 d. Listening skills

b. is correct.
Rationale: These children respond to stimuli at almost any place and time. They are not able to stop and think or control their responses to stimuli.

141. Social withdrawal, anxiety, depression, shyness, and guilt are indicative of:
 a. Conduct disorder
 b. Personality disorders
 c. Immaturity
 d. Socialized aggression

b. is correct.
 Rationale: These are all personality disorders.

142. Short attention span, daydreaming, clumsiness, and preference for younger playmates are associated with:
   a. Conduct disorder
   b. Personality disorders
   c. Immaturity
   d. Socialized aggression

c. is correct.
Rationale: These disorders show immaturity. The student is not acting age appropriately.

143. Truancy, gang membership, and a feeling of pride in belonging to a delinquent subculture are indicative of:
   a. Conduct disorder
   b. Personality disorders
   c. Immaturity
   d. Socialized aggression

d. is correct.
Rationale: The student is acting out by using aggression. This gives him a sense of belonging.

144. Temper tantrums, disruption or disobedience, and bossiness are associated with:
   a. Conduct disorder
   b. Personality disorders
   c. Immaturity
   d. Socialized aggression

a. is correct.
Rationale: These behaviors are designed to attract attention. They are conduct disorders.

145. Which of these is not true for most children with behavior disorders?
   a. Many score in the "slow learner" or "mildly retarded" range on IQ tests
   b. They are frequently behind their classmates in academic achievement
   c. They are bright but bored with their surroundings
   d. A large amount of time is spent in nonproductive, nonacademic behaviors

c. is correct.
Rationale: Most children with conduct disorders display the traits found in A, B, and D.

LEARNING DISABLED

146. Echolalia, repetitive stereotyped actions, and a severe disorder of thinking and communication are indicative of:
    a. Psychosis
    b. Schizophrenia
    c. Autism
    d. Paranoia

c. is correct.
Rationale: The behaviors listed are indicative of autism.

147. Teaching children functional skills that will be useful in their home life and neighborhoods is the basis of:
    a. Curriculum-based instruction
    b. Community-based instruction
    c. Transition planning
    d. Functional curriculum

b. is correct.
Rationale: Teaching functional skills in the wider curriculum is considered Community-based-instruction.

148. Disabilities caused by fetal alcohol syndrome are many times higher for which ethnic group?
    a. Native Americans
    b. Asian Americans
    c. Hispanic Americans
    d. African Americans

a. is correct.
Rationale: There is a very high incidence of this syndrome in Native American children on reservations.

149. Which of these would be the least effective measure of behavioral disorders?
    a. Projective test
    b. Ecological assessment
    c. Standardized test
    d. Psychodynamic analysis

c. is correct.
Rationale: These tests make comparisons, rather than measure skills.

150. Which behavioral disorder is difficult to diagnose in children because the symptoms are manifested quite differently than in adults?
    a. Anorexia
    b. Schizophrenia
    c. Paranoia
    d. Depression

d. is correct.

Rationale: In an adult, it may be displayed as age-appropriate behavior and therefore go undiagnosed. In a child, it may be displayed as not age appropriate, so it is easier to recognize.

References

Ager, C.L. & Cole, C.L. (1991). A review of cognitive-behavioral interventions for children and adolescents with behavioral disorders. *Behavioral Disorders,* 16(4), 260-275.

Aiken, L.R. (1985). *Psychological testing and assessment* (5th ed.). Boston: Allyn and Bacon.

Alberto, P.A. & Trouthman, A.C. (1990). *Applied behavior analysis for teachers: Influencing student performance.* Columbus, Ohio: Charles E. Merrill.

Algozzine, B. (1990). *Behavior problem management: Educator's resource service.* Gaithersburg, MD: Aspen Publishers.

Algozzine, B., Ruhl, K., & Ramsey, R. (1991). *Behaviorally disordered: Assessment for identification and instruction CED mini-library.* Renson, VA: The Council for Exceptional Children.

Ambron, S.R. (1981). *Child development* (3rd ed.). New York: Holt, Rinehart and Winston.

Anerson, V., & Black, L. (Eds.). (1987, Winter). National news: U.S. Department of Education releases special report (Editorial). *GLRS Journal* [Georgia Learning Resources System].

Anguili, R. (1987, Winter). The 1986 amendment to the Education of the Handicapped Act. *Confederation* [A quarterly publication of the Georgia Federation Council for Exceptional Children].

Ashlock, R.B. (1976). *Error patterns in computation: A semi-programmed approach* (2nd ed.). Columbus, Ohio: Charles E. Merrill.

Association of Retarded Citizens of Georgia (1987). *1986-87 Government report.* College Park, GA: Author.

Ausubel, D.P. & Sullivan, E.V. (1970). *Theory and problems of child development.* New York: Grune & Stratton.

Banks, J.A., & McGee Banks, C.A. (1993). *Multicultural education* (2nd ed.). Boston: Allyn and Bacon.

Barrett, T.C. (Ed.). (1967). *The evaluation of children's reading achievement. in perspectives in reading, No. 8.* Newark, Delaware: International Reading Association.

Bartoli, J.S. (1989). An ecological response to Cole's interactivity alternative. *Journal of Learning Disabilities*, 22 (5), 292-297.

Basile-Jackson, J. *The exceptional child in the regular classroom*. Augusta, GA: East Georgia Center, Georgia Learning Resources System.

Bauer, A.M., & Shea, T.M. (1989). *Teaching exceptional students in your classroom*. Boston: Allyn and Bacon.

Bentley, E.L. Jr. (1980). *Questioning skills* (Videocassette & manual series). Northbrook, IL: Hubbard Scientific Company. (Project STRETCH [Strategies to Train Regular Educators to Teach Children with Handicaps], Module 1, ISBN 0-8331-1906-0).

Berdine, W.H., & Blackhurst, A.E. (1985). *An introduction to special education*. (2nd ed.) Boston: Little, Brown and Company.

Blake, K. (1976). *The mentally retarded: An educational psychology*. Englewood Cliff, NJ: Prentice-Hall.

Bohline, D.S. (1985). *Intellectual and affective characteristics of attention deficit disordered children*. Journal of Learning Disabilities, 18 (10),604-608.

Boone, R. (1983). Legislation and litigation. In R.E. Schmid, & L. Negata (Eds.). *Contemporary Issues in Special Education*. New York: McGraw Hill.

Brantlinger, E.A., & Guskin, S.L. (1988). Implications of social and cultural differences for special education. In Meten, E.L. Vergason, G.A., & Whelan, R.J. *Effective Instructional Strategies for Exceptional Children*. Denver, CO: Love Publishing.

Brewton, B. (1990). Preliminary identification of the socially maladjusted. In Georgia Psycho-educational Network, Monograph #1. *An Educational Perspective On: Emotional Disturbance and Social Maladjustment*. Atlanta, GA Psychoeducational Network.

Brolin, D.E., & Kokaska, C.J. (1979). *Career education for handicapped children approach*. Renton, VA: The Council for Exceptional Children.

Brolin, D.E. (Ed). (1989). *Life centered career education: A competency based approach*. Reston, VA: The Council for Exceptional Children.

Brown, J.W., Lewis, R.B., & Harcleroad, F.F. (1983). *AV instruction: Technology, media, and methods* (6TH ed.). New York: McGraw-Hill.

Bryan, T.H., & Bryan, J.H. (1986). *Understanding learning disabilities* (3rd ed.). Palo Alto, CA: Mayfield.

Bryen, D.N. (1982). *Inquiries into child language.* Boston: Allyn & Bacon.

Bucher, B.D. (1987). *Winning them over.* New York: Times Books.

Bush, W.L., & Waugh, K.W. (1982). *Diagnosing learning problems* (3rd ed.). Columbus, OH: Charles E. Merrill.

Campbell, P. (1986). *Special needs report* [Newsletter]. 1(1), 1-3.

Carbo, M., & Dunn, K. (1986). *Teaching students to read through their individual learning styles.* Englewood Cliffs, NJ: Prentice Hall.

CArtwright, G.P., & Cartwright, C.A., & Ward, M.E. (1984). *Educating special learners* (2nd ed.). Belmont, CA: Wadsworth.

Cejka, J.M. (Consultant), & Needham, F. (Senior Editor). (1976). *Approaches to mainstreaming.* (Filmstrip and cassette kit, units 1 & 2). Boston: Teaching Resources Corporation. (Catalog Nos. 09-210 & 09-220).

Chalfant, J. C. (1985). *Identifying learning disabled students: A summary of the national task force report.* Learning Disabilities Focus, 1, 9-20.

Charles, C.M. (1976). *Individualizing instructions.* St Louis: The C.V. Mosby Company.

Chrispeels, J.H. (1991). *District leadership in parent involvement: Policies and actions in San Diego.* Phi Delta Kappa, 71, 367-371.

Clarizio, H.F. (1987). Differentiating characteristics. In Georgia Psychoeducational Network, Monograph #1, *An educational perspective on: Emotional disturbance and social maladjustment.* Atlanta, GA: Psychoeducational Network.

Clarizio, H.F. & McCoy, G.F. (1983). *Behavior disorders in children* (3rd ed.). New York: Harper & Row.

Coles, G.S. (1989). *Excerpts from the learning mystique: A critical look at disabilities.* Journal of Learning Disabilities, 22 (5), 267-278.

Collins, E. (1980). *Grouping and special students.* (Videocassette & manual series). Northbrook, IL: Hubbard Scientific Company. (Project STRETCH [Strategies to Train Regular Educators to Teach Children with Handicaps], Module 17, ISBN 0-8331-1922-2).

Craig, E., & Craig, L. (1990). *Reading In the Content Areas.* (Videocassette & manual series). Northbrook, IL: Hubbard Scientific Company. (Project STRETCH [Strategies to Train Regular Educators to Teach Children with Handicaps], Module 13, ISBN 0-8331-1918-4).

Compton, C., (1984). A Guide to 75 Tests for Special Education. Belmont, CA., Pitman Learning.

Council for Exceptional Children. (1976). Introducing P.L. 94-142. [Filmstrip-cassette kit manual]. Reston, VA: Author.

Council for Exceptional Children. (1987). The Council for Exceptional Children's Fall 1987. Catalog of Products and Services. Renton, VA: Author.

Council for Exceptional Children Delegate Assembly. (1983). Council for Exceptional Children Code of Ethics (Adopted April 1983). Reston, VA: Author.

Czajka, J.L. (1984). Digest of Data on Person With Disabilities (Mathematics Policy Research, Inc.). Washington, D.C.: U.S. Government Printing Office.

Dell, H.D. (1972). Individualizing Instruction: Materials and Classroom Procedures. Chicago: Science Research Associates.

Demonbreun, C., & Morris, J. Classroom Management [Videocassette & Manual series]. Northbrook, IL: Hubbard Scientific Company. Project STRETCH (Strategies to Train Regular Educators to Teach Children with Handicaps]. Module 5, ISBN 0-8331-1910-9).

Department of Education. Education for the Handicapped Law Reports. Supplement 45 (1981), p. 102: 52. Washington, D.C.: U.S. Government Printing Office.

Department of Health, Education, and Welfare, Office of Education. (1977, August 23). Education of Handicapped Children. Federal Register, 42, (163).

Diana vs. State Board of Education, Civil No. 70-37 R.F.P. (N.D.Cal. January, 1970).

Digangi, S.A., Perryman, P., & Rutherford, R.B., Jr. (1990). Juvenile Offenders in the 90's A Descriptive Analysis. Perceptions, 25(4), 5-8.

Division of Educational Services, Special Education Programs (1986). Fifteenth Annual Report to Congress on Implementation of the Education of the Handicapped Act. Washington, D.C.: U.S. Government Printing Office.

Doyle, B.A. (1978). Math Readiness Skills. Paper presented at National Association of School Psychologists, New York. K.J. (1978). Teaching Students Through Their Individual Learning Styles.

Dunn, R.S., & Dunn, K.J. (1978). Teaching Students Through Their Individual Learning Styles: A Practical Approach. Reston, VA: Reston.

Epstein, M.H., Patton, J.R., Polloway, E.A., & Foley, R. (1989). Mild retardation: Student characteristics and services. Education and Training of the Mentally Retarded, 24, 7-16.

Ekwall, E.E., & Shanker, J.L. 1983). Diagnosis and Remediation of the Disabled Reader (2nd ed.) Boston: Allyn and Bacon.

Firth, E.E. & Reynolds, I. (1983). Slide tape shows: A creative activity for the gifted students. Teaching Exceptional Children. 15(3), 151-153.

Frymier, J., & Gansneder, B. (1989). The Phi Delta Kappa Study of Students at Risk. Phi Delta Kappa. 71(2) 142-146.

Fuchs, D., & Deno, S.L. 1992). Effects of curriculum within curriculum-based measurement. Exceptional Children 58 (232-242).

Fuchs, D., & Fuchs, L.S. (1989). Effects of examiner familiarity on Black, Caucasian, and Hispanic Children. A Meta-Analysis. Exceptional Children. 55, 303-308.

Fuchs, L.S., & Shinn, M.R. (1989). Writing CBM IEP objectives. In M.R. Shinn, Curriculum-based Measurement: Assessing Special Students. New York: Guilford Press.

Gage, N.L. (1990). Dealing With the Dropout Problems? Phi Delta Kappa. 72(4), 280-285.

Gallagher, P.A. (1988). Teaching Students with Behavior Disorders: Techniques and Activities for Classroom Instruction (2nd ed.). Denver, CO: Love Publishing.

Gearheart, B.R. (1980). Special Education for the 80s. St. Louis, MO: The C.V. Cosby Company.

Gearhart, B.R. & Weishahn, M.W. (1986). The Handicapped Student in the Regular Classroom (2nd ed.). St Louis, MO: The C.V. Mosby Company.

Gearhart, B.R. (1985). Learning Disabilities: Educational Strategies (4th ed.). St. Louis: Times Mirror/ Mosby College of Publishing.

Georgia Department of Education, Program for Exceptional Children. (1986). Mild Mentally Handicapped (Vol. II), Atlanta, GA: Office of Instructional Services, Division of Special Programs, and Program for Exceptional Children. Resource Manuals for Program for Exceptional Children.

Georgia Department of Human Resources, Division of Rehabilitation Services. (1987, February). Request for Proposal [Memorandum]. Atlanta, GA: Author.

Georgia Psychoeducational Network (1990). An Educational Perspective on: Emotional Disturbance and Social Maladjustment. Monograph #1. Atlanta, GA Psychoeducational Network.

Geren, K. (1979). Complete Special Education Handbook. West Nyack, NY: Parker.

Gillet, P.K. (1988). Career Development. Robinson, G.A., Patton, J.R., Polloway, E.A., & Sargent, L.R. (eds.). Best Practices in Mild Mental Disabilities. Reston, VA: The Division on Mental Retardation of the Council for Exceptional Children.

Gleason, J.B. (1993). The Development of Language (3rd ed.). New York: Macmillan Publishing.

Good, T.L., & BROPHY, J.E. (1978). Looking into Classrooms (2nd Ed.). New York: Harper & Row.

Hall, M.A. (1979). Language-Centered Reading: Premises and Recommendations. Language Arts, 56 664-670.

Halllahan, D.P. & Kauffman, J.M. (1988). Exceptional Children: Introduction to Special Education. (4th Ed.). Englewood Cliffs, NJ; Prentice-Hall.

Hallahan, D.P. & Kauffman, J.M. (1994). Exceptional Children: Introduction to Special Education 6th ed.). Boston: Allyn and Bacon.

Hammill, D.D., & Bartel, N.R. (1982). Teaching Children With Learning and Behavior Problems (3rd ed.). Boston: Allyn and Bacon.

Hammill, D.D., & Bartel, N.R. (1986). Teaching Students with Learning and Behavior Problems (4th ed.). Boston and Bacon.

Hamill, D.D., & Brown, L. & Bryant, B. (1989) A Consumer's Guide to Tests in Print. Austin, TX: Pro-Ed.

Haney, J.B. & Ullmer, E.J. ((1970). *Educational Media and the Teacher.* Dubuque, IA: Wm. C. Brown Company.

Hardman, M.L., Drew, C.J., Egan, M.W., & Wolf, B. (1984). *Human Exceptionality: Society, School, and Family.* Boston: Allyn and Bacon.

Hardman, M.L., Drew, C.J., Egan, M.W., & Worlf, B. (1990). *Human Exceptionality* (3rd ed.). Boston: Allyn and Bacon.

Hargrove, L.J., & Poteet, J.A. (1984). *Assessment in Special Education.* Englewood Cliffs, NJ: Prentice-Hall.

Haring, N.G., & Bateman, B. (1977). *Teaching the Learning Disabled Child.* Englewood Cliffs, NJ: Prentice-Hall.

Harris, K.R., & Pressley, M. (1991). The Nature of Cognitive Strategy Instruction: Interactive strategy instruction. *Exceptional Children, 57,* 392-401.

Hart, T., & Cadora, M.J. (1980). *The Exceptional Child: Label the Behavior* [Videocassette & manual series], Northbrook, IL: Hubbard Scientific Company. (Project STRETCH [Strategies to Train Regular Educators to Teach Children with Handicaps], Module 12, ISBN 0-8331-1917-6). HART, V. (1981) *Mainstreaming Children with Special Needs.* New York: Longman.

Henley, M., Ramsey,R.S., & Algozzine, B. (1993). *Characteristics of and Strategies for Teaching Students with Mild Disabilities.* Boston: Allyn and Bacon.

Hewett, F.M., & Forness, S.R. (1984). *Education of Exceptional Learners.* (3rd ed.). Boston: Allyn and Bacon.

Howe, C.E. (1981) *Administration of Special Education.* Denver: Love.

Human Services Research Institute (1985). *Summary of Data on Handicapped Children and Youth.* (Digest). Washington, D.C.: U.S. Government Printing Office.

Johnson, D.W. (1972) *Reaching Out: Interpersonal Effectiveness and Self-Actualization.* Englewood Cliffs, NJ: Prentice-Hall.

Johnson, D.W. (1978) *Human Relations and Your Career: A Guide to Interpersonal Skills.* Englewood Cliffs, NJ: Prentice-Hall.

Johnson, D.W., & Johnson, R.T. (1990). *Social Skills for Successful Group Work. Educational Leadership. 47* (4) 29-33.

Johnson, S.W., & Morasky, R.L. Learning Disabilities (2nd ed.) Boston: Allyn and Bacon.

Jones, F.H. (1987). Positive Classroom Discipline. New York: McGraw-Hill Book Company.

Jones, V.F., & Jones, L. S. (1986). Comprehensive Classroom Management: Creating Positive Learning Environments. (2nd ed.). Boston: Allyn and Bacon.

Jones, V.F. & Jones, L.S. (1981). Responsible Classroom Discipline: Creating Positive Learning Environments and Solving Problems. Boston: Allyn and Bacon.

Kauffman, J.M. (1981) Characteristics of Children's Behavior Disorders. (2nd ed.). Columbus, OH: Charles E. Merrill.

Kauffman, J.M. (1989). Characteristics of Behavior Disorders of Children and Youth. (4th ed.). Columbus, OH: Merrill Publishing.

Kem, M., & Nelson, M. (1983). Strategies for Managing Behavior Problems in the Classroom. Columbus, OH: Charles E. Merrill.

Kerr, M.M., & Nelson, M. (1983) Strategies for Managing Behavior Problems in the Classroom. Columbus, OH: Charles E. Merrill.

Kirk, S.A., & Gallagher, J.J. (1986). Educating Exceptional Children (5th ed.). Boston: Houghton Mifflin.

Kohfeldt, J. (1976). Blueprints for construction. Focus on Exceptional Children. 8 (5), 1-14.

Kokaska, C.J., & Brolin, D.E. (1985). Career Education for Handicapped Individuals (2nd ed.). Columbus, OH: Charles E. Merrill.

Lambie, R.A. (1980). A systematic approach for changing materials, instruction, and assignments to meet individual needs. Focus on Exceptional Children, 13(1), 1-12.

Larson, S.C., & Poplin, M.S. (1980). Methods for Educating the Handicapped: An Individualized Education Program Approach. Boston: Allyn and Bacon.

Lerner, J. (1976) Children with Learning Disabilities. (2nd ed.). Boston: Houghton Mifflin.

Lerner, J. (1989). Learning Disabilities,: Theories, Diagnosis and Teaching Strategies (3rd ed.). Boston: Houghton Mifflin.

Levenkron, S. (1991). Obsessive-Compulsive Disorders. New York: Warner Books.

Lewis, R.B., & Doorlag, D.H. (1991). Teaching Special Students in the Mainstream. (3rd ed.). New York: Merrill.

Lindsley, O. R. (1990). Precision Teaching: By Teachers for Children. Teaching Exceptional Children, 22. (3), 10-15.

Linddberg, L., & Swedlow, R. (1985). Young Children Exploring and Learning. Boston: Allyn and Bacon.

Long, N.J., Morse, W.C., & Newman, R.G. (1980). Conflict in the Classroom: The Education of Emotionally Disturbed Children. Belmont, CA: Wadsworth.

Losen, S.M., & Losen, J.G. (1985). The Special Education Team. Boston: Allyn and Bacon.

Lovitt, T.C. (1989). Introduction to Learning Disabilities. Boston: Allyn and Bacon.

Lund, N.J., & Duchan, J.F. (1988)/ Assessing Children's Language in Naturalist Contexts. Englewood Cliffs, NJ: Prentice Hall

Male, M. (1994) Technology for Inclusion: Meeting the Special Needs of all Children. (2nd ed.). Boston: Allyn and Bacon.

Mandelbaum, L.H. (1989). Reading. In G.A. Robinson, J.R., Patton, E.A., Polloway, & L.R. Sargent (eds.). Best Practices in Mild Mental Retardation. Reston, VA: The Division of Mental Retardation, Council for Exceptional Children.

Mannix. D. (1993). Social Skills for Special Children. West Nyack, NY: The Center for Applied Research in Education.

Marshall, et al. vs. Georgia U.S. District Court for the Southern District of Georgia. C.V. 482-233. June 28, 1984.

Marshall, E.K., Kurtz, P.D., & Associates. Interpersonal Helping Skills. San Francisco, CA: Jossey-Bass Publications.

Marston, D.B. (1989) A curriculum-based measurement approach to assessing academic performance: What it is and why do it. In M. Shinn (Ed.). Curriculum-Based Measurement: Assessing Special Children. New York: Guilford Press.

McDowell, R.L., Adamson, G.W., & Wood, F.H. (1982). Teaching Emotionally Disturbed Children. Boston: Little, Brown and Company.
MCGINNIS, E., GOLDSTEIN, A.P. (1990). Skill Streaming in Early Childhood: Teaching prosocial skills to the preschool and kindergarten child. Champaign, IL: Research Press.

Mcloughlin, J.A., & Lewis, R.B. (1986). Assessing Special Students (3rd ed.). Columbus, OH: Charles E. Merrill.

MERCER, C.D. (1987). Students with Learning Disabilities. (3rd. ed.). Merrill Publishing.

MERCER, C.D., & MERCER, A.R. (1985). Teaching Children with Learning Problems (2nd ed.). Columbus, OH: Charles E. Merrill.

MEYEN, E.L., VERGASON, G.A., & WHELAN, R.J. (Eds.). (1988). Effective Instructional Strategies for Exceptional Children. Denver, CO: Love Publishing.

MILLER, L.K. (1980). Principles of Everyday Behavior Analysis (2nd ed.). Monterey, CA: Brooks/Cole Publishing Company.
MILLS VS. THE BOARD OF EDUCATON OF THE DISTRICT OF COLUMBIA, 348F. Supp. 866 (D.C. 1972).

MOPSICK, S.L. & AGARD, J.A. (Eds.) (1980). Cambridge, MA: Abbott Associates.

MORRIS, C.G. (1985). Psychology: An Introduction (5th ed.). Englewood Cliffs, NJ: Prentice-Hall.

MORRIS, J. (1980). Behavior Modification. [Videocassette and manual series]. Northbrook, IL: Hubbard Scientific Company. (Project STRETCH [Strategies to Train Regular Educators to Teach Children with Handicaps,] Module 16, Metropolitan Cooperative Educational Service Agency.).
MORRIS, J. & DEMONBREUN, C. (1980). Learning Styles [Videocassettes & Manual series]. Northbrook, IL: Hubbard Scientific Company. (Project STRETCH [Strategies to Train Regular Educators to Teach Children with Handicaps], Module 15, ISBN 0-8331-1920-6).

MORRIS, R.J. (1985). Behavior Modification with Exceptional Children: Principles and Practices. Glenview, IL: Scott, Foresman and Company.

MORSINK, C.V. (1984). Teaching Special Needs Students in Regular Classrooms. Boston: Little, Brown and Company.

MORSINK, C.V., THOMAS, C.C., & CORREA, V.L. (1991). Interactive Teaming, Consultation and Collaboration in Special Programs. New York: MacMillan Publishing.

MULLSEWHITE, C.R. (1986). Adaptive Play for Special Needs Children: Strategies to Enhance Communication and Learning. San Diego: College Hill Press.

NORTH CENTRAL GEORGIA LEARNING RESOURCES SYSTEM/CHILD SERVE. (1985). Strategies Handbook for Classroom Teachers. Ellijay, GA.

PATTON, J.R., CRONIN, M.E., POLLOWAY, E.A., HUTCHINSON, D., & ROBINSON, G.A. (1988). Curricular considerations: A life skills orientation. In Robinson, G.A., Patton, J.R., Polloway, E.A., & Sargent, L.R. (Eds.). Best Practices in Mental Disabilities. Des Moines, IA: Iowa Department of Education, Bureau of Special Education.

PATTON, J.R., KAUGGMAN, J.M., BLACKBOURN, J.M., & BROWN, B.G. (1991). Exceptional Children in Focus (5th ed.). New York: MacMillan.

PAUL, J.L. (Ed.). (1981). Understanding and Working with parents of Children with Special Needs. New York: Holt, Rinehart and Winston.

PAUL, J.L. & EPANCHIN, B.C. (1991). Educating Emotionally Disturbed Children and Youth: Theories and Practices for Teachers. (2nd ed.). New York: MacMillan. PENNSYLVANIA ASSOCIATION FOR RETARDED CHILDREN VS. COMMONWEALTH OF PENNSYLVANIA, 334 F. Supp. 1257 (E.D., PA., 1971), 343 F. Supp. 279 (L.D. PA., 19972).

PHILLIPS, V., & MCCULLOUGH, L. (1990). Consultation based programming: Instituting the Collaborative Work Ethic. Exceptional Children. 56 (4), 291-304.

PODEMSKI, R.S., PRICE, B.K., SMITH, T.E.C., & MARSH, G.E., IL (1984). Comprehensive Administration of Special Education. Rockville, MD: Aspen Systems Corporation.

POLLOWAY, E.A., & PATTON, J.R. (1989). Strategies for Teaching Learners with Special Needs. (5th ed.). New York: Merrill.

POLLOWAY, E.A., PATTON, J.R., PAYNE, J.S., & PAYNE, R.A. 1989). Strategies for Teaching Learners with Special Needs, 4th ed.). Columbus, OH: Merrill Publishing.

PUGACH, M.C., & JOHNSON, L.J. (1989a). The challenge of implementing collaboration between general and special education. Exceptional Children, 56 (3), 232-235.

PUGACH, M.C., & JOHNSON, L.J. (1989b). Pre-referral interventions: Progress, Problems, and Challenges. Exceptional Children, 56 (3), 217-226.

RADABAUGH, M.T., & YUKISH, J.F. (1982). Curriculum and Methods for the Mildly Handicapped. Boston: Allyn and Bacon.

RAMSEY, R.S. (1981). Perceptions of disturbed and disturbing behavioral characteristics by school personnel. (Doctoral Dissertation, University of Florida) Dissertation Abstracts International, 42(49), DA8203709.

RAMSEY, R.S. (1986). Taking the practicum beyond the public school door. Journal of Adolescence. 21(83), 547-552.

RAMSEY, R.S., (1988). Preparatory Guide for Special Education Teacher competency Tests. Boston: Allyn and Bacon, Inc.

RAMSEY, R.S., DIXON, M.J., & SMITH, G.G.B. (1986) Eyes on the Special Education: Professional Knowledge Teacher Competency Test. Albany, GA: Southwest Georgia Learning Resources System Center.

RAMSEY R.W., & RAMSEY, R.S. (1978). Educating the emotionally handicapped child in the public school setting. Journal of Adolescence. 13(52), 537-541.

REINHEART, H.R. (1980). Children I Conflict: Educational Strategies for the Emotionally Disturbed and Behaviorally Disordered. (2nd ed.). St Louis, MO: The C.V. Mosby Company.

ROBINSON, G.A., PATTON, J.R., POLLOWAY, E.A., & SARGENT, L.R. (Eds.). (1989a). Best Practices in Mental Disabilities. Des Moines, IA Iowa Department of Education, Bureau of Special Education.

ROBINSON, G.A., PATTON, J.R., POLLOWAY, E.A., & SARGENT, L.R. (Eds.). (1989b). Best Practices in Mental Disabilities. Renton, VA: The Division on Mental Retardation of the Council for Exceptional Children.

ROTHSTEIN, L.F. (1995). Special education Law (2nd ed.). New York: Longman Publishers.

SABATINO, D.A., SABATION, A.C., & MANN, L. (1983). Management: A Handbook of Tactics, Strategies, and Programs. Aspen Systems Corporation.

SALVIA, J., & YSSELDYKE, J.E. (1985). Assessment in Special Education (3rd. ed.). Boston: Houghton Mifflin.

SALVIA J., & YSSELDYKE, J.E. (1991). Assessment (5th ed.). Boston: Houghton Mifflin.

SALVIA, J. & YSSELDYKE, J.E. (1995) Assessment (6th ed.). Boston: Houghton Mifflin.

SATTLER, J.M. (1982). Assessment of Children's Intelligence and Special Abilities (2nd ed.). Boston: Allyn and Bacon.

SCHLOSS, P.J., HARRIMAN, N., & PFIEFER, K. (in press). Application of a sequential prompt reduction technique to the independent composition performance of behaviorally disordered youth. Behavioral Disorders.

SCHLOSS, P.J.., & SEDLAK, R.A.(1986). Instructional Methods for Students with Learning and Behavior Problems. Boston: Allyn and Bacon.

SCHMUCK, R.A., & SCHMUCK, P.A. (1971). Group Processes in the Classroom. Dubuque, IA: William C. Brown Company.

SCHUBERT, D.G. (1978). Your teaching - the tape recorder. Reading Improvement, 15(1), 78-80.

SCHULZ, J.B., CARPENTER, C.D., & TURNBULL, A.P. (1991). Mainstreaming Exceptional Students: A Guide for Classroom Teachers. Boston: Allyn and Bacon.

SEMMEL, M.I., ABERNATHY, T.V., BUTERA G., & LESAR, S. (1991). Teacher perception of the regular education initiative. Exceptional Children, 58 (1), 3-23.

SHEA, T.M., & BAUER, A.M. (1985). Parents and Teachers of Exceptional Students: A Handbook for Involvement. Boston: Allyn and Bacon.

SIMEONSSON, R.J. (1986). Psychological and Development Assessment of Special Children. Boston: Allyn and Bacon.

SMITH, C.R. (1991). Learning Disabilities: The Interaction of Learner, Task, and Setting. Boston: Little, Brown, and Company.

SMITH, D.D., & LUCKASSON, R. (1992). Introduction to Special Education: Teaching in an Age of Challenge. Boston: Allyn and Bacon.

SMITH, J.E., & PATTON, J.M. (1989). A Resource Module on Adverse Causes of Mild Mental Retardation. (Prepared for the President's Committee on Mental Retardation).

SMITH, T.E.C., FINN, D.M., & DOWDY, C.A. (1993). Teaching Students With Mild Disabilities. Fort Worth, TX: Harcourt Brace Jovanovich College Publishers.

SMITH-DAVIS, J. (1989a April). A National Perspective on Special Education. Keynote presentation at the GLRS/College/University Forum, Macon, GA.

STEPHENS, T.M. (1976). Directive Teaching of Children with Learning and Behavioral Disorders. Columbus, OH Charles E. Merrill.

STERNBURG, R.J. (1990). Thinking Styles: Key to Understanding Performance. Phi Delta Kappa, 71(5), 366-371.

SULZER, B., & MAYER, G.R. (1972). Behavior Modification Procedures for School Personnel. Hinsdale, IL: Dryden.

TATEYAMA-SNIEZEK, K.M. (1990.) Cooperative Learning: Does it improve the academic achievement of students with handicaps? Exceptional Children, 57(2), 426-427.

THIAGARAJAN, S. (1976). Designing instructional games for handicapped learners. Focus on Exceptional Children. 7(9), 1-11.

THOMAS, O. (1980). Individualized Instruction [Videocassette & manual series]. Northbrook, IL: Hubbard Scientific Company. (Project STRETCH [Strategies to Train Regular Educators to Teach Children with Handicaps]. Module 14, ISBN 0- 8331-1919-2).

THOMAS, O.(1980). Spelling [Videocassette & manual series]. (Project STRETCH [Strategies to Train Regular Educators to Teach Children with Handicaps]. Module 10, ISBN 0-83311915-X).

THORNTON, C.A., TUCKER, B.F., DOSSEY, J.A., & BAZIK, E.F. (1983). Teaching Mathematics to Children with Special Needs. Menlo Park, CA: Addison-Wesley.

TURKEL, S.R., & PODEL, D.M. (1984). Computer-assisted learning for mildly handicapped students. Teaching Exceptional Children. 16(4), 258-262.

TURNBULL, A.P., STRICKLAND, B.B., & BRANTLEY, J.C. (1978). Developing Individualized Education Programs. Columbus, OH: Charles E. Merrill.

U.S. DEPARTMENT OF EDUCATION. (1993). To Assure the Free Appropriate Public Education of all Children with Disabilities. (Fifteenth annual report to Congress on the Implementation of The Individuals with Disabilities Education Act.). Washington, D.C.

WALKER, J.E., & SHEA, T.M. (1991). Behavior Management: A Practical Approach for Educators. New York: MacMillan.

WALLACE, G., & KAUFFMAN, J.M. (1978). Teaching Children with Learning Problems. Columbus, OH: Charles E. Merrill.

WEHMAN, P., & MCLAUGHLIN, P.J. (1981). Program Development in Special Education. New York: McGraw-Hill.

WEINTRAUB, F.J. (1987, March). [Interview].

WESSON, C.L. (1991). Curriculum-based measurement and two models of follow-up consultation. Exceptional Children. 57(3), 246-256.

WEST, R.P., YOUNG, K.R., & SPOONER, F. (1990). Precision Teaching: An Introduction. Teaching Exceptional Children. 22(3), 4-9.

WHEELER, J. (1987). Transitioning Persons with Moderate and Severe Disabilities from School to Adulthood: What Makes it Work? Materials Development Center, School of Education, and Human Services. University of Wisconsin-Stout.

WHITING, J., & AULTMAN, L. (1990). Workshop for Parents. (Workshop materials). Albany, GA: Southwest Georgia Learning Resources System Center.

WIEDERHOLT, J.L., HAMMILL, D.D., & BROWN, V.L. (1983). The Resource Room Teacher: A Guide to Effective Practices (2nd ed.). Boston: Allyn and Bacon.

WIIG, E.H., & SEMEL, E.M. (1984). Language Assessment and Intervention for the Learning Disabled. (2nd ed.). Columbus, OH: Charles E. Merrill.

WOLFGANG, C.H., & GLICKMAN, C.D.(1986). Solving Discipline Problems: Strategies for Classroom Teachers (2nd ed.). Boston: Allyn and Bacon.

YSSELKYKE, J.E., ALGOZZINE, B., (1990). Introduction to Special Education (2nd ed.). Boston: Houghton Mifflin.

YSSELDYKE, J.E., ALGOZZINE, B., & THURLOW, M.L. (1992). Critical Issues in Special Education (2nd ed.). Boston: Houghton Mifflin Company.

YSSEDLYKE, J.E., THURLOW, M.L., WOTRUBA, J.W., NANIA, PA.A (1990). Instructional arrangements: Perceptions From General Education. Teaching Exceptional Children, 22(4), 4-8.

ZARGONA, N., VAUGHN, S., 7 MCINTOSH, R. (1991). Social Skills Interventions and children with behavior problems: A review. Behavior Disorders, 16(4), 260-275.

ZIGMOND, N., & BAKER, J. (1990). Mainstream experiences for learning disabled students (Project Meld): Preliminary report. Exceptional Children, 57(2), 176-185.

ZIRPOLI, T.J., & MELLOY, K.J. (1993). Behavior Management. New York: Merrill.

Resources

Organization	Audience	Mission
Autism Society of America 7910 Woodmont Avenue, Suite 300 Bethesda, Maryland 20814 www.autism-society.org 1-800-328-8476	Open to all who support the mission of ASA	To increase public awareness about autism and the day-to-day issues faced by individuals with autism, their families and the professionals with whom they interact. The Society and its chapters share a common mission of providing information and education, and supporting research and advocating for programs and services for the autism community.
Brain Injury Association of America 8201 Greensboro Drive Suite 611 McLean, VA 22102 http://www.biausa.org/ Phone: (703) 761-0750	Open to all	Provides information, education and support to assist the 5.3 million Americans currently living with traumatic brain injury and their families.
Child and Adolescent Bipolar Association (CABF) 1187 Wilmette Ave. P.M.B. #331 Wilmette, IL 60091 http://www.bpkids.org	Physicians, scientific researchers, and allied professionals (therapists, social workers, educators, attorneys, and others) who provide services to children and adolescents with bipolar disorder or do research on the topic	**educates** families, professionals, and the public about pediatric bipolar disorder; **connects** families with resources and support; **advocates** for and **empowers** affected families; and **supports research** on pediatric bipolar disorder and its cure.

TEACHER CERTIFICATION STUDY GUIDE

Children and Adults with Attention Deficit/Hyperactive Disorder (CHADD) 8181 Professional Place - Suite 150 Landover, MD 20785 www.chadd.org Tel: 301-306-7070 / Fax: 301-306-7090 Email: national@chadd.org	Open to all	providing resources and encouragement to parents, educators and professionals on a grassroots level through CHADD chapters
Council for Exceptional Children 1110 N. Glebe Road Suite 300 Arlington, VA 22201 www.cec.sped.org 1-888-232-7733 TTY: 1-866-915-5000 FAX 703-264-9494	Teachers, administrators, teacher educators, and related service personnel	Advocate for services for [disabled] and gifted individuals. A professional organization that addresses service, training, and research relative to exceptional persons.
Epilepsy Foundation of America 8301 Professional Place Landover, MD 20785 www.epilepsyfoundation.org/ (800) 332-1000	A non-membership organization	works to ensure that people with seizures are able to participate in all life experiences; and to prevent, control and cure epilepsy through research, education, advocacy and services
Family Center on Technology and Disability (FCTD) 1825 Connecticut Avenue, NW 7th Floor Washington, DC 20009 http://www.fctd.info/ phone: (202) 884-8068 fax: (202) 884-8441 email: fctd@aed.org	Non member association	a resource designed to support organizations and programs that work with families of children and youth with disabilities.

LEARNING DISABLED

Hands and Voices P.O. Box 371926 Denver CO 80237 www.handsandvoices.org Toll Free: (866) 422-0422 parentadvocate@handsandvoices.org	families, professionals, other organizations, pre-service students, and deaf and hard of hearing adults who are all working towards ensuring successful outcomes for children who are deaf and hard of hearing.	supporting families and their children who are deaf or hard of hearing, as well as the professionals who serve them.
The International Dyslexia Association Chester Building, Suite 382 8600 LaSalle Road Baltimore, Maryland 21286 http://www.interdys.org/ 410-296-0232 Fax: 410-321-5069	Anyone interested in IDA and its mission can become a member	Provides information and referral services, research, advocacy and direct services to professionals in the field of learning disabilities.
Learning Disabilities Association of America 4156 Library Road Pittsburgh, PA 15234 http://www.ldanatl.org/ Phone (412) 341-1515 Fax (412) 344-0224	Anyone interested in LDA and its mission can become a member	• provides cutting edge information on learning disabilities, practical solutions, and a comprehensive network of resources. • provides support to people with learning disabilities, their families, teachers and other professionals.

National Association of the Deaf (NAD) 8630 Fenton Street, Suite 820, Silver Spring, MD 20910-3819 301-587-1789 TTY, 301-587-1788 Voice, 301-587-1791 FAX Email: NADinfo@nad.org http://nad.org	Anyone interested in NAD and its mission can become a member	to promote, protect, and preserve the rights and quality of life of deaf and hard of hearing individuals in the United States of America.
National Mental Health Information Center P.O. Box 42557 Washington, DC 20015 http://www.mentalhealth.samhsa.gov/ 1-800-789-2647	Government Agency	developed for users of mental health services and their families, the general public, policy makers, providers, and the media.
National Dissemination Center for Children with Disabilities (NIHCY) P.O. Box 1492 Washington, DC 20013 (800) 695-0285 · v/tty (202) 884-8441 · fax nichcy@aed.org	Non membership association	a central source of information on: • disabilities in infants, toddlers, children, and youth, • IDEA, which is the law authorizing special education, • No Child Left Behind (as it relates to children with disabilities), and • research-based information on effective educational practices.

Resource	Type	Description
Office of Special Education and Rehabilitative Services US Department of Education http://www.ed.gov/about/offices/list/osers/index.html National Dissemination Center for Children with Disabilities (NIHCY) P.O. Box 1492 Washington, DC 20013 (800) 695-0285 · v/tty (202) 884-8441 · fax nichcy@aed.org	Government Resource Non membership association	Committed to improving results and outcomes for people with disabilities of all ages. a central source of information on: - disabilities in infants, toddlers, children, and youth, - IDEA, which is the law authorizing special education, - No Child Left Behind (as it relates to children with disabilities), and - research-based information on effective educational practices.
Wrights Law Wrightslaw.com webmaster@wrightslaw.com Office of Special Education and Rehabilitative Services US Department of Education http://www.ed.gov/about/offices/list/osers/index.html	Non membership organization Government Resource	Parents, educators, advocates, and attorneys come to Wrightslaw for accurate, reliable information about special education law, education law, and advocacy for children with disabilities. Provides parent Advocacy training and updates on the law through out the country. Committed to improving results and outcomes for people with disabilities of all ages.

TASH (Formerly **The Association for Persons with Severe Handicaps**) 29 W. Susquehanna Ave., Suite 210 Baltimore, MD 21204 www.tash.org Phone: 410-828-8274 Fax: 410-828-6706Wrights Law Wrightslaw.com webmaster@wrightslaw.com	Anyone interested in TASH and its mission can become a memberNon membership organization	**To create change and build capacity so that all people, no matter their perceived level of disability, are included in all aspects of society.**Parents, educators, advocates, and attorneys come to Wrightslaw for accurate, reliable information about special education law, education law, and advocacy for children with disabilities.
American Psychological Association 750 First Street, NE, Washington, DC 20002-4242 **Telephone: 800-374-2721; 202-336-5500. TDD/TTY: 202-336-6123** www.apa.orgTASH (Formerly **The Association for Persons with Severe Handicaps**) 29 W. Susquehanna Ave., Suite 210 Baltimore, MD 21204 www.tash.org Phone: 410-828-8274 Fax: 410-828-6706	Psychologists and professors of PsychologyAnyone interested in TASH and its mission can become a member	Provides parent Advocacy training and updates on the law through out the country. Scientific and professional society working to improve mental health services and to advocate for legislation and programs that will promote mental health; facilitate research and professional development.**To create change and build capacity so that all people, no matter their perceived level of disability, are included in all aspects of society.**

Organization	Audience	Purpose
American Psychological Association 750 First Street, NE, Washington, DC 20002-4242 **Telephone: 800-374-2721; 202-336-5500. TDD/TTY: 202-336-6123** www.apa.org	Psychologists and professors of Psychology	Scientific and professional society working to improve mental health services and to advocate for legislation and programs that will promote mental health; facilitate research and professional development.
Association for Children and Adults with Learning Disabilities 4156 Library Road Pittsburgh, PA 15234 http://www.acldonline.org/	Parents of children with learning disabilities and interested professionals	Advanced the education and general well-being of children with adequate intelligence who have learning disabilities arising from perceptual, conceptual, or subtle coordinative problems, sometimes accompanied by behavior difficulties.
The Arc of the United States (Formerly the National Association of Retarded Citizens) 1010 Wayne Avenue Suite 650 Silver Springs, MD 20910 www.the arc.org (301) 565-3842 FAX: (301) 565-3843Association for Children and Adults with Learning Disabilities 4156 Library Road Pittsburgh, PA 15234 http://www.acldonline.org/	Parents, professionals, and others interested in individuals with mental retardationParents of children with learning disabilities and interested professionals	Work on local, state, and national levels to promote treatment, research, public understanding, and legislation for persons with mental retardation; provide counseling for parents of students with mental retardation. Advanced the education and general well-being of children with adequate intelligence who have learning disabilities arising from perceptual, conceptual, or subtle coordinative problems, sometimes accompanied by behavior difficulties.

National Association for Gifted Children 1707 L Street, NW Suite 550 Washington, DC 20036 http://nagc.org Phone: (202) 785-4368 FAX: (202) 785-4248 Email: nagc@nagc.org	Parents, educators, community leaders and, other professionals who work with Gifted children. Parents, professionals, and others interested in individuals with mental retardation	To address the unique needs of children and youth with demonstrated gifts and talents. Work on local, state, and national levels to promote treatment, research, public understanding, and legislation for persons with mental retardation; provide counseling for parents of students with mental retardation.
The Arc of the United States (Formerly the National Association of Retarded Citizens) 1010 Wayne Avenue Suite 650 Silver Springs, MD 20910 www.thearc.org (301) 565-3842 FAX: (301) 565-3843		
National Association for Gifted Children 1707 L Street, NW Suite 550 Washington, DC 20036 http://nagc.org Phone: (202) 785-4368 FAX: (202) 785-4248 Email: nagc@nagc.org	Parents, educators, community leaders and, other professionals who work with Gifted children.	To address the unique needs of children and youth with demonstrated gifts and talents.

Organization	Members	Purpose
Council for Children with Behavioral Disorders CEC Two Ballston Plaza 1110 N. Glebe Road Arlington, VA 22201 ccbd.net 800-224-6830 (business) 888-232-7733 (membership line) 703-264-9494 fax.	Members of the Council for Exceptional Children who teach children with behavior disorders or who train teachers to work with those children	Promote education and general welfare of children and youth with behavior disorders or serious emotional disturbances. Promote professional growth and research on students with behavior disorders and severe emotional disturbances.
Council for Educational Diagnostic Services, CEC Two Ballston Plaza 1110 N. Glebe Road Arlington, VA 22201 Council for Children with Behavioral Disorders CEC Two Ballston Plaza 1110 N. Glebe Road Arlington, VA 22201 ccbd.net 800-224-6830 (business) 888-232-7733 (membership line) 703-264-9494 fax.	Members of the Council for Exceptional Children who are school psychologists, educational diagnosticians, [and] social workers who are involved in diagnosing educational difficultiesMembers of the Council for Exceptional Children who teach children with behavior disorders or who train teachers to work with those children	Promote the most appropriate education of children and youth through appraisal, diagnosis, educational intervention, implementation, and evaluation of a prescribed educational program. Work to facilitate the professional development of those who assess students. Work to further development of better diagnostic techniques and procedures. Promote education and general welfare of children and youth with behavior disorders or serious emotional disturbances. Promote professional growth and research on students with behavior disorders and severe emotional disturbances.

Council for Exceptional Children Two Ballston Plaza 1110 N. Glebe Road Arlington, VA 22201Council for Educational Diagnostic Services, CEC Two Ballston Plaza 1110 N. Glebe Road Arlington, VA 22201	Teachers, administrators, teacher educators, and related service personnelMembers of the Council for Exceptional Children who are school psychologists, educational diagnosticians, [and] social workers who are involved in diagnosing educational difficulties	Advocate for services for [disabled] and gifted individuals. A professional organization that addresses service, training, and research relative to exceptional persons. Promote the most appropriate education of children and youth through appraisal, diagnosis, educational intervention, implementation, and evaluation of a prescribed educational program. Work to facilitate the professional development of those who assess students. Work to further development of better diagnostic techniques and procedures.
Council of Administrators of Special Education Two Ballston Plaza 1110 N. Glebe Road Arlington, VA 22201Council for Exceptional Children Two Ballston Plaza 1110 N. Glebe Road Arlington, VA 22201	Members of the Council for Exceptional Children who are administrators, directors, coordinators, or supervisors of programs, schools, or classes for exceptional children; college faculty who train administrators Teachers, administrators, teacher educators, and related service personnel	Promote professional leadership; provide opportunities for the study of problems common to its members; communicate through discussion and publications information that will facilitate improved services for children with exceptional needs. Advocate for services for [disabled] and gifted individuals. A professional organization that addresses service, training, and research relative to exceptional persons.

Division for Children with Communication Disorders Two Ballston Plaza 1110 N. Glebe Road Arlington, VA 22201 Council of Administrators of Special Education Two Ballston Plaza 1110 N. Glebe Road Arlington, VA 22201	Members of the Council for Exceptional Children who are speech-language pathologists, audiologists, teachers of children with communication disorders, or educators of professionals who plan to work with children who have communication disorders Members of the Council for Exceptional Children who are administrators, directors, coordinators, or supervisors of programs, schools, or classes for exceptional children; college faculty who train administrators	Promote the education of children with communication disorders. Promote professional growth and research. Promote professional leadership; provide opportunities for the study of problems common to its members; communicate through discussion and publications information that will facilitate improved services for children with exceptional needs.

LEARNING DISABLED

TEACHER CERTIFICATION STUDY GUIDE

Division for Early Childhood Two Ballston Plaza 1110 N. Glebe Road Arlington, VA 22201Division for Children with Communication Disorders Two Ballston Plaza 1110 N. Glebe Road Arlington, VA 22201	Members of the Council for Exceptional Children who teach preschool children and infants or educate teachers to work with young childrenMembers of the Council for Exceptional Children who are speech-language pathologists, audiologists, teachers of children with communication disorders, or educators of professionals who plan to work with children who have communication disorders	Promote effective education for young children and infants. Promote professional development of those who work with young children and infants. Promote legislation and research. Promote the education of children with communication disorders. Promote professional growth and research.
Division for the Physically Handicapped Two Ballston Plaza 1110 N. Glebe Road Arlington, VA 22201Division for Early Childhood Two Ballston Plaza 1110 N. Glebe Road Arlington, VA 22201	Members of the Council for Exceptional Children who work with individuals who have physical disabilities or educate professionals to work with those individualsMembers of the Council for Exceptional Children who teach preschool children and infants or educate teachers to work with young children	Promote closer relationships among educators of students who have physical impairments or are homebound. Facilitate research and encourage development of new ideas, practices, and techniques through professional meetings, workshops, and publications. Promote effective education for young children and infants. Promote professional development of those who work with young children and infants. Promote legislation and research.

LEARNING DISABLED

Division for the Visually Handicapped
Two Ballston Plaza
1110 N. Glebe Road
Arlington, VA 22201

Division for the Physically Handicapped
Two Ballston Plaza
1110 N. Glebe Road
Arlington, VA 22201

Members of the Council for Exceptional Children who work with individuals who have visual disabilities or educate professionals to work with those individuals

Members of the Council for Exceptional Children who work with individuals who have physical disabilities or educate professionals to work with those individuals

Work to advance the education and training of individuals with visual impairments. Work to bring about better understanding of educational, emotional, or other problems associated with visual impairment. Facilitate research and development of new techniques or ideas in education and training of individuals with visual problems.

Promote closer relationships among educators of students who have physical impairments or are homebound. Facilitate research and encourage development of new ideas, practices, and techniques through professional meetings, workshops, and publications.

Division on Career Development
Two Ballston Plaza
1110 N. Glebe Road
Arlington, VA 22201

Division for the Visually Handicapped
Two Ballston Plaza
1110 N. Glebe Road
Arlington, VA 22201

Members of the Council for Exceptional Children who teach or in other ways work toward career development and vocational education of exceptional children

Members of the Council for Exceptional Children who work with individuals who have visual disabilities or educate professionals to work with those individuals

Promote and encourage professional growth of all those concerned with career development and vocational education. Promote research, legislation, information dissemination, and technical assistance relevant to career development and vocational education.

Work to advance the education and training of individuals with visual impairments. Work to bring about better understanding of educational, emotional, or other problems associated with visual impairment. Facilitate research and development of new techniques or ideas in education and training of individuals with visual problems.

Division on Mental Retardation Two Ballston Plaza 1110 N. Glebe Road Arlington, VA 22201 Division on Career Development Two Ballston Plaza 1110 N. Glebe Road Arlington, VA 22201	Members of the Council for Exceptional Children who work with students with mental retardation or educate professionals to work with those students Members of the Council for Exceptional Children who teach or in other ways work toward career development and vocational education of exceptional children	Work to advance the education of individuals with mental retardation, research mental retardation, and the training o professionals to work with individuals with mental retardation. Promote public understanding of mental retardation and professional development of those who work with persons with mental retardation. Promote and encourage professional growth of all those concerned with career development and vocational education. Promote research, legislation, information dissemination, and technical assistance relevant to career development and vocational education.

Organization	Audience	Purpose
Gifted Child Society P.O. Box 120 Oakland, NJ 07436 Division on Mental Retardation Two Ballston Plaza 1110 N. Glebe Road Arlington, VA 22201	Parents and educators of children who are gifted Members of the Council for Exceptional Children who work with students with mental retardation or educate professionals to work with those students	Train educators to meet the needs of students with gifted abilities, offer assistance to parents facing special problems in raising children who are gifted, and seek public recognition of the needs of these children. Work to advance the education of individuals with mental retardation, research mental retardation, and the training o professionals to work with individuals with mental retardation. Promote public understanding of mental retardation and professional development of those who work with persons with mental retardation.
National Association for the Education of Young Children 1313 L St. N.W. Suite 500, Washington DC 20005 (202) 232-8777 || (800) 424-2460 || webmaster@naeyc.org http://www.naeyc.org/ Gifted Child Society P.O. Box 120 Oakland, NJ 07436	Parents and educators of children who are gifted	Promote service and action on behalf of the needs and rights of young children, with emphasis on provision of educational services and resources. Train educators to meet the needs of students with gifted abilities, offer assistance to parents facing special problems in raising children who are gifted, and seek public recognition of the needs of these children.

National Association for Retarded Citizens 5101 Washington Ave., N.W. Washington, D.C www.thearc.org .National Association for the Education of Young Children 1313 L St. N.W. Suite 500, Washington DC 20005 (202) 232-8777 || (800) 424-2460 || webmaster@naeyc.org http://www.naeyc.org/		Work to promote the general welfare of persons with mental retardation; facilitate research and information dissemination relative to causes, treatment, and prevention of mental retardation.Promote service and action on behalf of the needs and rights of young children, with emphasis on provision of educational services and resources.
National Easter Seal Society 230 West Monroe Street, Suite 1800 Chicago, IL 60606 800-221-6827 (toll-free) 312-726-4258 (tty) 312-726-1494 (fax) http://www.easterseals.com/National Association for Retarded Citizens 5101 Washington Ave., N.W. Washington, D.C www.thearc.org .	State units (49) and local societies (951); no individual members	Establish and run programs for individuals with physical impairments, usually including diagnostic services, speech therapy, preschool services, physical therapy, and occupational therapy. Work to promote the general welfare of persons with mental retardation; facilitate research and information dissemination relative to causes, treatment, and prevention of mental retardation.

Organization	Members	Purpose
National Easter Seal Society 230 West Monroe Street, Suite 1800 Chicago, IL 60606 800-221-6827 (toll-free) 312-726-4258 (tty) 312-726-1494 (fax) http://www.easterseals.com/	State units (49) and local societies (951); no individual members	Establish and run programs for individuals with physical impairments, usually including diagnostic services, speech therapy, preschool services, physical therapy, and occupational therapy.
The National Association of Special Education Teachers 1201 Pennsylvania Avenue, N.W., Suite 300 Washington D.C. 20004 **Call us at:** 800-754-4421 **Fax us at:** 800-424-0371 **Or email us at:** contactus@naset.org	Special Education Teachers	to render all possible support and assistance to professionals who teach children with special needs. to promote standards of excellence and innovation in special education research, practice, and policy in order to foster exceptional teaching for exceptional children.
The National Association of Special Education Teachers 1201 Pennsylvania Avenue, N.W., Suite 300 Washington D.C. 20004 **Call us at:** 800-754-4421 **Fax us at:** 800-424-0371 **Or email us at:** contactus@naset.org	Special Education Teachers	to render all possible support and assistance to professionals who teach children with special needs. to promote standards of excellence and innovation in special education research, practice, and policy in order to foster exceptional teaching for exceptional children.

XAMonline, INC. 21 Orient Ave. Melrose, MA 02176

Toll Free number 800-509-4128

TO ORDER Fax 781-662-9268 OR www.XAMonline.com

MICHIGAN TEST FOR TEACHER EXAMINATION - MTTC - 2007

PO#   Store/School:

Address 1:

Address 2 (Ship to other):

City, State Zip

Credit card number _____-_____-_____-_____   expiration_____

EMAIL _____

PHONE   **FAX**

13# ISBN 2007	TITLE	Qty	Retail	Total
978-1-58197-968-8	MTTC Basic Skills 96			
978-1-58197-954-1	MTTC Biology 17			
978-1-58197-955-8	MTTC Chemistry 18			
978-1-58197-957-2	MTTC Earth-Space Science 20			
978-1-58197-966-4	MTTC Elementary Education 83			
978-1-58197-967-1	MTTC Elementary Education 83 Sample Questions			
978-1-58197-950-3	MTTC English 02			
978-1-58197-961-9	MTTC Family and Consumer Sciences 40			
978-1-58197-959-6	MTTC French Sample Test 23			
978-1-58197-965-7	MTTC Guidance Counselor 51			
978-1-58197-964-0	MTTC Humanities& Fine Arts 53, 54			
978-1-58197-972-5	MTTC Integrated Science (Secondary) 94			
978-1-58197-973-2	MTTC Emotionally Impaired 59			
978-1-58197-953-4	MTTC Learning Disabled 63			
978-1-58197-963-3	MTTC Library Media 48			
978-1-58197-958-9	MTTC Mathematics (Secondary) 22			
978-1-58197-962-6	MTTC Physical Education 44			
978-1-58197-956-5	MTTC Physics Sample Test 19			
978-1-58197-952-7	MTTC Political Science 10			
978-1-58197-951-0	MTTC Reading 05			
978-1-58197-960-2	MTTC Spanish 28			
978-158197-970-1	MTTC Social Studies 84			
FOR PRODUCT PRICES GO TO WWW.XAMONLINE.COM			SUBTOTAL	
			Ship	$8.25
			TOTAL	

www.ingramcontent.com/pod-product-compliance
Lightning Source LLC
Chambersburg PA
CBHW080536300426
44111CB00017B/2758